Paradise Under the Knife
A Wild Adventure in
Tropical Medicine and International Intrigue

M. Allan Daly

First published by Dog Ear Publishing
4010 W. 86th Street, Ste H
Indianapolis, IN 46268
www.dogearpublishing.net

ISBN: 978-145753-101-9

Library of Congress Control Number: has been applied for

This book is printed on acid-free paper.

Printed in the United States of America

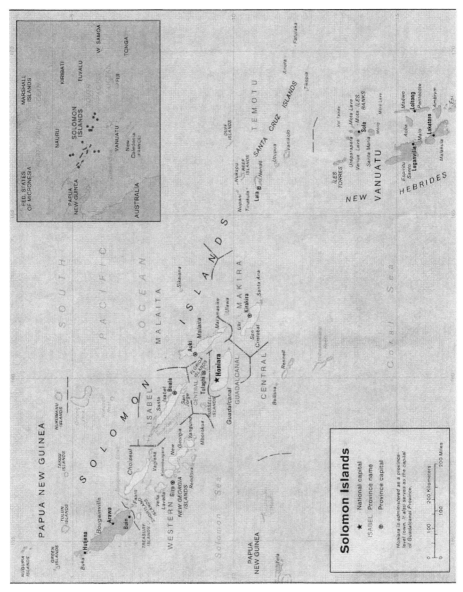

Courtesy of http://en.wikipedia.org/wiki/File:SolomonIslands_1989.jpg

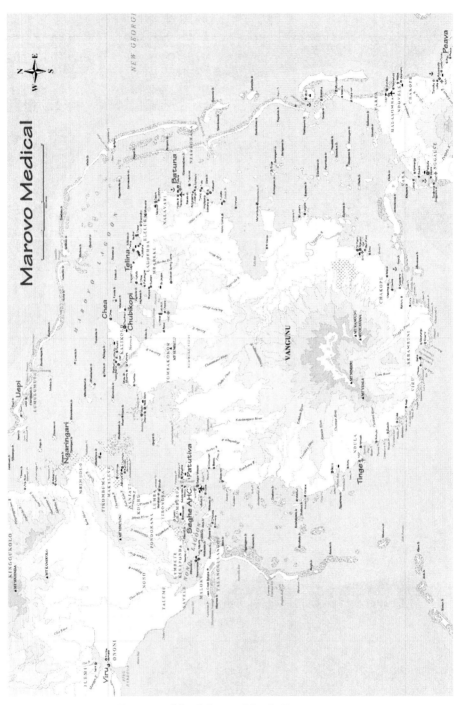

Courtesy of the Solomon Islands Government

Acknowledgments

To everyone who has played a role in helping to increase the level of healthcare available to the people of the Marovo Lagoon, Solomon Islands, I thank you with the most sincere thanks I can offer. Suzanne, Jason, Grant, Jill, Gordon, Kate, and the board of Marovo Medical Foundation, we've had good success, but let's not stop here!

CHAPTER

1

"*A*re you kidding? They burned down Chinatown?" My facial contortions would have made circus folk proud. "We just booked our tickets yesterday. This was supposed to be a once-in-a-lifetime vacation. … What are we supposed to do now?" I begged the travel agent in real horror, terrified of potentially losing the thousands of dollars that this trip had already cost.

"Allan … I want you to relax. The Solomon Islands have been in a serious state of flux since the civil war ended in 2002. These were the first real free elections that have taken place since the civil war, or tension, as they call it," Phil said as he tried not to lose the business that I had given him the day before. Some would consider free elections only four years after the end of a civil war pretty good progress. Surprisingly, altruism was failing me at this point.

As Phil had mentioned, the problem had begun when Chinese money had influenced members of parliament away from the candidate who was preferred by the people. Most of the retail businesses in Honiara, the capital of the Solomon Islands, were owned by the Chinese. The political bribe money had tipped the balance in parliament to guide the votes away from the people's choice candidate to the Chinese choice candidate. The vote had been immediately rejected by the masses, and they had directed their fury on Chinatown in Honiara. An entire hotel-casino was burned to the ground in the melee.

After learning about the destruction in Chinatown, I started looking at the text in our travel insurance policy. I even called the company to discuss how it would work if the tenuous situation in Honiara prevented us from traveling or from feeling safe enough to travel. I received a fair bit of nebulous

1

information … sort of surprising, since it was an insurance company. The insurance industry is known for dealing in absolutes and for making sure those absolutes are articulately, if not craftily, conveyed throughout its policies. In effect, the insurance company was telling me that it was too soon to be able to make any decisions regarding our travel plans.

With no clear course of action available at that moment, receiving reimbursement, or not, from the insurance company wasn't going to dissuade my wife—Suzanne—and I from following through with the trip. If, near the time of departure, the US government had serious concerns about our safety, then we would make a decision on how to proceed.

The *Sydney Morning Herald* was reporting that the Diggers, as they are called, were being deployed into Honiara to try to restore order. I learned that the Diggers are some of Australia's finest army soldiers, but I didn't care who they were. My selfishness just wanted them to get a handle on the volatility in Honiara before our trip, which was planned for September, just five months away.

My wife and I had just spent a boatload of money on this trip, and now I had to tell her the news about the fluid situation in Honiara. In reality, this wasn't for her to worry about, though. I had become the house husband and travel planner since we had moved to Salt Lake City. My job at the University of Maryland had been the ultimate in career satisfaction for me, but Suzanne's career as a gastroenterologist trumped mine as a natural resources extension agent. Unfortunately, there weren't many jobs like that, and at the time, Utah State University didn't have any openings for me. Thus, I had landed myself in the grocery aisle, behind the vacuum, and in the kitchen in my new role.

It was this newfound career as a domestic stallion that had given me the time to find a little gem of a vacation locale in the South Pacific. Initially in the trip-planning process, the Solomon Islands had not been the planned destination for our vacation. My Internet searches had led me to a small island gem located in the Torres Strait in Australia. It was an area that held a lot of intrigue in my mind, as it was at the crosscurrents of the area between the tip of Cape York Peninsula in northern Queensland, Australia, and the wild unknown of Papua New Guinea.

By now, fall of 2006, Suzanne and I had taken many trips since we married in 2002. We had really started to enjoy visiting ecotourism lodges in various places. Most of my master's degree, in Parks, Recreation, and Tourism, had focused on the fledgling ecotourism industry as it was at the time. A great vacation day for us was strolling through a rainforest with our binoculars, trying to identify as many new birds as we could. We loved experiencing the local cuisine of wherever we happened to be visiting. Throw in a sea kayak trip or canoe adventure down a tropical rainforest-lined river and that was a fantastic getaway for us. We never had much desire to visit a large, sterile, "poodled," beach resort in the Caribbean, or anywhere else, for that matter. We loved comfort, but we didn't want sterility in the surrounding environment.

At the time, the growing trend in ecotourism and eco-lodges carried a focus on sustainability of the natural environment and culture surrounding the accommodation. This related to all aspects of the operation, from sourcing local materials and local labor to ensuring that the construction of the facility was planned to promote conservation in the surrounding landscape. Ecotourism was focused on smaller, nature-related travel offerings, not mass tourism in the form of mega-hotels and massive cruise ships. It was this type of adventurous travel, focused on the natural environment, that I was searching for in the wilds of the Torres Strait Islands. I found it in a little eco-lodge that only had two rooms and was situated on a remote and sparsely populated tropical paradise of an island. The surrounding waters were alive with coral and fish. I knew it hadn't been trashed like much of the Caribbean, or man-made like Waikiki. Knowing there would be adventure at every step and discovery around every bend was the draw. The island had been able to accommodate us for the dates that I had requested. The booking had been made and the deposit paid.

We were going to add this on to an already planned trip to Australia. We couldn't get enough of the island continent. Our honeymoon had been spent driving the entire coast of Western Australia. Suzanne thought she'd had enough of Australia, until I planned a trip to the rainforests and coral reefs of far north Queensland. A new love had been found. The upcoming trip would be our second to far north Queensland. On the trip I was planning, we would continue our exploration of Australia by flying to the top of Cape York and taking an adventurous boat ride to the paradise I had found online.

A week after I had made the booking for the Tores Strait eco-lodge, I was figuring out what airlines or charters serviced Cape York. It was during this search that I stumbled upon a news article concerning our small island paradise. The article caught my eye immediately because it mentioned the island and sea level rise. Uh … wait a minute. The news claimed that higher high tides had been washing over the island. Hmm. I was not in a place mentally where I wanted to think about the potential issues surrounding a stay on the island. This had to change. I immediately went into damage-control mode and contacted the eco-lodge to cancel my reservation. I didn't mention the news article, and thankfully, they were very kind to completely refund our entire reservation. Now, the quest for an Australia trip extension continued.

Papua New Guinea was out. The Torres Strait was out. What else was there in that neck of the woods? I loved maps and geography, so I grabbed my world map and gazed at the area in detail. Immediately, a group of islands jumped off the map at me. They were adjacent to the south east of Bougainville Island, Papua New Guinea. The islands belonged to the Solomon Islands.

The first fact that piqued my interest was the number of tourists who visited the country each year. At the time, it was one of the least visited countries in the world, with roughly 15,000 tourists a year. That's not a lot of people visiting a country containing more than 990 islands. Of those 990 islands, only a third were supposedly inhabited. Interesting. I was still engaged. Uninhabited tropical islands sounded like they would have idyllic scenery with seclusion and adventure around every corner. That's what I wanted. Throw in a little comfort and this could turn into the most ultimate "comfortable adventure" that we had experienced since we had tied the knot.

Upon searching the Internet for accommodations in the Solomons, it didn't take me long to figure out where we were headed: Uepi Island Resort, on an island named Uepi (pronounced "oopee"). There was one place that captivated my imagination after I visited the website. It was isolated, far from any town, but it had all the amenities we were looking for in a comfortable adventure. Not only did the website provide alluring photos of the pristine waters, but it assured me that the resort was adept in catering to new divers. This would be our first adventure into the world of scuba. "Dive the dream" was the slogan on Uepi Island Resort's website. Looked like we couldn't go wrong.

The place seemed to have it all—serenity, wild discovery, pristine natural resources, friendly locals, nice amenities, and food to beat the band. The only problem was how far it was from the United States. From the States, there were only two travel options for getting to the Solomon Islands: through either Australia or Fiji. Going through Fiji was a little cheaper, but the itinerary would have us travel nonstop with a couple of long airport layovers. It was likely this remoteness of the Solomon Islands that contributed to the "off the beaten path" nature the islands offered.

With our plans finally made, all I could do was wait. It was inevitable: whenever I planned a trip, it always seemed like time stopped moving. But finally, a few weeks later, experiencing the dank dinginess of LAX, I realized that time had flown and there was no going back now. We were off on the next adventure, and I couldn't have been more excited, though my enthusiasm waned every time I thought of being sequestered in a cramped coach seat for fourteen hours nonstop. Settling into our tight coach seats en route to Brisbane, all I could think about was the wheels touching down on Australian soil … as soon as possible, please!

CHAPTER

2

*A*t the time of our departure from Brisbane to Honiara, Solomon Airlines didn't own its own jet aircraft. It owned smaller aircraft for domestic travel, but to make the three-and-a-half-hour flight to Honiara, they were leasing an aircraft. The plane we boarded was a nondescript Boeing 737 without any markings on it.

The flight attendants were beautiful young ladies and good-looking young men. The ladies had white tropical flowers tucked behind their ears. They were immaculately dressed and full of smiles. Their attire and demeanor made me feel welcome and gave me a thought, however temporary, that we would likely see a lot of similar-looking people when we landed in Honiara.

During the flight, I noticed a couple close to our age sitting across the aisle. The flight wasn't full, so each had a window seat, with the man sitting behind the woman. They seemed almost giddy throughout the flight. As we initiated our descent, they kept looking at one another and the guy kept touching the woman on the shoulder as he pointed out the window. Their behavior made me think they had been to the Solomon Islands before. Their level of excitement seemed promising.

After we had descended for about ten minutes, land came into view. Honiara sits on the northern end of Guadalcanal. The southern end of the island looked like an untouched tropical rainforest paradise. I couldn't believe the massive waterfall that was emptying into a beautiful pool several thousand feet below us. As far as I could see, the mountainous forest was completely intact. Most of the higher mountains were shrouded in clouds, including the highest point in the Solomon Islands, Mt. Popomanaseu, which climbs to an impressive 7,661 feet.

Before long, the uninterrupted rainforest came to an end. Forest clearings began to emerge, which then gave way to almost no forest at all. Brown patches that were burning or had recently burned seemed to be the only color on the landscape that was not green. Gardens of some sort gave way to scattered palm trees, and then we were back out over the ocean. A gradual left-hand 360-degree turn gave us a fairly good glimpse of Honiara. The city didn't look too big. It was evident that the main part of town clung to a narrow strip of flat land along the water, with lots of houses pasted on the hillsides above and behind town.

Upon our arrival, the Diggers from the Australian military were fanned out on the tarmac, providing security for the Solomon Airlines flight. I looked out the window and thought, *Hmm, this trip just started to get interesting.* We haven't traveled anywhere else where armed military were standing outside the aircraft alert and ready to address any potential issue that may arise.

Upon exiting the door of the airbus, I was hit by a humidity bat like never before. The walk across the tarmac was one of the hottest, most humid walks I can ever remember taking. It didn't take Suzanne long to put her long red hair up in a clip. How in the world were those soldiers standing there in dark green head-to-toe battle fatigues with large automatic weapons in their arms in those sweltering conditions? It was beyond me. Nevertheless, I was happy they were there. I wasn't sure what the alternative would have been, but they made me feel a little more comfortable.

I watched as the line of passengers passed the soldiers. I could see the soldiers talking on their radios, snickering about the looks or shapes of the passengers walking across the tarmac. I'm sure this was their form of leisure because, obviously, there wasn't an imminent threat to the airport.

Bottom line, the international terminal wasn't pretty. It was a classic South Pacific leaf house design, but the inside wasn't attractive in the least. Seventy years earlier, the airport had been an airstrip built by the Japanese and later taken over by the Americans during the Guadalcanal campaign of WWII. It had been named Henderson Field by the Americans, and the name has stuck to this day.

The rafters were full of spider webs. The state of the ceiling gave the impression of a culture that didn't quite know what to do with maintenance and management of a building. While waiting in line to clear immigration, I figured life in the Solomons was probably pretty laid back. The immigration officers were about as interested in their jobs as I am in a craft fair. They walked up to their booths with the urgency of walking in to register for a colonoscopy.

On the other side of immigration, we had to wait for our luggage on the carousel. As bags started heading around the small carousel, the electricity went off in the building. The carousel stopped, and most of the obviously nonlocal passengers looked around with a puzzled look as to what was next. Eventually, a door next to the carousel opened to the whirling noise of a jet engine from the aircraft sitting outside. The plane was being serviced to send a group of passengers back to Brisbane.

The baggage handlers started bringing bags in the door and stacking them on the floor. Of course this quickly turned into a major cluster, as a lot of the bags belonged to passengers who were yet to clear immigration. After we spent several minutes watching the baggage circus, our luggage emerged. We grabbed the bags and proceeded through customs unmolested.

Exiting an airport in a foreign land is inevitably full of unknowns. We found at least a dozen cab drivers waiting outside the door. A couple of them approached and asked if we needed a taxi. We declined and continued to walk to the domestic terminal. During the four-hundred-yard walk from the international terminal, we saw random fires burning outside the airport grounds. The travel agent hadn't painted too scary of a scene, but he also hadn't filled me in on the stark realities of life around Henderson Field. People were standing behind makeshift booths selling various items that I was unable to make out from a distance. Whatever they were selling, I was not interested. I saw terribly skinny, mangy-looking dogs wandering about, and it was at that point my irrational brain jumped straight to thinking about the prevalence of rabies in the Solomon Islands.

It quickly became evident that roller suitcases don't roll very well on gravel roads with deep potholes. Some of the potholes were big enough to swallow an entire suitcase. It became easier at certain spots to just carry the heavy bags full of scuba gear.

As we approached a building that must have been the domestic terminal, we started to see more and more bloody red stains along the white gravel. We had read about betel nut and how it was chewed throughout the South Pacific and well into Southeast Asia and beyond. It provides the chewer a serious caffeine-like stimulation and, as we would come to find out, also destroys the mouth, teeth, and throat. The juice color closely resembles blood. The red splotches on the ground looked disgusting and rather repulsive. It literally looked like someone had a serious bleeding wound and decided to stand in one spot to let it bleed for a few minutes before moving on to a new spot to continue the drainage.

There wasn't any signage on the outside of the building that was being used as the domestic terminal. Taxis were parked outside, and other people were walking in and out of the building, so we figured it must be the spot. Upon entering, we looked upon a building that was roughly forty feet squared and dingy as dingy gets. My initial thoughts were that the best way to improve the building would be to introduce it to the blade of a large bulldozer.

There were four or five rows of wooden benches sitting in the middle of the room. Two old scales were positioned in the gaps between the ticket counters. The scales were definitely from another era. Their metal was rusty, and it seemed more appropriate to lay a large slab of beef than a piece of luggage on the scales.

No one staffed the counter upon our arrival to the terminal. We sat on one of the benches for close to twenty minutes before someone resembling an airline employee appeared. The gentleman in a lackluster blue uniform stood at the counter, looking through some papers as I approached.

"Hello, we are going to Seghe," I told him.

"Plane isn't going to Seghe," the person, who, I'm pretty sure, was a Solomon Airlines agent, said to me as he continued looking at his paperwork.

"Um … we are on the flight to Seghe scheduled for three o'clock," I gingerly replied.

The agent looked up and said, "Plane isn't going to Seghe. … It's going to Ramata."

This was getting interesting. "I don't know where Ramata is, but we need to land at Seghe to go to Uepi Island Resort," I replied, knowing that was about all the information I could provide the gentleman in what seemed to be a pretty cut-and-dry case. Our plane tickets were printed with Honiara to Seghe on them, and not having a map of the Solomon Islands handy, I was at a loss for where Ramata was in relation to Seghe.

I wasn't sure as to whether the agent was getting perturbed with my insistence or whether he was showing pity on me for not knowing Solomon Islands geography off the top of my head. "Your plane is going to Ramata. … Boat will be there to pick you up." Those were his last words regarding our flight plans, and I figured I'd better just trust what the man said and get on the flight to Ramata.

As we turned around to return to our seats, I noticed the same couple from the earlier flight also sitting in the domestic terminal. After we had eyed one another several times and seen that we were all interested in this supposed flight to Seghe, the gentleman asked us if we were going to Uepi. We engaged in some small talk, but before long, a door to the left of the counter opened and the ticket agent announced, "Ramata now boarding!"

Off we went. There were no boarding passes at the time, so we just gave the gentleman our names as we passed and he checked them off the list. At this point, it was three in the afternoon, and the walk across the tarmac to the awaiting Twin Otter was just as hot as it had been a couple of hours before.

I didn't need to be an aviation expert to determine that this Twin Otter had a few flights under its wings. As we approached the aircraft, I noticed that our luggage had been wheeled out to the plane by hand and was being loaded into the rear storage compartment. The stairwell was toward the back of the aircraft, and Suzanne and I climbed aboard and found two empty seats. I sat in the window seat, and Suzanne was next to me, in the aisle seat. The other couple was not far from us, both sitting in window seats as they had done on the international flight.

The seats were a plastic-leather amalgam of some sort and didn't scream cleanliness at first inspection. As we were sitting there waiting for the next step, the sweat started to pour out of our bodies because it was very hot and humid and there was no airflow inside the fuselage. Then … he climbed aboard and the plane seamed to jostle a little as he moved about the aircraft. He made sure the rear door closed securely and then tried to navigate his large frame down the very narrow aisle. This rotund man was the copilot. He gave an ever so brief safety talk about the airplane and then squeezed into the seat next to the captain and continued with the preflight checks. He was so fat that I was hoping the stick was far enough in front of his belly that he could pull back enough to make the plane take off. You don't want your pilot dropping dead of a heart attack during the flight, but first, he needs to have the room to pull the stick back to at least get the plane off the ground. The concern I felt at seeing the copilot's girth wasn't a good start to the flight.

The engines revved, and we began to lurch toward the runway. I had a perfect view of the engine and landing gear assembly. It wasn't nearly as clean as I would have liked. I recall a piece or two of some sort of tape wrapped around what looked like brake lines. I just hoped it was some good-quality tape.

The De Havilland Twin Otter is an STOL aircraft, which stands for short takeoff and landing. It held true to its classification, as we were airborne in no time. We veered left over Iron Bottom Sound and slowly started flying to the northwest. We past Honiara and Point Cruz on our left and before long had passed the northern tip of Guadalcanal with nothing but the deep blue ocean in front of us.

Twenty minutes later, my eyes were greeted with unbelievable beauty as we flew over the Russell Islands. I was snapping pictures right and left through a window that was so scratched it was probably due for a replacement. The color contrasts below were mind-boggling. The cobalt blues of the deep ocean meeting the light greens of the shallowest reef waters were the sweetest of eye candy. Some islands had beautiful cream-colored beaches surrounded by dense green rainforest canopy. The intense beauty was almost too good to be true. Suzanne kept leaning over me to see the reason for my continued bursts of excitement.

As all good things in life come to an end, the eye candy of the Russells was gobbled up by the deep cobalt blue of more open ocean. The next twenty minutes were rather mundane, until another set of islands began to appear toward the front of my window. I knew this had to be part of the Marovo Lagoon. The islands were situated in nearly parallel rows. I knew this was the Marovo because the southeastern part of the Marovo had been described to me as having one of the best examples of a double barrier island chain separating the sea from the lagoon. This was the best aerial geography lesson I could have ever asked for.

Over the next fifteen minutes, islands appeared and disappeared from my window. I could see small houses here and there. Most of the structures were built along the water's edge.

A change in the whirr of the engines and a downward pitch of the aircraft signaled our initial descent. We didn't know what to expect at the Ramata Airport—if it could even be called an airport. As we flew lower and lower, the pilot banked the airplane in a gradual circle to the left. Looking across the aisle to the other side of windows, we could see a long, skinny island with a strip cut out of the forest—must be Ramata, I figured. The pilot circled to get a good look at the strip. We came in low over some trees for our final approach.

Prior to the wheels hitting the weed-strewn runway, I saw a chicken barely miss the tires on our side of the plane. One also does not need to be an aviation expert to know that large fowl and airplanes don't make good bedfellows. Boom, the wheels hit the runway like they hadn't been meant to leave the ground in the first place. Up and down we bounced along the runway as the pilot gained more and more control of the aircraft. There's always a point in the landing when I breathe a sigh of relief. Seeing the chicken cheat death delayed my sigh on this landing an extra five seconds, but before long, I was confident we weren't going to launch off the other end of the strip and land in the lagoon.

The final few hundred feet of the taxi were slow and deliberate. Suzanne and I were sitting on the right side of the aircraft, and as the pilot turned to the left to park the plane, we saw a large group resembling a welcoming committee come into view. There must have been twenty to thirty people standing in formation, almost like they were posing for a group photo. Behind them was a small, dilapidated building that must have been the terminal building.

Maybe it was my naivety, but I didn't know if the villagers would be wearing clothes or not, though I should have known better. The people were all fully clothed, and their very dark complexions were devoid of smiles. The initial looks of intimidation from our vantage inside the aircraft made me reassure myself that headhunting had died out about ninety-five years earlier. I knew they weren't looking for a couple of white heads to harvest, but my mind did wander a little bit at that point. This was our first venture into an area that was normally only viewed in the pages of *National Geographic*. I truly didn't know what to expect from the villagers as we disembarked the airplane.

We exited the plane before the Australian couple that we had spoken to in the domestic terminal. In the sea of dark-complected faces before us, one individual stepped out from the group and approached us. "Uepi, are you going to Uepi?"

"Yes, we are going to Uepi," I said with a sigh of relief, knowing that the Solomon Airlines ticket agent had been correct in that someone would meet us at Ramata. The Australian couple from the plane seemed to know the gentleman and were excited to see him. I couldn't tell if he truly remembered them or not. His English, through a thick Solomon Islands accent, wasn't easy to decipher.

Only four of us got off the eighteen-seat plane at Ramata. I made sure our luggage got off the airplane before it took off to who knew where. We waited about ten minutes to see the plane safely take off. After the plane left the runway and veered off to the right, the gentleman from Uepi started to pick up some luggage and walk down the hill to the right of the terminal building. We quickly followed so as to not be left behind in this wild foreign land.

The earth beneath my feet was a deep, dark red interspersed with chunks of coral that had seemingly been smoothed over by bare feet traversing this area for many years. Instantly, I learned that suitcase wheels were never designed to go off a sidewalk for the most part. My bag wanted to twist and turn, and I struggled to keep it directly behind me without twisting too far right or left. The next thing I noticed, my suitcase levitated off the ground, and I turned around to see a beautiful cadre of children who were smiling at me while they helped carry my suitcase. I thanked them for the help, and they continued to smile and giggle at the funny white people with all the stuff.

The trail took us through some gardens and past a few houses that didn't look good compared to western standards. They were raised well off the ground and had partial thatch and wood walls with open windows and thatch roofs. The ground was damp and the trail slick. I was glad I had the local welcome wagon acting as a good rudder for my heavy suitcase. I knew it would have been quite the hit for the kids had I slipped and gone down the hill on my backside. Suzanne took some photos at this point, helping to solidify some great memories of our initial arrival to the Marovo Lagoon.

The trail abruptly ended at the bottom of the hill. Two boats were parked alongside a homemade rock jetty that was only about fifteen feet long. The boat driver from Uepi started to put the luggage in one of the boats. I thanked the children for helping to carry the bags, and Suzanne showed them their photos on the camera. They were giddy with excitement after seeing their pictures, and before long, a few of them started to climb a big tree overhanging the jetty. They climbed higher and higher with ease. As we pulled away in the boat, they were up in the canopy, shaking the limbs with grand smiles and deliberate waves. Wow, what a first experience with the local people. They were delightful, and all it seemed to take to break the tough-looking facades was a simple smile.

Mainly the heat, but also some of the humidity, seemed to melt away as we scooted down the lagoon at probably twenty-five knots. On our left were the outer barrier islands of the lagoon, and on our right, the long and mountainous island of New Georgia. Logging scars could be seen all over this northwestern portion of New Georgia. The barrier islands, from what we could see, didn't seem to have many man-made scars, or if they did, the forests hid the evidence pretty well.

Other than the surprisingly pleasant hum of a Honda four-stroke motor, all five of us in the boat passed the ninety-minute ride to Uepi without much conversation. By the end of the boat ride, the sun was getting very low on the horizon. As we neared Uepi, the lagoon opened up to its widest point. It was a gorgeous area, and the sunset over New Georgia was most memorable.

The cabins of Uepi Island Resort were in plain view off to our left as we continued around the island. We turned left into a channel, made obvious by red and green maritime markers. Another thirty seconds, and a small wooden dock came into view. Two people were standing there, seemingly prepared to greet us. The woman was tall, with long blonde hair, and the man was just as tall with short red hair.

The driver pulled the boat up to the dock like he had done it a thousand times. The woman on the dock welcomed us to Uepi Island Resort and told us to get off the boat and leave our luggage, as it would be transferred directly to our cabins.

Standing on the welcome dock, or jetty, as they call it, I looked over the edge briefly in sheer amazement with the life I saw under the surface. It was getting dark, but I could easily tell the water was crystal clear, and I noticed a black-tipped reef shark swim by the jetty. Directly below the shark, in about six feet of water, were several beautiful giant clams.

Introductions were made before we left the jetty. The couple who greeted us were named Ian and Gayle, and the couple who we had been basically traveling with from Brisbane were Dave and Jo. I realized we should have introduced ourselves earlier, as it had started to get awkward, looking at one another without speaking on the ninety-minute boat ride.

The tropical nature of the island was smack-dab in front of us as we walked from the welcome jetty to the dining hall-bar area. Tree trunks and branches were covered in orchids, some blooming while others simply hugged their host trees, waiting for the opportune time to send out stalks of flowers. To our left was a volleyball court that was empty at the time, as it was getting close to dark. Prior to reaching the steps to the dining hall, I noticed several rainforest plants in various pots near the steps. Two of the planters were old bombs from World War II. It was evident we were in a place that saw major battles during the war in the Pacific.

Gayle had us sit in the chairs to listen to the welcome speech. She clearly outlined various things about the resort that we needed to know. We each received a welcome drink, cold and delicious. It must have been a concoction of banana, papaya, and something else I couldn't figure out. I could have had three more of those drinks, they were so good. Since I was in vacation mode, it even crossed my mind that the welcome drink would be fantastic with a shot of vodka. Patience, I reminded myself, there would be plenty of time on this trip to enjoy more drinks.

We didn't have long to settle in to our cabin, which was at the far end of the developed area of the island. We needed to get ready to return to the main house, as they referred to it, for dinner. On the menu for dinner was someone who was large and formerly in charge of his/her subsurface mangrove lair. As we approached the dinner seafood buffet, we beheld massive mud crab bodies and claws. The trip was going just fine at this point. Suzanne was first in line and picked the largest mud crab claw off of the plate. She held it up to her hand to compare the size; the crab claw was unbelievably larger. If the resort was going to serve this every night, we might not leave this place.

Along with the mud crab were battered fish, or batta fish, as was written on the menu board. A pasta dish and some fish in a banana leaf also adorned the table. Freshly barbecued chicken was there to complete the surf-and-turf offering. I'll use the term "barbecued" loosely, as most of the time, Australians do not actually barbecue their meat over a flame. They typically have a metal flat-top skillet on top of a grill and throw some oil on the skillet, actually frying the food, not barbecuing or grilling it. I mention Australians because Uepi was owned and managed by Australians. It was obvious, however, that the majority of the workers at the resort were local Solomon Islanders.

The dinner was fantastic. We got to know Dave and Jo a little better. Dave worked selling steel in Brisbane, and Jo was in the financial industry. They were a delightful couple and had been to Uepi once before. After a couple of cocktails, we all loosened up, and they shared their first Solomon Islands experience with us. Dave and Jo were avid divers. They had been diving all over the east coast of Australia but had never traveled outside of the country prior to their first trip to the Solomons a year or two before. Incredibly, they had won their first trip to Uepi through a contest from an Australian dive magazine. Their story was full of laughs, and it was a great end to the evening.

After dinner and hearing Dave and Jo's tale, Suzanne and I navigated our way down the path to our cabin. The night sky was alive with a variety of bats, big and small. The sounds of the forest that night were new to me, but not intriguing enough to prevent my eyes from closing for the evening.

CHAPTER

3

*W*aking up to the splendor and awe of the Marovo Lagoon was surreal. The crystal water gently lapped the beach in front of our cabin. The forested islands dotted the lagoon like green puffballs on a turquoise carpet. As far as the eye could see, nothing but true paradise was visible. From our cabin, we were looking across the widest part of the lagoon. Two main islands interrupted the horizon. On the right was New Georgia, and the left, Vangunu. The mountains on Vangunu were striking, looking like the remnant of a massive volcano. Too many islands to count filled our field of view.

All the cabins at the resort faced the Marovo Lagoon. A narrow beach of white sand in front of the cabins sloped gently into shallow water. I could have walked close to one hundred yards before the water was over my head. Not so on the other side of the island, which faces the Slot, as it's called. Along there, from one step off the shore, the water can be as deep as 600 to 1,000 feet. It was the deepwater upwelling that brought nutrients and sea life to the shores of Uepi. The Slot is the name given to the long channel that runs between several major islands in the country. The Slot was the passage used by Japanese and American ships in World War II. Hundreds of ships lay on the bottom of the slot from the fierce battles that took place.

Our first dives at Uepi were incredible. In hindsight, I'm not sure if engaging in our first real scuba diving experience at Uepi Island Resort was a smart thing. I'm sure every dive site around the world has its own selling points, but Uepi has the complete package. It's one of the best spots on Earth. It took us only a couple of dives to realize that it might all be downhill from Uepi.

Dinner blew us away for the second night in a row. We enjoyed more conversation with Dave and Jo. They gave us some pointers on diving, which really helped. They seemed like seals in the water. Their movements were effortless, and they didn't seem to struggle at all.

That evening, the news came out that Suzanne was a doctor. In contrast to the glamour and respect that doctors often receive in conversation, I received the usual laughs when I announced that I was currently a domestic stallion. Normally, people either exhibit signs of envy or look down their noses at me as an inferior male who is not able to be the breadwinner in the family. The crowd this night seemed to show some envy, which always made me feel better than the alternative.

The next day, Suzanne and I were sitting on the deck, enjoying our lunch of breaded wahoo sandwiches, which had been delivered to our cabin. The crystal-blue waters of the lagoon contained the most beautiful colors my eyes had ever seen.

"Hello … Suzanne, Allan?" Gayle said as she walked up the path toward our cabin.

"Hey, Gayle. What's going on?" I replied.

"Suzanne, I know you are on holidays, and I don't want to disturb you."

"That's okay. … What, Gayle?" Suzanne inquired.

"There's no doctor in the lagoon, and we have two workers who are feeling very ill. Would you be willing to see them for a few minutes?"

"Sure, no problem. I don't have a stethoscope or anything else, but I'd be happy to sit down with them."

"Thank you very much! Most doctors who come here don't want to be bothered, so this means a lot to us that you are willing to talk to these two."

As Gayle walked away, her words struck a chord with me in a bad way. Why would doctors not be willing to talk to a couple of people during their holiday? At first I couldn't see how there were two sides to this coin. How could someone not help if asked to help? I also knew how hard Suzanne worked and the tremendous weight that was on her shoulders every day.

For me, the question Gayle posed would have triggered a mental tug-of-war. Do we turn our backs on those in need so our batteries can be completely recharged, or bend just a little to help someone who doesn't have a good alternative for medical care? I could see both sides of the argument, but one side was definitely winning in my mind. It was easier for me because I hadn't gone to medical school. My place was not to encourage Suzanne one way or another. At the end of the day, it was her vacation, and she had earned the money so we could get to Uepi. I needed to be comfortable with her decision either way.

The resort typically offers two scuba dives a day. After the second dive that afternoon, Suzanne sat down with the two workers separately on the deck of our cabin. I made myself scarce for about an hour while she plied her trade.

After exploring the island for a while, I figured Suzanne must have had enough time to examine the two workers. Strolling back to our cabin gave me the opportunity to look at all the different orchids lining the pathway. There were all shapes and sizes to behold. One had long petals with brown splotches. It made me think of a giraffe, at closer inspection. The folks at Uepi had transplanted orchids from various places to the pathway. They had cut posts out of palm trees and lined them up along both sides. At least four or five species were in bloom on the walk from the boat jetty.

I passed the second patient on the trail after she had left our cabin. As I approached the cabin, Suzanne was sitting on the deck in a plastic chair. "How was it?" I asked.

Suzanne looked at me with a sense of gratification and satisfaction. She obviously had done the right thing in agreeing to see the two patients. "It was really good. It's different when you don't have any tools to do a thorough physical exam."

"A stethoscope would have been nice, huh?"

"Yeah, but I think I figured out what their problems are. The first has a bleeding ulcer."

"What are the chances? That's right up your alley. If they only knew that they had their own gastroenterologist here at Uepi."

"Well, you are going to have to contribute to the treatment. I need your PPI to treat the bleeding ulcer."

PPI stands for proton pump inhibitor. It's a class of medicine designed to stop the stomach from producing acid, then allow the stomach to heal itself from ulcers and erosions. An overwhelming urge to give whatever I could to help this individual came over me. I had so much, and physically, I felt so good that at that moment, I would have offered all my clothes, my camera, my toothbrush, and everything else I had with me if it would have helped. "Take it, give it to them. My reflux will be fine for a week without it. What's the other person have?"

"She has a urinary tract infection. I'm going to give her the ciprofloxacin that we brought for traveler's diarrhea."

"Great, do it!"

"Allan, that was a really special interaction. That right there … was why I went into medicine. It was just me and the patient. There was no HIPAA or insurance paperwork to wade through. I didn't have anything but a conversation, my hands, and knowledge to figure out what their problem was. That was the pure doctor-and-patient relationship I learned about in medical school and up until now had been unable to find."

"Did you like it?"

"It was fantastic! That was the essence of why I went into medicine, right there."

That day, I witnessed a side of Suzanne I hadn't seen since we had been married four years earlier. She was a very caring doctor and probably the most in-demand gastroenterologist in Salt Lake City. I saw an altruistic approach in her to these two patients that seemed to reach philanthropic status in my mind. The patient consulations had passed quickly, but the depth of gratification she had received from the consultations would last her quite a while.

Dinner that evening was just as awesome as the previous two nights, but something was different. Before the menu was read aloud by the kitchen staff, they brought out several plates of fresh yellowfin tuna sashimi. I had enjoyed different types of sushi in the States, but nearly all sushi in the United States is previously frozen before it's served in a restaurant, to help minimize the risk of parasite infections. The tuna before us was straight out of the ocean, and even though there was a slight risk of parasites, we couldn't stop eating the sashimi. The juice of the fresh-squeezed limes, picked off the trees at Uepi, helped to partially cook the fish. To finish the proper preparation technique, we mixed some soy sauce and real wasabi together on the plate. It was maybe the best tasting seafood I had ever put in my mouth, it was so smooth and delicate. I could have devoured all the sashimi brought out from the kitchen that evening. One more way Uepi was ruining us forever.

Gayle and Ian sat near us, and they immediately thanked Suzanne for seeing the patients. The conversation then gravitated toward the health care situation in the Marovo Lagoon. Suzanne questioned why there wasn't a doctor in the lagoon.

The hospital at Seghe, the village surrounding the airstrip, had been built in 2000 and had yet to receive a permanent posting of a physician from the government. The only daily personnel at the hospital were a few nurses and a couple of malaria technicians. Gayle wasn't sure how large of a population relied on the facility for their health care needs. She didn't know a lot about the facility because she and Ian were filling in for the resort's full-time managers, Jill and Grant. Unfortunately, Jill and Grant were not there during our stay, so we didn't get all the answers we were after.

The situation at the hospital, both known and unknown, piqued our curiosity. We inquired whether we could see the hospital before our departure. Gayle assured us that wouldn't be a problem, so we planned to leave thirty minutes early for a quick tour of the facility on our way to the airport.

We had only one more day to enjoy with Dave and Jo. They were leaving the next day for Gizo, another island in the Solomon Islands, to dive some shipwrecks and see some new underwater sites. We had really enjoyed our time together and vowed to stay in touch. Suzanne and I had a love affair with Australia, so the chances of seeing this couple again were good.

The remainder of our stay at Uepi was surreal. We had never visited such a paradise through all our travels around the world, but we knew that all the joys of Uepi had to come to an end at some point. Without having quite perfected how to make time stop, we had to leave and head back to the States. We left our bags on the deck of our cabin and headed down the trail one last time for breakfast.

The usual suspects were singing loud in the rainforest canopy. The brilliant Cardinal Lorikeets were a sight for sore eyes but could be a little hard on the tympanic membranes. We heard the loud wing beats of a Blythe's hornbill, a prehistoric-looking bird, but never actually spotted the bird. The beautiful white-and-blue beach kingfisher could sometimes be spotted perched on branches overhanging the water. The one bird we could count on hearing and seeing every day at Uepi was Willy Wagtail. The bird field guide actually listed the bird's name as willy wagtail, part of the fantail family. I viewed Willy as the ambassador of Uepi, as the bird helped us get out of bed in the morning with his/her melodious song, a catchy tune. Then, Willy would always be along the pathway, grabbing insects and wagging its tail back and forth in a very exaggerated motion. Whoever gave willy wagtail its name had a sense of humor but was also very observant.

The breakfast spread of fresh fruits was in full splendor that morning. The pineapple was one of the highlights for me. It was so good, it should have come with a warning label. Another fruit in the spread was papaya, or paw paw, as they called it. Although the fruit is very attractive, Suzanne and I didn't acquire the taste for it. The flavor and texture combination was a turn-off for us. The massive jack fruit, on the other hand, made me feel like I was eating candy. Why couldn't apples be that inviting to the palette? The jack fruit was almost too candy-like to indulge in too voraciously. The small bananas or plantains (I was never sure which they were) were half the size of the bananas we buy in the States, but they had so much more flavor than our bananas. There were evidently more than a dozen varieties of bananas in the area. I'm not sure it would have the allure of wine tasting in Sonoma, but maybe the Solomon Islands could market executive or boutique banana tastings at private leaf huts with fresh coconut water in between tastings to cleanse the palette. The idea probably wouldn't go far.

During breakfast, Gayle told us she was going to accompany us to the hospital because she had yet to tour the facility. As we stood on the welcome jetty after breakfast, the sharks slowly swam around and under our feet.

They swam away as the transfer boat approached and tied up to the jetty. Suzanne and I said good-bye to Ian and a couple of other members of the staff who had come down to wish us farewell. Oh, why did we have to leave paradise?

4

*S*truggle was a good word to describe the difficultly I had in watching the pristine waters and swaying palm trees of Uepi Island slowly fade away. Our experience in the Marovo Lagoon had been fabulous, and my stock had gone up with Suzanne in terms of her trusting me to find cool places to travel. I reflected on this idea on the peaceful twenty-minute ride across the lagoon to Seghe.

The warm, humid air in my face engendered a feeling of re-creation and relaxation within. The water was so clear, I could watch coral reef structures whiz by underneath the boat. Occasionally, I'd see a good-sized fish dart away to avoid the speeding vessel. Ten minutes from Seghe, we passed a couple of small villages off our starboard side. Thin plumes of smoke rose through the tree canopy in places. In the distance, we could barely make out a woman washing clothes near the water's edge. Children splashed in the water nearby. It was a simple way of life, yet very distant in many ways from our lives in the United States.

Before reaching Seghe, we passed Patutiva, Seghe's closest neighbor. The village was on a small peninsula that stuck out of Vangunu Island. Across the narrow body of water from Patutiva was Seghe, situated on the southeastern tip of New Georgia Island. Gayle mentioned to us that Patutiva was one of the largest villages in the lagoon, with close to one thousand inhabitants.

Shortly after passing Patutiva, the driver throttled back as we approached a wooden wharf along the shore. Beyond the wharf on the righthand side was a red wooden building with people sitting on a balcony. Behind the red building was a lighter-colored building that looked like it had been there for decades. Moss was growing over the roof, and the sides of the building were stained green and brown. It was not in pristine condition, to say the least.

We disembarked at the wharf and started to follow Gayle up the little hill as the driver reversed the boat and took our bags down to the airport. It was evident that the red building on our right was a little store of some sort. A woman was standing behind the counter, and I could see various merchandise stacked on shelves behind her.

The run-down-looking building had a sign on the front that indicated it was a library. The sign out front had obviously been there for a while, without much cleaning. It welcomed readers to Seghe Theological Seminary for the United Church of the Solomon Islands.

Suzanne and I followed Gayle to the left, and then we saw a concrete block building painted a light turquoise green. Two solar panels were on a post out front that had wires running into the roof. On the main wall above the panels was a sign that read, "Seghe Hospital."

The front right portion of the hospital had an overhanging eave supported by several steel posts. As we stepped onto the concrete pad, we saw a long wooden bench outside of a door. The words on the door indicated that the room was the outpatient clinic. Gayle led the way as we walked inside. There were a couple of nurses milling about in white uniforms. Gayle told the nurses that Suzanne was a doctor and that we were interested in touring the hospital. The nurse told Gayle to feel free to walk around the facility. We did our best to understand what we were seeing without having a formal guided tour of the facility.

Florescent light fixtures dotted the ceiling, but none of the lights were on. Several of the light bulbs had mud daubers' nests on them. The linoleum floors had not been thoroughly cleaned in some time. There was mud on the floors, and the remnants of betel-nut spit could be seen in some areas. It looked like the two solar panels in front of the hospital were powering the radio located next to the outpatient clinic table.

The counters in the outpatient area were anything but clean. Dirty instruments lay around, both in and out of the sink. Every surface looked like it needed severe and thorough disinfecting. The walls were dingy, and the corners of the walls were disgustingly dark from being rubbed up against and seemingly never cleaned.

We walked back out of the outpatient area and entered the open-air wait-ing room, which had a roof over it. The area connected to a hallway that held some offices and a room with a dental chair. In the corner of the wait-ing room was a wooden sliding window that read, "Malaria, Knock and Wait"—the door to the malaria lab. Inside the lab sat one of the malaria technicians. The windows in the lab, as throughout the hospital, were devoid of screens. The technician had what looked like a decent micro-scope on the counter. The scope was attached to a car battery below his feet. The battery was connected to two other small solar panels positioned outside of the lab.

Continuing down the back hall, we saw the dental chair, which didn't actu-ally look too bad. The room it was in seemed to be lacking any dental tools or other things one would expect to see in a dentist's office, however.

One door beyond the head nurse's office was a staff toilet for men. It was in horrendous condition, and the smell was almost unbearable. Spider webs, mud dauber nests, dirt, urine, probably feces, and water were all over the ceiling, walls, and floor. I couldn't even figure out where one would begin cleaning the bathroom to make it respectable. I was glad none of the lights were on, as the room would have been that much scarier to see in good light.

Turning right out of the hallway led us into another covered open-air path-way. This path led between two ward buildings. On the left was the main ward, and on the right, the maternity ward. Alongside the pathway, in the grass, were all sorts of medical-waste items. It was not piled high, but used gauze, food waste, trash, and other items were strewn about.

Approaching the main ward, we saw a chicken walk into the maternity ward. I don't think it takes an MD to come to the conclusion that you don't want poultry mixing with mothers delivering babies. Shocked would have been a mild depiction of my horror.

The condition in the main ward was one of pure despair. The beds caught my immediate attention. The frames were completely rusted and looked like they were from WWII. After seeing a few of the mattresses, I almost forgot how bad the frames looked. Some of them were open-cell yellow foam that had all sorts of bodily fluid stains covering them. In addition to being stained, they were picked apart and had big holes and indentations in various places. Suzanne said she couldn't imagine what bugs were growing on those mattresses as a result of years of bodily fluids soaking into the foam. The mattresses were, without a doubt, a pathogen breeding ground. They were likely making people more sick than when they arrived at the hospital.

At the end of a few of the beds were tall sticks jammed into the frames. These sticks had forks at the top. They were obviously being used as IV poles. Some of the beds had ratty-looking mosquito nets draped over them, but the more I thought about it, the more I thought how crazy it was to have a hospital in a malaria hot zone with no screens on the windows. At some point, someone or some organization had obviously spent some time and money to build the facility but hadn't thought to include screens on the windows.

The patient bathrooms at the end of the ward were as bad as the men's staff toilet. It was painful to just look at it without having to physically use it. I couldn't get out of the main ward fast enough. I found myself holding my breath and trying not to smell the air in general. I turned on self-preservation mode, and I was only touring the facility. Thankfully, I was not a patient.

We walked fifteen feet across a walkway to the maternity ward. Along the walkway were a couple of buckets of discarded hospital waste. I saw fluids that I could not and did not want to identify. There were plenty of bandages and possibly human excrement in the buckets.

The table in the delivery room had a sobering look to it. It was a large rectangle of solid stainless steel. The table had a crank on the side that could make the center of the table rise up so fluids would not pool, thus running off the sides of the table. Not only did it resemble something out of a meat packing plant, but the table's legs were not made out of stainless steel. They were rusting to pieces because of all of the birthing fluids that had run down them over the years.

At this point, I wanted the tour to be over. I was disturbed and needed to leave. Fortunately, we had seen everything. We walked past the outpatient clinic and thanked the nurses for allowing us to see the hospital. I don't remember a lot about the walk to the airport, other than that there wasn't a lot of conversation between Gayle, Suzanne, and me.

We passed a couple of small schools before we came to the main wharf at Seghe. There was a small market in progress, with people selling fruits and vegetables. People smiled and looked at us. I didn't know how often white people strolled through Seghe.

Inside the dank terminal building, Suzanne and I weighed ourselves and our luggage on another antiquated scale. Gayle sat with us as we waited for the airplane. The still, humid conditions were not comfortable. A half hour later, the relative quiet of the area was broken by the distinctive high-pitched wine of the Twin Otter's engines alerting us to its arrival. The pilot circled the airstrip once before making his final approach.

The airstrip at Seghe had been surreptitiously constructed in a week by the US Navy Seabees during WWII. It had lasted for more than sixty years by the time we were about to fly out. We had discovered that the reason we hadn't been able to land at Seghe on our arrival was because over time, a low spot had developed at one end of the runway. When it rained heavily, a large puddle formed, which didn't allow the planes to safely take off or land. Fortunately for us, it had been dry for the past few days.

The Twin Otter bounced a couple of times while touching down, and then the pilot hit the brakes to gain control. The aircraft pulled up in front of the terminal shack and proceeded to turn the near engine off while the far engine kept running. Suzanne and I hugged Gayle and said our good-byes as a much skinnier pilot walked off the plane for an inspection. We climbed through the small door and waved good-bye to Gayle.

What happened next had never before happened in my life and has never happened since. Suzanne and I looked at one another and had a mutual understanding and feeling that we were being called into action right at that very moment. It was without a doubt a divine lightning bolt coming down from heaven to give us direction. The divine calling was unmistakable. We were the lightning rods, and our feet were planted firmly on the ground at Seghe. We both shared Christian faith, but this moment made it more real than ever. It was as if we were being given explicit instructions. We looked at one another, and I said, "We have to do something about the hospital." Without any hesitation, Suzanne agreed.

The plane sped down the runway. Suzanne and I took off with a new purpose in life. We knew we were going to act, but we weren't sure about how to take the next step.

CHAPTER

5

*S*urplus energy was flowing out of our bodies upon returning home. The stories we told of our trip kept friends and family engaged for quite some time. Not only had the Australian portion of the trip been a spicy adventure, including a 4x4 adventure through the Australian rainforest, but we had found something much bigger than the two of us in the Solomon Islands. This newfound calling required immediate action. The drive propelling me forward was unprecedented in my life. A force beyond my control was directing us back to the Solomon Islands.

Our initial plan, in response to our experience at Seghe, was to help alleviate the current dearth of medical care. Our return trip would allow Suzanne to be a doctor and to treat patients who needed to be seen. Our initial plan was a knee-jerk reaction to what we had seen over there, but it was also somewhat logical. Although we wanted to do more, we couldn't do much more right away. We needed to gather more information about the hospital before we could make improvements. Information such as who owned the facility and who was accountable for the day-to-day management were critical pieces of the puzzle. Before we could begin to know what was truly needed to increase the level of cleanliness and healthcare options of the hospital, we had to have the basics.

We didn't know what we were getting ourselves into. We'd never done anything like this. I had an overwhelming desire to make some sort of positive change at Seghe Hospital. My logistical side switched into high gear. Only a few weeks after we got home, I looked at flights for the next trip to the Marovo Lagoon. We were scheduled to depart nearly twelve months after our return from our first visit.

The task of collecting medical supplies and medicines began almost immediately after we arrived home. Suzanne was able to get sample medications from her office, other offices, and some drug representatives. A major unknown facing us was what treasures existed or didn't exist in the pharmacy at Seghe Hospital. Without knowing the drug inventory, we were forced to cover a lot of bases. An online information search of the medical scene in the Solomon Islands yielded very little information. The Centers for Disease Control and World Health Organization had information that pertained to malaria, but anything more than that was unavailable. The Solomon Islands Ministry of Health (MOH) website had not been updated in quite some time and offered very little statistical information. It seemed like a medical information vacuum had enveloped the country. I didn't know if this was a casualty of the civil war or just how things were in a developing country.

I was able to find an e-mail address for one of the health ministers in Honiara. I contacted him to figure out what steps Suzanne needed to take to legally practice medicine in the country. The reply didn't take long, and I was glad to have made an initial contact with the MOH. The health minister's reply stated that Suzanne needed to supply her curriculum vitae, current medical license, and certification of a clean criminal record. I tracked down these items in short order and sent them off to my contact at the MOH. Unfortunately, the quick response to my first e-mail had conditioned me to expect a quick response this time. What I wasn't expecting was to never hear back from my contact. My repeated tries were met with no returned e-mails. What was going on over there?

While I waited for the reply that would never materialize, I discovered a website created by a Swiss surgeon who had helped to create the surgery program in the Solomon Islands. The website provided information for medical and surgical residents who were planning to do a rotation at the National Referral Hospital (NRH) in Honiara. One important piece of information suggested that applicants not fret if they didn't hear back from the MOH regarding credentialing approval. The site instructed the incoming doctors to notify immigrations and customs officials upon their entry into Honiara that the paperwork was waiting for them at the MOH. Armed with that information, I felt a little better about not receiving a reply from the MOH, though it would have been nice to have received word that Suzanne would in fact be practicing medicine legally.

The time between the two trips passed quickly. As we neared our return trip to the Solomons, our luggage ensemble consisted of two large roller suitcases. One of our suitcases was completely full of medicines and supplies. I was rather nervous with the idea of transporting a suitcase full of pills. All one had to do was shake the bag a little and it sounded like it was full of small candies.

Before we could even try to enter the Solomon Islands with medicines, we first had to get them into Australia. Australia's customs website was thorough in explaining what was allowed and what was prohibited. The website had an extensive list of prohibited medicines; fortunately, we didn't have any of those items. Australia seemed to be concerned mainly with anabolic steroids, not antibiotics. Nevertheless, I created an inventory list of what we were carrying with us so we didn't look completely like drug mules. We didn't have anything to hide, but I didn't know what to expect after notifying the customs officials of the small pharmacy in our luggage. We had two countries through which we had to run the customs gauntlet.

At the time, Suzanne and I were attending a Presbyterian church in Salt Lake City. We had mentioned to several people at church that we were heading back to the Solomons. A couple of days before we left, the prayer team at church asked us to come to the Wednesday-night prayer meeting so they could pray over us. At the meeting, I expressed concerns about traveling with all the medicines. I didn't want any of the medicines to be taken from us, and I didn't want to get in trouble for having the medicines, either. Suzanne also expressed concerns about having to potentially deal with a wide range of medical issues that she either hadn't ever encountered or hadn't encountered in quite a while. The trip was rife with uncertainty, and it was nice to share our feelings about those uncertainties with friends at church. My faith was strong, but I hadn't conquered my issues with worry, either. I knew the big picture was out of my hands, but I knew I had to be proactive and on guard as well.

We left the prayer meeting with a feeling of reassurance that one way or another, everything was going to work out. It was comforting, knowing that a group of people in Salt Lake City were thinking about us. Their prayers for our safety and for our effectiveness in easing some of the suffering at Seghe Hospital were very important to us.

As the massive 747-400 touched down at Brisbane International a couple of days later, my nerves began to kick in. I didn't know what to expect at customs. We filled out the immigration card and checked "yes" for the box that denoted we were carrying medicines that may be prohibited. I had learned from traveling internationally that as long as you declare the item and it is not against the law, customs has a harder time legally taking it from you. We also showed, by checking the box, that we were open to inspection and were not trying to hide anything from the authorities. I hoped it would immediately start us off on the right footing with customs officials.

We gathered our backpacks from the overhead bins. Exiting the plane under the foggy spell of a fourteen-hour flight was always welcome yet strange. I still couldn't believe the airplane could stay in the air for fourteen hours. It was surely a feat of modern engineering.

The immigration stop was first. Those folks allow you or deny you legal access into the country. After that point, if we hadn't had any luggage, we would have been free to walk out the door and enjoy Australia. Because we did have luggage, it was going to be x-rayed and potentially searched. Most pieces of luggage were being x-rayed coming into Australia. The Australian customs program had evolved to be a hyper-vigilant machine against the importation of exotic species and illegal goods.

We waited for our bags to come off the carousel. I watched the customs area as one bag after another entered the x-ray machine. Unfortunately, my mind often went to extremes. I thought that either we were going to get through there without too much fanfare or we were going to be sleeping in a federal jail cell that evening. I tried to work on a more middle-of-the-road approach to emotional issues, but sometimes it just didn't pan out for me.

With two roller suitcases in tow and two backpacks strapped to our backs, Suzanne and I got in the customs line. We had our cards out to give to the pre-card screener. This person was telling travelers where to take their bags. My heart was pounding as we approached her station. We needed to remain calm, and I hoped my nerves weren't going to indicate the need for a severe dog-sniffing and follow-up cavity search. One thing was for sure, customs officials around the world were hired to be as deadpan as possible. The woman we were about to encounter fit the bill. She didn't crack a smile with anyone in front of us. I was too nervous to try to turn on the charm, so I just handed her our cards with a smile.

"What do you have today?" she asked as she looked at our cards.

I took the lead and replied, "Medicines for the Solomon Islands. We are going there tomorrow on a medical trip."

"Go straight ahead to x-ray line number four."

We walked ahead, about to venture into one of the mazes of moveable partitions, but before we could make the first turn, a woman in a supervisor's uniform appeared out of nowhere. She stopped us and put her hand out for our cards. "What are you declaring?" she asked.

"Medicines that we are taking to the Solomon Islands tomorrow on a medical tour," I responded.

She kept the cards in her hand and turned around to the pole and opened the retractable belt barrier, pulling off the clasp that was holding the strap to the pole. "You are alright. Go ahead and exit."

"Thank you," I said normally. I wanted to jump for joy and yell to the entire airport, "Yes, yes, we made it through with all of our drugs!" Obviously, that would have been counterproductive. I was truly in awe at what had just happened. Where had that woman come from? What were the chances that she would stop us and tell us to walk through without being x-rayed? I was dumbfounded. Everyone was being x-rayed … except us. The hair was standing up on the back of my neck as we walked out. Prayers had been answered! I couldn't stop saying, "Thank you, Lord, thank you, Lord," under my breath.

As we exited customs into the passenger reception area, two big smiles awaited us. Dave and Jo were standing along the railing as we came through the sliding glass doors. There were big hugs all around, as we were all so happy to see each other.

The drive to Dave and Jo's house was about forty-five minutes. They lived south of Brisbane in the Springfield area. It was a delightful spot, and their home was very nice. I'm not sure if it is one of the great mysteries of the world, but Suzanne and I can never figure out why we come off of a long flight without really moving much yet feeling so scummy. It had to do with the dryness, I'm sure. Inevitably, the first order of business for both of us was a shower to return to the land of the living.

Dave and Jo had two Staffordshire terriers that, upon first inspection, seemed like they might remove one of my legs. The little female, Verity, was outside the kitchen screen door, licking and licking and licking the screen. At the rate she was going, she might get through that screen before I could escape to safety. After a jumpy licking introduction, Verity and I were buds. Verity and her brother, Costa, ran around the backyard at warp speed, chasing a rugby football. Watching Costa grab the ball and shake it viciously in his powerful jaws was somewhat troubling. I couldn't imagine being an intruder in their backyard. A burglar might be able to get out of the yard, but not with both calf muscles intact.

I had a challenge for Dave during our visit. We both enjoyed table tennis, and while we had been at Uepi, Dave had destroyed me. Dave was definitely a better player, because he had been able to overcome the fact that the Uepi table was shorter and narrower than a regulation table. On this visit, Dave opened the door to their back shed to reveal a beautiful professional-grade table tennis table. It didn't take long before we were going at it! Dave was wiping the table with me. It wasn't pretty from my side of the table. I couldn't make excuses, but it wasn't easy trying to focus on that little white ball after fourteen hours on an airplane. I gave it my best shot, but Dave was the champion yet again. It drove me crazy to lose, but I lost to a great player, which was a slight consolation for my ego.

Dave and Jo had learned of our interest in bird watching when we'd met them at Uepi. Incidentally, "bird watching" to Australians means looking at women. Upon our arrival, they had a new pair of binoculars and a field guide for the birds of Australia. After I lost the second US–Australian Table Tennis Tournament, we headed out to Tamborine National Park for a day trip of hiking and birding.

Dave and Jo shared our excitement for getting back to Uepi. They were jealous that we were heading back, but they were only three and a half hours from Uepi, so they could make a visit much more easily than we could. Throughout the few days with them, we could not have had better hosts. They didn't let us pay for anything and went into the airport with us while we checked in to leave. At the top of the stairwell leading to security and customs, we said our good-byes and walked down the stairs. There were a couple of watery eyes in the bunch. It was a good feeling, knowing they would be there for us upon our return from the Solomons. Having a familiar face greet you halfway around the world is always welcome.

Part two of the drug mule-fueled nerves started to kick in for me as we boarded the plane to Honiara. One customs clearance was down, and a potentially more uncertain experience lay ahead. The immigration-customs forms we were given on the plane had a place for declaring medicines or prohibited items. I checked the boxes, and Suzanne and I signed the forms prior to landing. Hopefully, our signing the forms would prohibit any cavity searching since we had been honest, but that fear was probably just my tendency to jump to extremes.

The strip at Henderson Field wasn't the longest in the world, so when the pilot landed, he or she normally punched the brakes pretty hard and without delay. Because the strip had only one runway, the plane had to go all the way to the end to have room to turn around and slowly taxi back to the terminal.

Boom, the heat and humidity bat struck again as I walked off of the plane. They didn't have jet bridges in Honiara, so we exited down the moveable stairway that was bolted to the back of a truck. People stood on top of the terminal building on a large viewing platform. It must not have gotten old, watching a fast and loud jet aircraft land at the airport.

One thing different about landing in Honiara this time was that we were not greeted by the Australian Army. The only show of law enforcement on the tarmac included a couple of Caucasian police officers, likely part of the international police/stabilization force called RAMSI. The Regional Assistance Mission to the Solomon Islands had been in place since the civil war and comprised several countries throughout the South Pacific, including Australia, New Zealand, Fiji, and others. They were assisting in all areas of the government to help rebuild and stabilize various institutions that had lost their footing after the civil war. Visitors typically only identified the face of RAMSI with the police officers who carried guns. Guns had been taken away from the Solomon Island police officers after order had been restored post-civil war. Evidently, one of the factions fighting in the war had stormed a couple of police barracks and stolen all their weapons. As a result, the Solomon Islands government and RAMSI had collectively decided that the Solomon Islands police force should not have guns for the foreseeable future.

Suzanne and I made our way into the terminal and stood in line to clear immigration. The only difference between being here and being outside was that the sun was not beating down on us here. The air was just as hot and humid inside.

The power was on that day, and the luggage carousel worked without a hitch. Thankfully, the bags made it. Now it was go time again. My heart started to pound as we lined up in the "something to declare" line. One more checkpoint, and we would be home free.

The young Solomon Islands woman waved us ahead after her station became vacant. In typical Solomon Islands fashion, she said in a very soft, barely audible voice, "What do you have to declare?"

"We have medicines for the Seghe Hospital. My wife is a doctor, and we are going to the Marovo Lagoon to treat patients … at the Seghe Hospital."

She looked at us and then motioned to her supervisor to come over.

"Oh shit," were the first words that popped into my head … "not the supervisor." The guy walked over with a clipboard and looked at the young customs official. They communicated without really saying many words.

He pointed at the bags. "What do you have?"

"Medicines for the Seghe Hospital. My wife is a doctor, and we are here to treat patients in the Marovo."

"Do you have paperwork from the Ministry of Health to bring these medicines into the country?"

"The ministry told us the paperwork would be waiting for us in their offices."

The pause seemed like an hour. Did he feel the need to make a power play to prove he was a big man, as was the term in the Solomon Islands? I hoped he wasn't planning to use us as his stepping-stone to achieve his next promotion. Please just say something…

"Okay, go ahead," he said with a seemingly reluctant wave of his hand.

We had made it! In an instant, a flood of gratefulness and relief escaped my soul. Amazingly, no one in Australia or the Solomon Islands had wanted to see the medicines that we had declared. Had I been shaking the suitcase full of meds prior to meeting the customs officials, it may have turned out differently. I'm thankful that, yet again, prayers were answered.

On this trip, the Seghe airstrip was open. After a long day of traveling, the twenty-minute boat ride from Seghe to Uepi was a lot more enjoyable than the ninety-minute ride from Ramata to Uepi. Returning to a foreign place for the second time was exciting yet comforting because a lot of the unknown was eliminated.

The warm, humid air filling my lungs was a welcome contrast with the desiccating, recycled air on the jet. The complexity of the travel from Salt Lake to Uepi was serious, and I was truly thankful that we had arrived safely and unmolested by Australian and Solomon Islands customs officials.

Familiar faces were standing on the welcome jetty as we arrived at the resort. Gayle and Ian were still helping out with management duties at Uepi and were happy that we had returned. There was an additional person on the dock whom we did not know. She introduced herself as Jill. We had heard about Jill Kelly. She and her husband, Grant, were the full-time managers of the resort.

Sitting down at the main house, Suzanne and I sipped our delicious welcome drinks. Gayle ran through an abbreviated orientation because we had heard it less than a year earlier. A large, strapping man walked up on the deck of the main house and approached us. He introduced himself as Grant, Jill's husband. He was very cordial, but I could tell immediately he was a no-nonsense kind of guy.

Our goal was to visit Seghe Hospital for three days and a village for one day. We didn't want to bite off more than we could chew. All the weight was on Suzanne's shoulders, and I was there to be her support staff. The folks at Uepi were aware that our trip was more business than pleasure. The only uncertainty remaining was to figure out what days of the trip would be best to visit the hospital and the village.

We learned that the vast majority of Uepi's staff were from two villages, Chubikopi and Vakabo. Each village scattered throughout the lagoon was dominated by a specific Christian denomination. Uepi tended to employ people only from United Church of the Solomon Islands' villages, to which Chubikopi and Vakabo belonged. Seventh-day Adventist villages did not allow people to work on Saturdays; thus, Seventh-day Adventists were not suited to working at a resort where work is required over a seven-day shift.

Grant determined that we should visit the hospital on Wednesday, Thursday, and Friday. Grant and Jill had one of the staff members notify Chubikopi that we would be in that village on Saturday. Without much pre-trip communication with the hospital, the nurses were not aware that Suzanne was coming. We didn't want to step on toes, so we hoped they wouldn't mind us showing up to treat patients. The MOH had never responded to me when I had asked for verification of medical privileges, so I highly doubted that it had notified the staff at Seghe that a doctor was about to arrive.

We arrived at Uepi on a Monday, and the next day, we had time to do two dives. Like riding a bike, maintaining my buoyancy came back to me without too much tweaking. We still had a long way to go before we were pro divers, but our skill level seemed to be improving after our second dive of the day. Pinching myself wasn't enough to get it through my head that I was back in paradise after nearly a year in the Great Basin. The Marovo Lagoon was slowly taking a piece of my heart. I couldn't imagine a more incredible place on Earth.

On Tuesday night, Suzanne and I sorted the medicines and supplies we had brought. Hoping the hospital had dressings and general supplies, we had decided to fill our backpacks with some medicines and specialty supplies. We had a blood pressure cuff, a stethoscope, and a blood glucose monitor to test sugar levels. A urologist colleague of Suzanne's had given us a tube of urinalysis test strips that would likely come in handy. That was the extent of our diagnostic testing. Suzanne would have to rely on her clinical skills and medical knowledge to get her through the rest of it. She had brought a tropical medicine text with her. Neither of us knew what we would encounter from a medical perspective, but I knew without a doubt that I was traveling with the best doctor in the entire South Pacific region. That Suzanne had done her residency and gastroenterology fellowship at the University of Virginia wouldn't matter one bit to these people. Snobs in the United States might care about those things, but right now, the word "doctor" was all that mattered to the people Suzanne was about to see. These people didn't have the luxury of perusing airline magazine advertisements showcasing downright creepy photos of the "best" lips, nose or butt doctors in the United States. Thankfully, Suzanne did not need to advertise in Salt Lake, and the locals in the Marovo were about to advertise her presence without her even knowing it.

CHAPTER

6

*F*anfare was nonexistent as Suzanne and I walked into the hospital. There was no welcome committee with outstretched hands to shake. It didn't seem as though anyone cared that we were there. We entered the outpatient clinic with our backpacks on and with our hearts ready to serve. I knew it took a special type of person to work in a hospital. No other profession or vocation earned the amount of respect from me as people who worked in hospitals. I wasn't fond of hospitals and never had been. I chalked it up to some experiences I had when I was young, visiting family members in hospitals. I remember a lot of old people seemingly rotting away in hallways, and there was one scary woman who gave me the stink eye and mumbled some scary gibberish in my face. That had stayed with me, and I was still not comfortable being in a hospital. To be there for Suzanne, I had to put all those uneasy hospital feelings in the backseat. This wasn't about me. It was about how I could facilitate Suzanne treating people who may be dying or have traumatic wounds. I felt strangely calm entering the hospital. My nerves had gone away, and for the next few days, I would be a hospital volunteer and I wasn't going to let anyone else know any different. An incredible sense of peace coupled with the need to be a purposeful servant enveloped my heart and soul. I was ready.

Heads turned as we walked through the door. Two female nurses sat behind the triage table. A patient was in the process of being worked up. The nurses knew something was amiss. First, two white people had walked through the door, and second, Suzanne was wearing scrubs. We introduced ourselves and asked to speak with the head nurse. A few minutes later, a man walked into the clinic and introduced himself as Francis, the head nurse. Suzanne explained to him that we were there for three days to see patients. Francis had been unaware that we were coming, and we were not surprised. Fortunately, he spoke good English, as neither of us was proficient in Pidgin.

Francis asked Suzanne to have a look at some of the inpatients. The walkway outside the main ward had just as many unidentifiable waste items strewn about on our walk through this time as it had a year earlier. The lights were still covered in mud daubers, and the lights were still not on. I couldn't hear a generator running; thus, there was still no electricity.

The first patient Suzanne saw was a woman, brought to the hospital three days before with a couple of complaints. Her daughter, who was probably in her twenties, was sitting next to her on the bed. On the floor were all sorts of pots, dishes, and food items. It was evident that if a patient showed up at the hospital without a family member or advocate of some sort, they were not going to eat.

The woman lay on one of the disgusting yellow foam mattresses. A thin sheet was the only thing between her and a lot of badness festering in the foam. Francis presented the case to Suzanne. The woman complained of a problem with one of her eyes. Suzanne knew she couldn't do anything about that, but then Francis finished the story. Because the woman's eye had bothered her, she had missed a step while walking out of her house and had fallen. She was unable to walk due to a leg injury.

I was taking notes as Suzanne started to examine the patient. As she moved down the woman's body, Suzanne had a disturbed look on her face. I knew that look, and I knew we had a problem. Standing at the foot of the bed, I was unable to smell what Suzanne had wafting into her nostrils.

As the woman winced at Suzanne's touch, the tenderness of her leg was not in question. The woman was lying on her back, and a visual inspection did not reveal anything out of the ordinary. Where was the smell coming from? Suzanne asked Francis to help her roll the patient over on her side. Watching a doctor's face can tell you all you need to know about the severity of a situation. After seeing Suzanne's eyes open wide, I moved to my right to see what had her so concerned. The silver dollar-sized abscess on the back of the woman's thigh was the source of the smell.

We were looking at a fractured femur that had gotten infected and was draining out of a large wound. It was draining directly into the yellow foam mattress that we knew was a problem. Francis said he had been unaware of the wound. He was visibly embarrassed. This was atrocious because the woman had been in the bed for three days and no one had done a thorough exam on her to find this life-threatening wound.

Suzanne knew this was totally unacceptable care, but she was a visitor and wasn't going to let Francis have it, because the timing and circumstances weren't right. She reached straight for her antibiotic resource guide. She questioned Francis about the type of IV antibiotics available at the hospital. Her next question to Francis was about the availability of a medical evacuation because this woman had an excellent chance of losing her leg and a good chance of losing her life if they didn't get her to a surgeon immediately. Wow, this was quite an introduction to the medical scene at Seghe.

Francis explained that they would need to speak to the doctor in charge at the headquarters of the Western Province Health Service in Gizo. The MOH in Honiara was in charge of the over all health care picture in the country, but each province was given jurisdiction over health matters within its boundaries.

Determined to get this woman evacuated, Suzanne asked Francis to show her how to use the radio. He did the legwork to get the folks in Gizo on the line, and then Suzanne took over. "My name is Dr. Suzanne Daly, and I am a physician from the United States." I could tell from the doctor's voice when he answered that he knew he had a serious case to deal with. Suzanne made her case for the woman to be evacuated at the earliest opportunity. She pushed to have the Western Province Health Service pay for an airplane seat for the patient's husband as well. The woman definitely needed his support. After several minutes of Suzanne describing the situation, the head of the Western Province Health Service assured her that they would evacuate the woman on the next flight. It was a small victory, but the woman had a long way to go before she was out of the woods.

For the next step, Francis and Suzanne coordinated the administration of a full barrage of IV antibiotics. They needed all microscopic musclemen on deck to fight an epic battle if this woman had any chance at survival. It took well over an hour for them to assess and execute a plan for the first patient.

As we moved to the second patient, so did all the family members and children in the hospital. We seemed to be a novelty act, and obviously, they wanted to see what Suzanne was going to pull out of her hat next.

Obviously, there were no HIPAA laws in the Solomon Islands. Anyone was able to insert themselves into another person's medical care without cause for concern.

Still in the female section of the main ward, Suzanne and Francis addressed the next patient. She was a frail little lady who looked like she was in her early seventies. It was obvious that she'd had one of her legs amputated below the knee. Her primary reason for being in the hospital was a skin infection on her other leg. She and her family were pleasant to speak with. The patient wanted to go home. Suzanne was not satisfied with the short course of antibiotics that had been prescribed for the woman. She explained the importance of the patient staying in the hospital for two more days to fully eradicate the infection.

I stood in the only place that was out of the way—the foot of the bed. I was looking at the bottom of the woman's only foot. It was obvious to me that something was wrong with the tips of her toes. They had black circles on them, as if she had experienced frostbite. I let Suzanne finish and then asked her to ask the family about the black circles. Instantly, the woman's face changed from being happy to expressing some embarrassment or shame. She spoke very little English, so her son explained the situation to Suzanne. Her other leg had been amputated as a result of diabetes. Now she was beginning to lose feeling in her other leg and foot. Not looking Suzanne in the eye, the woman's son explained that a rat would come into her room at night and chew on her toes. Because the woman was losing feeling in her foot, she would not react in her sleep to shake the rats off. Suzanne didn't miss a beat; she told the son to wrap the woman's foot up at night so the rat could not get to her toes.

As we walked to the next patient, I had to confirm with Suzanne what I thought I had heard. There hadn't been anything lost in translation. The woman was slowly being eaten alive at night as she slept. That experience made me immediately thankful for what I had, and it also hardened me toward people back home who bitched and whined about the need for pain pills. Oh no, you had to wait forty-five minutes at the doctor's office. Poor baby! Right then, I knew the poor in the United States had it much better than the poor in the third world with regards to access to healthcare.

While assisting Suzanne, I began to think of what the hospital was really lacking, besides a doctor, of course. Francis told us that there was no money available for diesel fuel, and thus it became obvious why the generator was never running. Nearly $10 US dollars per gallon for diesel seemed crazy expensive; it was no wonder the lights were never on. No money for fuel had led to a downward spiral, negating other critical services at the hospital such as water, sanitation, and personal safety at night. I didn't need to be more than a domestic stallion to know that the hospital needed a reliable source of electricity.

While Suzanne discussed a couple of items with the nurses, I did a thorough accounting of all the light fixtures and air conditioners in the hospital. Ten dollars a gallon would require around $73,000 a year if the generator burned only twenty gallons a day. That was a lot of money. Entertaining a long-term fundraising scenario to support that kind of energy expenditure was pure folly. Obviously, there was no power grid at Seghe, so the hospital needed a power plant that didn't require any fuel inputs. Solar power was the first option that popped into my mind.

Before I started doing the "American power play," I needed to find out who was in charge of the hospital and have a discussion regarding a new electric system. That would have to wait, however, because it was nearly time for us to leave for the day.

Suzanne and I knew Gayle and Ian better than Jill and Grant, but Gayle and Ian weren't the primary decision makers at Uepi. My idea of installing a solar power system on the hospital didn't receive the warmest of receptions at Uepi. Jill and Grant were not opposed to the idea, but they were not rolling out the red carpet, either. They provided us with a little background information on the hospital. Nothing they shared seemed to be the smoking gun for why they were cold to the idea. I didn't consider that the fact that they didn't really know us probably played a big part in their hesitancy and tepid response.

Playing my cards at the most opportune time has not always been my strong point. Self-control had never been my best friend. I queried Grant on his thoughts about incorporating a wind turbine into a power system at Seghe. He explained that we were sitting smack-dab in the middle of the doldrums at eight degrees south of the equator. Although there were winds from time to time, reliable winds were not available. A solar/wind hybrid system often worked well for off-grid power applications in other parts of the world, but unfortunately, wind wasn't an option here.

I was in pure help mode. My mindset for the first time had really changed from looking out for me, me, me, to figuring out how I could help the people of the Marovo Lagoon. For some reason, I wanted to do anything and everything I could to help a community of people of whom I knew no one. Saving the world was not on my radar screen, and I did not think it was possible. We were sitting in an area with a tremendous need for health care, and Suzanne and I had the means, whether personally or with the help of friends, to follow through and change Seghe Hospital. We knew we'd be able to turn it into a facility that people would actually want to go to if they needed health care.

My brain started to jump to scenarios and outcomes for which I wasn't able to connect the dots. My focus was on figuring out a way to improve the hospital, and installing a solar power system seemed like a great first step. The end seemed perfect, but in reality, the means were unknown, and our only logistical connection thus far, Uepi Island Resort, didn't seem interested in helping.

*   *   *

We started day two at the hospital, and we were welcomed with a sight that didn't make Suzanne happy. The woman with the broken infected leg was still in her bed.

"Francis, why is this woman still here?" Suzanne probed with eyes of steel, intently focused on hearing a response that she could adequately accept. I doubted Solomon Islanders were aware of the stereotypical feistiness and fierceness innate within redheads.

"Too much rain yesterday; the plane couldn't land," he responded with the Solomon Islanders' customary lack of eye contact. His response seemed hollow, but it was probably more a function of "Solomon time" than actual lack of caring, or so we hoped. We were learning that things in the South Pacific didn't happen with much urgency, not even health care issues.

"What's the plan for getting her to Honiara?"

"If the plane comes today, she'll go. If not, she'll have to go to Ramata tomorrow and get the plane to Honiara."

I was hoping that wouldn't have to happen. Ramata was two hours from Seghe by boat. I couldn't imagine bouncing up and down on a boat for two hours with a broken and infected leg.

Suzanne reexamined the patient. As she sat, leaning over the patient, I could tell she wasn't happy about something. Her face was cold, yet I could sense anger brewing within her. At closer inspection, she had noticed that the leg's dressing had not been changed as she had asked. At this point, I was pretty sure Solomon Islanders were not aware of the sayings Americans had about redheads. I knew this redhead really well, and I was glad I was not the nurse who had not followed her orders. The tongue-lashing Suzanne gave Francis was more subdued than the one she would have given a nurse in America. She had said more than one time that the dressing needed to be changed every so many hours. Suzanne demanded accountability when she gave an order, and that was one of the reasons why she was so respected as a physician.

After the examination of the patient, we met Jimmy, a malaria tech, who showed us the malaria lab. Suzanne had little experience with malaria, so she wanted to learn as much as she could from Jimmy. A blood smear test for malaria was the only diagnostic test offered at the hospital. A patient suspected of having malaria would first have their finger pricked. The blood was smeared on a slide, and it was the patient's responsibility to walk the sample over to the lab and "knock and wait," as the sign read. The little wooden door slid open, and the tech took the slide from the patient and told the patient to wait. The tech added a fixing agent to the blood on the slide and then dried the slide. Then the slide was ready to be analyzed. The techs had a book next to the microscope that was open to a page full of drawings of different malarial strains. Jimmy explained that there were three strains of malaria prevalent in the Marovo. Plasmodium vivax, Plasmodium ovale, and the really bad one, Plasmodium falciparum were the usual suspects. Jimmy explained that the majority of cases occurred at the end of their wet season, typically in March, April, and May. It was September at this point, so they weren't seeing a ton of cases, but the disease was surely present. Suzanne was in her element. She loved looking through the microscope at a couple of samples. This was the tropical medicine rubber hitting the road right in front of us.

During our discussion, I asked Jimmy who was in charge of the hospital. He motioned up behind him with his finger as he said the bishop was. The bishop lived on top of the hill on the grounds of the theological seminary, also owned by the United Church of the Solomon Islands. He was the man I needed to speak with regarding my solar power idea. I gently asked Jimmy if he would be able to ask the bishop to come down and meet with me for a few minutes. Jimmy agreed and walked out of the lab to find the bishop.

I moved to the small office room next door. There were a desk and chair that didn't seem to be getting much use. Opening my notebook, I quickly wrote down my thoughts in the form of a proposal. I had no idea what to expect from the bishop. The American confidence in me suggested that there was no way he was not going to be interested in my idea. How could anyone from the third world not be interested in a flashy new project from an American? These very thoughts were problematic in many ways. I've since learned that it was the wrong attitude to start with when considering a rural development project in the third world.

Twenty minutes later, Jimmy returned. "The bishop will be here soon."

"Thank you, Jimmy, for getting him for me," I responded, hastily finishing my proposal. It wasn't pretty, but it cut to the chase and spelled out my offer. I was high on discovering the incredible feeling of unselfishly serving my fellow man. Comparatively, Suzanne and I had the moon and stars when looking at the socioeconomic status of residents of the Marovo Lagoon. I was ready to give and ready to serve more and more. The experience was changing the very core of my being. Up until now, traveling around the world had been just for us, but this trip was about other people. It was liberating to shed the chains of self-indulgence. The thought of an entire community benefiting from our desire to help was a feeling that a week at a five-star resort couldn't touch, in my mind.

A very dark face peered around the doorframe. The bishop was dressed in a beautiful purple oxford shirt with a white clergy collar. The black ebony-wood cross around his neck popped in contrast to the stunning nautilus-shell inlay throughout the piece. He seemed young to be a bishop in the church, but I wasn't quite able to interpret age in the Solomon Island population. I stood and introduced myself as we shook hands.

We sat down across from one another, and the bishop started the conversation. "I have to apologize that I did not know you and your wife were coming."

"That's okay. I'm sorry the Ministry of Health did not notify the hospital of our plans. Thank you for coming to meet me on short notice."

He nodded in acknowledgment, and I gave him some background on us before I shared my thoughts on a solar power system. "I understand that funds are not available to pay for diesel to run the generator. Electricity is obviously essential to a functioning medical facility. I have written up a proposal that outlines an offer to install a solar power system in the hospital. This will provide the hospital with electricity twenty-four hours a day. The system would be a gift and would belong to the hospital."

He didn't interrupt me and sat there for most of the conversation without changing his facial expression. "Your proposal sounds interesting. The hospital is governed by a medical board. I will have to present your proposal to the board for consideration. After they have decided, I will contact you and share their response. I see you have included your contact information. Thank you."

Suzanne and I had brought two duffle bags full of donated clothing from neighbors and people at our church. I figured the local head of the church would be the best person to give the donations to. As I gave him the bags, he looked somewhat in distress, as if I had created a burden for him. I wasn't aware of local customs with regards to providing items to people for free. His expression left me hoping I wasn't creating a problem for him in figuring out the proper way to distribute the clothes, but I couldn't dwell too much on that. We had hauled those two duffle bags all the way from the States, and hopefully, they were going to be used by someone, somewhere. At the time I gave the solar power system proposal to the bishop, I had no clue about the problems associated with international aid projects, but I would soon learn.

Prior to ending my meeting with the bishop, I wrote down an e-mail address and mailing address for Bishop Wilfred. He was a nice gentleman, and I expressed my sincere wishes to hopefully see him again in the near future. He said his good-byes and headed back to the seminary.

After my meeting with the bishop, Francis requested a short meeting with us. He said there was something at the hospital that had been bothering him for some time. He asked us to follow him to a spot down by the edge of the lagoon. I had not yet become desensitized to disturbing images from being in the dirty hospital for a couple of days, though I doubt anything could have prepared me for what I was about to see. Francis led us between two small, dilapidated houses and toward the water. The grass was high and moist. I was uneasy walking anywhere around the hospital, as I didn't know if I was walking on medical waste, human excrement, or dog crap. Guaranteed, whatever it was would be something muddy because of the amount of rain the island received.

I was third in line as we came closer to the water. "Oh no!" I heard Suzanne gasp. Before I had enough time to respond to her words, my eyes saw the heinous pile. Francis held out his hand and told us not to get too close. My brain didn't want to accept the information my eyes were sending. We were standing five feet away from the water of the Marovo Lagoon and were looking at all of the waste that had been generated from the hospital over the past six years. It was brought out to this pile and periodically lit on fire, but the fire failed to reach temperatures high enough to melt sharps. Needles were everywhere. The entire pile was full of needles, scalpel blades and broken glass slides from the malaria lab. Our faces were rife with horror. This was one of the worst scenes my eyes had ever witnessed. Children played along the edge of this lagoon, and fish were readily consumed from the adjacent waters. There was no fence or barrier around the pile to prevent children, dogs, or chickens from wandering onto the sharps-laden, disease-infested heap.

Francis couldn't answer why the hospital did not have an incinerator. He had heard speculation about one sitting on the docks in Honiara and waiting to be transferred, but that was just talk. The absence of an incinerator was an utter failure on so many levels, but the blame could be spread out to every institution, organization, and government entity involved in Seghe Hospital. Six years of hospital waste just thrown on a pile alongside the water was borderline criminal in my mind.

Another interesting thing I noticed in the pile were yellow sharps containers provided by the MOH. The containers were made from, of all things, cardboard. Plastic would likely repel penetrations from sharps better than cardboard, but I can see using cardboard if that is all that's available. Neither cardboard nor plastic would matter in a real medical-waste incinerator; either type of container, along with all the sharps in it, would burn adequately. In this case, some of the cardboard sharps containers had disintegrated in the rainy conditions, thus exposing the sharps within. I also saw the remnants of sharps containers that hadn't made it through the small fires, yet all their sharp contents had survived unscathed. The scene was as unacceptable as unacceptable gets.

The hospital had been built in 2000, without any consideration given to the appropriate disposal of medical waste. There were other considerations that had clearly not been taken into account, such as a plan to address continual maintenance and cleaning of the facility. The aid organizations had done a great job building the hospital, which was an incredible gift to the community. The structure had solid bones and was built for the long run. However, simply building a new health care facility and walking away without providing the locals with any training, tools, or finances epitomized many of the problems associated with third-world aid projects. This was why so many aid projects around the world crumble shortly after the first-world saviors have finished their construction, along with patting themselves on the back for a job well done. Most of these projects fail because long-term planning for the continual operation and maintenance of the facility never enter the equation. Building a relatively sophisticated structure for a culture that doesn't have the means and knowledge to care for it is a recipe for absolute failure.

It wasn't much longer into this trip that I realized there was no sex appeal in talking about the long-term viability of a project. It's only sexy to talk about building a new clinic, bridge, or power plant. It's a downer to ever talk about what happens after the project is finished. As a result, most often, that conversation doesn't take place—or it takes place and the answer is "Oh, the locals are going to take care of it because it will be their clinic now." That line of thinking is myopic and is pure hogwash. For instance, in the Marovo Lagoon, western ideas and interactions have been sparse and slow to infiltrate since Christianity first arrived in 1911. South Pacific cultures in general lack a sense of haste with regard to doing most things. The concept of cleaning or maintaining a new structure is also new. These cultures evolved in an area that had climatic conditions and food availability that negated the need to do anything in a hurry. It's always warm, and food has never been far away for South Pacific islanders; thus, there has never been an urgency to complete any one task at any given time.

It is also unreasonable to think that if an aid organization builds a facility, members of the community will volunteer to maintain it in the future. The problem with that line of thinking in the Marovo Lagoon is that probably more than ninety percent of the people living in the lagoon are living a subsistence lifestyle. A lot of their time is spent in their gardens or out on the water, fishing to put food on their plates. Most of them do not have the luxury of discretionary income to enable them to volunteer to clean or maintain a new community facility. They spend the majority of their day doing what is necessary to survive.

One problem inherent in the international-aid world is that people are sent to a foreign land by USAID, AUSAID, UNDP, or any other aid organization with one primary objective: spend the money that has been allotted for the area or initiative. Their mandate is to spend money, not to follow up to make sure the projects have a long-term viability and are actually beneficial for the local inhabitants in the long run. That is not part of the wiring of these large international-aid organizations. The thinking is "We are only responsible for building the structure; taking care of it will be their problem." The recipients are often not equipped to take care of it, however. Therein lies the problem.

The boat driver was ready to take Suzanne and me back to Uepi at the end of our second day at Seghe. The relatively cool wind was a great relief after we had been sweating in the hospital all day. Two days at the hospital were in the books, and although tiring, the experience was actually recharging our batteries.

We had in our minds that if the medical board accepted our offer of solar panels, we were going to be committed to Seghe Hospital for years to come. "One and done" was not going to be our motto; we knew that, but part of the battle would be convincing Jill and Grant of our level of commitment. They lived in the lagoon full time. They were the only people who could offer the support we would need to get the job done, and we knew their participation with logistics, transportation, and labor would be key to getting this project off the ground.

CHAPTER

7

*A*rriving at the hospital on the third day yielded a different scene from the previous two. Word had spread around the lagoon that Suzanne was seeing patients at Seghe. Opportunities to see a doctor, without having to travel to one of the larger towns, didn't happen often. It was obvious many people had health concerns they wanted addressed.

Francis greeted us with good news. The woman with the infected broken leg was being transferred to Ramata. The Seghe airstrip was still too wet for planes to land, but as we knew from experience, the airstrip at Ramata didn't have drainage issues, so unless the weather was really bad, planes could always land there. If all went to plan, the woman would be in Honiara in several hours. Even with the two-day delay, it was a major victory for us. She was still alive, and upon closer inspection, Suzanne felt as though the antibiotics were at least keeping the infection from getting worse.

Through a couple of conversations with hospital staff, I learned why the hospital was so dirty. The church did not have enough money to pay for dedicated cleaning staff. It was a terrible situation. Not only were the nurses short staffed and operating the hospital without the guidance and support of a doctor, but they also had to assume the cleaning responsibilities for the entire facility. They weren't being compensated to clean the hospital but felt like they didn't have a choice because it was where they had to work every day. Obviously, they weren't able to spend the time necessary to keep the place as clean as it should be. My hat went off to them for doing their best with severely limited resources.

Suzanne loved taking care of patients without the burden of excessive paperwork. The rudimentary health care system dictated that people carry their own health care records with them. An individual's health record was a small book that the person typically received at birth. Each visit to a clinic would add additional information regarding any conditions or pertinent changes in the person's health. It was Suzanne's job to write down the details of the visit so the health record remained up to date. She also used the books to write prescriptions. For chronic diseases such as diabetes, Suzanne's notes in the book served as orders to recheck sugar levels and to receive any necessary refills of medicine.

I continued to assist Suzanne with measuring blood sugars and taking notes. The pace had really picked up. Fortunately, there weren't many inpatients to see. All the business that day was from the outpatient clinic. As midday approached, I could sense that Suzanne was not going to be able to address all the patients' needs. This last day at the hospital fell on a Friday, and we had only a half day because Fridays were staff changeover days at Uepi, meaning all of the resort's boats were needed to shuttle workers back to their villages. The staff members worked one week on and one week off. The two of us knew this ahead of time, but the villagers didn't know we couldn't stay the entire day. I wasn't sure what to do about the situation. Maybe the best thing to do would be to briskly walk out the door. We definitely wouldn't be able to walk by furtively, because we were the two most conspicuous people at the hospital.

Right before we had to leave, one gentleman was excited to tell me that he was looking forward to seeing the doctor. He shared that he was having prostate problems and could barely pass urine. I looked him in the eye, but I couldn't bring myself to tell him that we had to leave. Suzanne would not get a chance to address his condition. I felt terrible. We didn't actually have any medicine to help his condition. I imagine that if it got bad enough, the nurses would insert a catheter into his bladder so he could pass urine.

The morning flew by. The boat driver came to get us. We barely had a chance to say good-bye to the nurses as we left. The line of people waiting to see Suzanne was close to twenty in number. Without looking at them, we had to walk past and get in the boat. It probably created a burden for the nursing staff, as they likely had to tell the patients that the doctor was gone and not coming back. It was a gut-wrenching experience. The walk to the wharf was insanely painful. In the boat, Suzanne put her head down and covered her face. She shed tears of sorrow the entire way back to Uepi. The boat ride seemed to go on forever. Those patients may have paddled their dugout canoes for miles to see her. Knowing that we couldn't treat all of them was excruciating. That moment solidified Suzanne's resolve to return with more doctors.

Although our time at the hospital was over, our commitment to treating patients on this trip was not. We still had to go to Chubikopi Village the next day. There, we wouldn't have any support from the nurses at the hospital. It would just be Suzanne and me and a village of more than five hundred people. I had an uneasy feeling. Images of being trampled in a stampede seeped into my brain. Chubikopi had close ties to Uepi, so I hoped we'd be in safe hands.

*   *   *

We hadn't yet grown accustomed to sleeping in the heat and humidity of the Marovo. At bedtime, we lay down with barely anything on, under a ceiling fan on full blast. Around three or four each morning, we would eventually be cool enough to pull the one sheet partially over us. I didn't want to think about what would happen if the fan cut out.

After a night of tossing and turning, I awoke to willy wagtail belting out his melodious tune. We could set our watches by him. I wished he could have slept in a little, but the choral notes beat any alarm clock on the market. I walked out on the deck to find Suzanne doing some yoga. It was a great scene, watching her stretch with the stunning azure waters lapping the shore behind her. What a way to start the morning. I was so thankful to be in this wild place, doing some good, however little it was. It was a start, and that was all that mattered.

Grant had told us the night before that the boat would leave at nine in the morning for Chubikopi. We would be gone the better part of a full day, as we were to come back around three or four. Because we had briefly visited a village on the first trip, our apprehension levels weren't too high, but we didn't know how many people were going to come looking for care. As we had found out the day before, Suzanne could see only so many people in a given amount of time. It was obvious we needed ten doctors to meet the needs of the lagoon.

Pulling away from the boat jetty, we headed left. If we had been going to Seghe, we would have gone straight across the widest part of the lagoon. This way took us a direction we had yet to experience. We skimmed along the water at a good clip. My eyes were glued to the water rushing by. The fish and coral below could only be seen for a split second, but the variety and quantity of reef bommies and fish were impressive.

On the point of Marovo Island was the Seventh-day Adventist village Chea. From a distance, it looked well taken care of. I could see grass and trimmed hedges around some of the houses. A large church was perched above the village.

Not far from Chea, the large green church of Chubikopi came into view. It, too, sat perched above the village. Chubikopi was a United Church village. Evidently, the two villages weren't getting along because of a long-simmering land dispute. As long as the machetes didn't come out, I'd be happy.

A short, stocky gentleman, Fred, met us as we tied up the boat at Chubikopi. He led us to a building built on stilts at the water's edge. It was the village guesthouse. Sea kayakers paddling through the lagoon would pay to spend the night here. It was a rectangular building of wood with a corrugated metal roof. The people of the Solomon Islands refer to the roofing material simply as "iron."

We conveyed to Fred that we would like him to try to filter or triage patients. We wanted the most ill patients or patients with injuries first. Then we left our shoes at the front door and walked into the room. The floor was covered in a material that seemed like thin linoleum, but it wasn't securely fastened to the floor. A couple of posters describing fishing practices and conservation adorned the walls. One compact fluorescent bulb hung from a wire out of the ceiling. There must have been a small solar panel on the roof.

We had our suitcase full of supplies and medicines. Fortunately, we hadn't had to use a lot at the hospital, so we were still well stocked. Opening the suitcase, I heard a loud bell ringing. Uh-oh, this must be for us. Some people brought several plastic deck chairs in and placed them around a large square table. The table was too short for my legs to go under, so I had to straddle a corner as I set out medicines and supplies.

Before long, the room started to fill up with villagers. They sat along the walls, male and female, young and old. Holy cow, this was going to be big.

Fred called up a couple of the older folks. The first woman was generally not feeling well. She was overweight, and Suzanne asked me to get a sugar level while she took the woman's blood pressure on her other arm.

"It says 490," I said.

"What? Do it again," Suzanne replied.

"It just says high now."

"Her blood pressure is really high as well. She's about to have a stroke right in front of our eyes."

I wasn't entirely sure what would happen next if the woman stroked in front of us. It had been a long time since I had certified in CPR and first aid. That wasn't my area of expertise, so I just had to do what Suzanne told me and hope that everything would be okay. Fortunately, the woman didn't stroke out, and although she obviously wasn't feeling well, it was a condition she had been living with, and the status quo seemed more or less okay in her mind.

Alarm bells were going off in our minds with the number of overweight diabetics we were seeing. Something must be happening with the islanders' food choices and lack of exercise. There were too many patients to see for us to stop and have a conversation with the villagers about these concerns. In addition, most of the patients claimed to smoke cigarettes, which likely complicated and exacerbated most of the chronic conditions we were seeing. An in-depth conversation with the Kellys regarding village eating and living habits would have to wait until dinner.

I filled prescriptions, dispensing them in small brown paper envelopes as fast as Suzanne could write them. We continued to tell the patients to stop smoking. Fred was interpreting for us and at one point said that we were trying to take away their culture. Not being familiar with anyone in this village, I should have responded with kid gloves, but I called him out right there. Without a hint of ambiguity in my voice, I sternly told him that smoking kills people all over the world and we were not taking away their culture. My response may have been heavy-handed, but I wasn't about to let him try to defend one of the scourges of society by attaching a cultural necessity to it. That was bogus.

After we had seen many older patients, a young man in his early twenties walked in and showed Suzanne his hand. Fred explained that the man had been spear fishing a few days prior and a fish spine had broken off inside his knuckle. It was obvious something was festering in there, because the man's knuckle was nearly the size of a golf ball. Suzanne examined the knuckle; gauging from the young man's reaction, it was tender to the touch.

Suzanne asked for the one disposable scalpel that we had in the suitcase. She explained to the guy that she didn't have any medicine to numb the knuckle. He maintained that he wanted her to try to clean it up. We had Fred track down a bucket to place on the floor to catch the fluids likely trapped in the boil. Suzanne cleaned all around the knuckle with a couple of alcohol swabs. She didn't have safety glasses, and thus I told her to be careful in the event the abscess was under pressure.

The man chose to stand instead of sit. "Are you ready?" Suzanne asked as she unsheathed the scalpel. He nodded, and then something strange happened. Prior to Suzanne touching his knuckle with the scalpel, the young man balled his other fist and raised it above Suzanne's head. Was he going to punch her in the head? I watched with great concern as she began to cut. He squeezed his fist and started to sing in a high pitch.

Suzanne was aware there were tendons that she had to miss. Thankfully, the abscess didn't spew under high pressure. She continued to cut and manipulate the abscess to drain more puss. It wasn't easy to watch, but I had it much easier than the guy getting his finger cut open. Suzanne never found a fish spine, but she determined that she had cut enough and didn't want to risk hitting a tendon. I filled a prescription of antibiotics for the young man as Suzanne dressed the wound. We gave him extra dressing so he could continue to keep it clean throughout the healing process.

The next patient was in a similar situation. He was eighteen years old and couldn't walk into the building by himself. His knee was blown up from an infection that had resulted after he had wiped out on the soccer field. Evidently, the soccer field was chock-full of coral boulders sticking up throughout the pitch. It was obvious from looking at this boy's knee that the coral won every time.

We didn't have another scalpel to slice his knee open, so Suzanne's only option was to prescribe a hefty dose of antibiotics to try to eliminate the infection from within. I think the young man was probably happy with that after seeing his friend's finger cut open without anesthetic.

Suzanne and I had been noticing a little difference in the treatment Fred was giving to the men and women, but we were very unknowledgeable about Solomon Islands customs and cultural quirks. His explanations were more thorough with some patients than with others, and some of the women didn't seem happy to be sharing their health issues with Fred. Suzanne wasn't completely sure he was giving her correct information from the patients. I doubt he was blatantly misinforming Suzanne, but he may have been giving more credence to certain people's complaints over others. We should have asked for a female interpreter as well, but the craziness of the day prevented us from thinking that through.

As our time to leave got closer, Fred kept saying, "One more, one more." It had been a long day and we wanted to treat everyone we could, but we also had a schedule by which to abide. A young baby was the final patient of the day. We went to the new mother's house to see the child. The mother was the wife of our boat driver and also was the daughter of the village chief.

We entered the wooden house, which was perched on stilts. The living space was very small, with a thin partition dividing the two rooms. There were no mattresses inside. The residents of the house slept on woven grass mats on either the floor or an elevated wooden frame. Mom was holding the baby as we walked in. The baby was hot to the touch, obviously feverish. She had not been sleeping well and wasn't feeding well on her mom's milk. The mother said they had not been sleeping under a mosquito net. Suzanne suspected malaria in the child, but we did not have a way of testing for malaria. We gave the baby some children's acetaminophen in a suspension to relieve some of the symptoms. Suzanne told the mother it was very important to go to Seghe to get the baby checked for malaria. Fortunately, the hospital had medicine to treat the baby if it turned out to be a positive malaria test.

Back at Uepi that evening, Suzanne and I mentioned the diabetes issue to the Kellys. Living at Uepi for more than fifteen years, Jill had a lot of experience with the locals and had been watching their diet change before her eyes. She thought the prevalence of diabetes at Chubikopi was probably very representative of the rest of the lagoon. For centuries, the Solomon Islanders had eaten a variety of fruits, vegetables, and fish. Eventually, other protein items such as chicken and pork had slowly made their way into the islands through contact with the outside world. Jill mentioned that these proteins were not consumed nearly as often as fish, however. Chicken and pork seemed to be reserved for special occasions such as birthdays.

The problem was that fast food had arrived in the Marovo Lagoon. It wasn't in the form of western-style fast food. It wasn't in the form of hamburgers, French fries, and milk shakes. There were no buildings with playrooms for kids or even drive-thru windows. The people were making a quick change from fruits, vegetables, and fish to white rice, white flour, and soft drinks. White rice seemed to be the biggest culprit. Just adding white rice to one's diet wasn't necessarily a bad thing; the problem arose when they almost completely substituted white rice for the fruits, vegetables, and fish. Jill explained that the islanders would mound an entire plate full of rice and that would be one person's dinner. They may put a little tuna or canned beef on top. She estimated that each person was consuming around four to six servings of white rice per meal. That boiled down to a large plate of sugar multiple times a day.

I consider this their version of fast food because villagers could quickly feed themselves without having to toil in the garden or spend hours out on the water, trying to catch fish. Replacing traditional foods with white rice was also leading to a more sedentary lifestyle, thus exacerbating the problem associated with increased sugar intake from white rice. As a result, obesity was on the rise in a community that didn't have all the first-world trappings like automobiles, television, and junk food that have made us westerners fat. There were also reports of an increase in hemorrhoids. This was a population that had probably never dealt with hemorrhoids in the past because they were always getting enough fiber in their diet. Now, the huge amounts of white rice were not providing the fiber they needed, and rice actually acted as a binding agent and made it harder to have bowel movements.

Jill also mentioned that people who gained weight were viewed as being successful in the community. Around the world, diabetes is more or less a rich man's disease. Most people who come down with Type II diabetes have the luxury of ingesting a lot of sugar without their pancreas being able to produce enough insulin to protect the body from the increased sugar levels in the bloodstream. Without proper education about the perils of diabetes, people in the Marovo Lagoon would likely not take the disease seriously. This was an area that had no health infrastructure or health education programs available to handle an onslaught of new diabetes cases. These people will slowly and painfully rot from the disease. Eliminating white rice isn't necessarily the solution, of course. Educating villagers about portion size and about the need to continue eating fruits, vegetables, and fish in proper proportion to one another is what is needed to stem the growing tide of diabetes in the Marovo Lagoon.

The overall experience of this trip was life altering. Suzanne had an idea of what we wanted to do next in the lagoon, but we needed some time to talk it over. We needed Jill and Grant's support to make a difference at Seghe. Without it, we didn't have the logistical support and local know-how to help us implement change at the hospital. For now, we were leaving Uepi without their vital support.

As we said our good-byes and shoved off from the welcome jetty, Jill, Grant, Gayle, and Ian all performed a farewell dance. Their arms moved in unison, left and right, like in a typical Polynesian dance. Then their arms went over their heads back and forth, and finally, they jumped in the air and then turned around and scratched their backsides. It was quite funny and a very nice send-off. Uepi Island is a magical place, and after visiting twice, we had begun to create memories to last a lifetime.

CHAPTER

8

*T*hree months had passed since we had returned from our second trip to the Solomon Islands. It was the beginning of February 2008, and we had not heard a response from the bishop at Seghe regarding the solar power proposal. Together, Suzanne and I decided that a good next step would be to assemble a medical team and return in November for our first group trip because Suzanne had not been able to care for everyone by herself. We needed to take several practitioners with us so everyone who needed to see a doctor would have the opportunity.

It was new territory for us, to say the least. Neither of us had ever led a group of people overseas, let alone to the wilds of the Solomon Islands. What would it entail? I had no idea how many people we would be able to entice to go on the trip. There was a lot to think about, and getting a group of people there was only half the equation. The other half would have to be coordinated by Uepi. Unfortunately, I wasn't in direct contact with Jill and Grant. I could only communicate with them through the travel agent. Many unknowns floated around the planning process. We hoped we could pull it off.

Another issue we needed to figure out was how to work the trip through a nonprofit so people could get a tax deduction for going. It would be a charity-driven trip and thus should be tax deductible for participants, but we needed a nonprofit entity to sponsor us. I didn't know where else to turn but to our church.

Suzanne and I were in a care group, as it was called. It was basically a small group of people from church who got together roughly once a month to discuss events in one another's lives as well as have a time for fellowship. We happened to be in a care group with a few members of the church leadership.

Once a month, Suzanne and I would highlight what was happening with regard to our homegrown efforts to help the people in the Marovo Lagoon. We poured out our hearts to the group about the struggles the Marovo community faced with health care. We shared this newfound passion for moral support from fellow believers and to try to help bolster additional health care resources for Seghe Hospital. I was unable to gauge if our goals to provide assistance had struck a chord with anyone in the group.

I approached the session at church for assistance. In Presbyterian circles, the session is the group of church members or elders who make big decisions for the church. The session serves as the church's supervisory board, in effect. I gave a brief presentation to the session, asking for the church to sponsor our first group medical trip to the Solomon Islands. I didn't ask for money. I simply asked for the church to stand behind our mission so our participants could receive a tax deduction for their participation. In effect, we would be serving the people of the Marovo Lagoon as a mission or outreach arm of the church.

A week or so later, I received word that a member of the church had cautioned the church not to sponsor our trip because the IRS might have objections. His conclusion made no sense to me. Churches all over the United States sent teams to various places with various goals in mind. Maybe some factions in the church didn't want the church to be involved in a place so far away from the United States, I figured. Who knew? I had explained to the session that at the time, there were no churches from the United States involved in any mission or aid work in the Marovo Lagoon— none! What an opportunity for the church to establish a relationship with the United Church of the Solomon Islands and sponsor our next trip. Again, I hadn't asked for a dime. I had simply asked them to officially sponsor us, which would allow medical team participants to write off however much the IRS would allow.

I didn't feel as though we were being treated fairly. Power was being exerted from different places within the church, and I wasn't willing to cause divisions to get my way. We loved worshipping there and wanted to continue to do so; many members of the congregation were near and dear to our hearts.

Suzanne and I didn't have children in church and thus we were not part of the, in my mind, overly powerful youth ministry. From my vantage, the youth ministry was guiding the international mission opportunities of the church, and we weren't part of that club to receive many of the benefits. Suffice it to say that my philosophy of international aid and mission was totally different from what the leaders at church proposed for their mission programs. They were initially engaged in fundraising to subsidize their travel costs for mission work. We were about to engage in fundraising to invest in infrastructure improvements for Seghe Hospital. We couldn't have been further apart, in my view. I saw them as a group of traveling Christians. It was my Christian faith in action that caused me to want to effect change at Seghe in a positive way. Seghe needed physical improvements, not simply smiling Christian tourists coming in to play with children and say, "Hello, and may God bless you."

Strangely enough, shortly after they denied my request, the session supported the youth ministry team taking a large group of kids to Kenya. How was a youth trip to Kenya allowable by the IRS and a medical trip to the Solomon Islands not? I'll never know the answer. The denial was difficult to stomach. It was our faith that was propelling us to help in the first place. It was painful to realize that our church didn't feel the project was worthy of its support. I didn't have the luxury of having other people pay for our travel or the travel of any of our prospective participants. I hadn't even asked the church for that type of support. All I had asked for was a sponsorship indicating on paper that our project would be part of the church so participants would receive tax benefits from their participation—nothing more, nothing less. Asking someone to lay down several thousand dollars to go to an unknown place and treat patients for free was a big deal. Yes, there were intrinsic benefits from that type of experience, but receiving a tax deduction for one's charity work would really help with recruitment. I didn't agree with the session's decision, but that's the way it goes.

Now what were we going to do? We were about to do a major charity project, and we needed a charity sponsor. I wasn't about to ask interested folks to participate without having the ability to get a charity deduction for their service.

Not long after the session's decision, we had our yearly meeting with our accountant. We shared our experience from the Solomons, and he was touched. I explained that we had offered to purchase and install a solar power system on the hospital and that although we hadn't heard anything from the bishop yet, we needed a way to figure out how to coordinate all this through a nonprofit of some sort. We didn't have time to apply and be approved for nonprofit status before the planned group trip. What the accountant said next blew us away: "You can work under my nonprofit. We'll sponsor your endeavors." Now I felt like we had a chance to make a difference. This was the first major hurdle for the trip, and we had finally jumped it.

About a week later, toward the end of February 2008, I received a letter from the bishop at Seghe. The letter stated that the medical board overwhelmingly supported my proposal. He finished his letter with a statement saying that they were looking forward to the installation of the solar power system. Oh boy … what had I gotten myself into? I had just promised these people 8,000 miles away that I would install a solar power system on their hospital.

I had to take a step back. After I read the letter, my face was flushed and I felt warm all over. It's one thing to offer to help someone, but they had just accepted an offer that was a little more involved than mowing my neighbor's lawn while the neighbor was away on vacation.

When Suzanne came home from work that evening, I told her the news. She seemed to react the same way I had. "So what do we do now?"

"Um … well, I guess I need to figure out how much this thing is going to cost. I was thinking to ask Gordon at church if he would be interested in helping us. He installed a solar power system for some folks in the Philippines. If he can tell us what type of a system we're going to need, then I'll figure out how much it's going to cost."

I switched into high gear like never before in my life. I shed my domestic-stallion uniform and jumped straight into a new career. I could vacuum, shop, and clean house with the best of them, but now there was a more important, higher calling beckoning for my attention. I needed a moniker equal to the catchy ring of domestic stallion. Hmm, I'd have to think about that one for a while.

Gordon had oodles of experience with both electrical and medical issues. He had degrees in both electrical and biomedical engineering. He was a big part of the original team that had created the electronic medical record system for the Veterans Administration medical system. He was definitely going to be my go-to guy for this project.

I met him at his office one day, and we walked next door to have some pizza for lunch. I had come well prepared with photos of the hospital and a list of all the electrical needs, or load, of the facility. I drew an aerial sketch of the facility and gave him rough dimensions. Gordon asked great questions for which I often didn't have the answers. One question of his concerned the security around the hospital: Did we need to worry about the solar panels walking off the roof and disappearing? I made notes throughout the meeting. Another inquiry I had to ask of the equipment suppliers: Do solar panels come with locking devices?

Gordon needed to do some calculations to figure out how big the solar power system needed to be. Until he had those figures, he wouldn't speculate on how much it was going to cost. He did offer me solace when he said solar is a beautiful thing because it can be scaled up if needed. Depending on how much money we would be able to raise, we could essentially purchase the system in phases and install the pieces incrementally. That news alleviated some of the weight starting to grow on my shoulders. I shared our plans with him to take a medical team to the Marovo later that year. We both acknowledged that it was an ambitious timeline to raise the money, assemble a team, and install the system in roughly nine months' time.

Gordon and I spoke regularly. A few days after our initial meeting, he called with some sizing information. He calculated a 10.5-kilowatt (KW) off-grid system. The system would be designed and installed as a stand-alone power station that relied on solar panels to convert the sun's energy into electricity. The electricity would be channeled through a couple of charge controllers that would allow power to enter into a bank of batteries and the inverters. The inverters would then convert the power from direct current (DC) to alternating current (AC) and make it useable throughout the hospital in the form of lights or power sockets for other appliances requiring electricity.

We could get to 10.5 KW with multiple sizes of solar panels. It depended upon the prices of the panels to figure out the number of panels needed to reach 10.5 KW. Panels around 200 watts were significantly more expensive per watt than panels at 175 watts.

We agreed that it would be the best plan, for multiple reasons, to source the solar power system from the Solomon Islands. I liked the idea of injecting the local economy with foreign investment, and I also didn't want to think about shipping. I found two solar power businesses operating in Honiara.

Only one of them was able to handle the intricacies of putting together a system of this size. I e-mailed the specifications so the business could provide me with a price.

I knew it would probably take a couple of weeks to receive a bid from Honiara. There were two other logical places at which to inquire about bids. Brisbane, Australia, was the closest, most developed city near Honiara. Also, I found an Internet-based solar power sales company based in New Mexico. I requested bids from both outfits and waited for their responses. The bids from Brisbane and New Mexico would involve shipping, but I needed to know the layout of the playing field to make an informed decision.

Sticker shock was never a happy concept. It's an even worse thing when you have promised someone to purchase the items that cause the sticker shock. I would equate sticker shock to having all the wind knocked out of you in an instant. This was maybe the first time I had all the wind knocked out of me just by opening an e-mail. The first company to respond was the one from New Mexico. The price without shipping was nearly $90,000. Each solar panel was listed at nearly $800. At that moment, I stopped moving and put my head down in pure despair. How were we going to raise that kind of money in six months? We hoped to return in September of 2008 to install the system. After a few minutes of anguish, I remembered Gordon's words about being able to purchase half the system now and the other half after we raised the remainder of the money. Still, $45,000 in six months ... Suzanne was going to freak out. We had committed to doing this project, and we were going to be on the hook for whatever amount we were unable to raise. I did have two potential aces in the hole—the chance that the bids from Honiara and Brisbane might be cheaper. There wasn't time to wait for that possibility, though.

We had to figure out a plan to start raising money. Suzanne was a doctor, and I had been a natural resources educator. Neither of us had any training or experience in asking people for money. Personally, I detested being asked for money. It also didn't help that I had developed some sort of "booth phobia." I couldn't stand going to festivals, other than wine festivals. Festivals always had people sitting behind booths, wanting me to get invested in their worthwhile causes. I did have a deep sense of care and responsibility when it came to natural-resource stewardship and my fellow man, but I wanted to find out about it on my own, not by someone giving me a sales pitch from behind a booth.

Incredibly, I had just thrust myself into that role of the booth people at festivals whom I tried to avoid with all my being. I would rather chew on my arm than go to festivals and be approached by people peddling this or trying to convince me of that. Well, move over booth people, because you have competition for those already scarce donations. I was about to see how they feel, always trying to bend a sympathetic ear or to sift some cash out of a wallet.

I knew from the get-go that Suzanne's professional colleagues and contacts were going to be more fruitful than my own personal contacts. Her professional circles had the potential to donate more money than my lower-paid colleagues in parks and recreation. I hoped her outstanding reputation in Salt Lake City was going to help with our fundraising efforts. Unfortunately, there was a definite propensity for snobbery in the medical community. I had been to multiple doctor-type events where people hadn't shown any interest in talking to me because I'm not a doctor. I had thought being married to a doctor would have given me a full-access pass into the club, but I had found that not to be the case. Part of it is that a lot of doctors are socially awkward. I think it goes with the territory. Understandably, they also try to avoid being put in social situations where people use them for free consultations. Admittedly, being used for free consultations has happened to Suzanne many times, and I can see how it drives doctors crazy. They want to relax in a social situation just like everyone else, without someone they're speaking to lifting up a shirt for the doctor to examine a growth, or discussing a terrible medical story that happened to their mother's best friend. I think all doctors should have a standard response for medical questions asked in social situations. They should say to people asking for advice, "Fortunately, I brought a pair of gloves, because that is going to require an immediate rectal exam." Problem solved.

Suzanne and I mentioned the need to do a fundraiser to our neighbor Betsy. She is a fantastic social dynamo of a woman who seems to produce fun at every turn. Oddly enough, she also attended the same church as us. I'm sure we were in some secret database somewhere because we were two of the three Presbyterian households on the same street in a Mormon-dominated neighborhood. Another neighbor two doors down in the opposite direction also attended our church. Betsy's house had a great backyard, very conducive to entertaining. She offered to host the event with the assistance of her friend Marina. The two of them were a social force to be reckoned with. Whenever they were together, good times were guaranteed. Our fundraising was in good hands.

A friend of ours, Brooke, had experience cooking for large groups and offered to coordinate the food. We planned a couple months in advance to hold the event in June 2008. Suzanne and I agreed to pay for all the food and drink for the event. I was able to surreptitiously secure tables and chairs for free from church. We had no costs associated with the event other than food and beverages. Between Suzanne, myself, Betsy, and Marina, we were able to put together a list of roughly one hundred people to invite. We decided not to charge for admission. Our plan was to have people come and enjoy a nice evening. Suzanne and I would describe the situation at Seghe and would convey our plan and financial needs for the solar power system.

Shortly before the fundraiser, we received the other two bids, from Brisbane and Honiara. Initially, I hadn't wanted to deal with having to ship all the supplies from the United States. After I received the other bids, though, my worries about the potential headache associated with international shipping quickly faded. The bid from the company in Brisbane was almost exactly double the bid from the New Mexico company—$175,000. Each solar panel was double the cost, and the inverters were nearly double as well.

After receiving the quote from the company in Honiara, I asked for a clarification that it was correct. In my response, I asked the guy to break down his bid of $300,000 so I could see the details of what he was going to provide. I explained that it was three times the amount of the quote I had received from the United States, and he told me to take it or leave it. The price was insanely high, and after communicating with the guy, I decided he may have been insane as well. Obviously, I didn't have a hard decision to make.

The fundraiser was a great success. Everyone involved did a great job, and Suzanne and I were very thankful for the assistance. We had roughly thirty people in attendance and collected approximately $11,000 in donations. We were on cloud nine after that, but we still needed a lot more money to reach our goal. Time was running short because we needed to purchase the system and have it shipped in time to arrive prior to the November trip.

A couple of weeks after the fundraiser, we received a donation that blew us away. A ninety-year-old patient of Suzanne's made a $10,000 donation. We were elated. We went down to the retirement community where she lived. It was a great visit; she was thrilled to be able to help us. She was very grateful for the medical care Suzanne had provided her and looked forward to being kept up to date on happenings with the project.

Prior to the fundraiser, the children's ministry leader at our church, Stefanie, approached me about incorporating a Solomon Island's project into the children's summer camp. I was thrilled to have the help. The church as a whole had decided not to sponsor us, so when Stefanie, who was sympathetic to our cause and was already planning to conduct a summer camp, suggested a joint project, I was on board. We put together a couple of events to weave the Solomon Islands project into the camp. I led a half-day trip for the middle-school kids to the local library, where they spent a couple of hours researching various aspects of the Solomon Islands, including geography, culture, economics, and World War II, which in Pidgin is called Hem Big Fella Fight. I also presented a lot of photos and stories about the Solomon Islands and asked the students to research renewable-energy projects, specifically solar power. Each group presented its findings. The benefits of the exercise were evident. Collectively, the kids had a sense of excitement and decided to try to help us raise money to purchase solar panels. Their efforts in the end were praiseworthy. We were able to purchase several more panels thanks to their grassroots fundraising campaign. Stefanie and her kids really came through for us!

After we received the acceptance of our solar power proposal from the bishop, Suzanne and I also spent a lot of time recruiting participants to join us on the first group trip scheduled for September of 2008. We had secured seven physicians, two nurse practitioners, and three nurses to join us. Good friends of ours, Kirk and Jenny, decided to join us for their honeymoon trip to help out in the pharmacy. Gordon and Terry, both engineers, were in charge of the solar power installation.

It was estimated to take nearly three months for the solar supplies to sail from Los Angeles to Honiara. There wasn't much time left to order the solar equipment and get it on its way. We had only raised enough money to purchase half of the system, so in July, I ordered the equipment. At least the hospital would have power for lights until we could secure the funds for the other half of the system.

Upon nearing the July shipping deadline, I checked back with the solar equipment supplier in New Mexico. I needed to pull the trigger and get the stuff on the ship. It was obvious the solar power business was taking off, because the guy had forgotten about our order. When I explained to him about the urgency of the shipment, his response didn't fill me with confidence, so I bailed.

In a stressed-out frenzy, I searched the Web for another company that hopefully wouldn't drop the ball. I came across an outfit called Wholesale

Solar located in northern California. I called with an impassioned plea for last-minute assistance. Fortunately, I had the owner, Mark Coleman, on the phone, and he immediately attended to my needs. Mark began to diagram a system for us based on Gordon's power calculations. His company was able to pre-wire the power panel, which was a big help. He also designed the appropriate racking system to make sure the panels would fit securely to the roof. Mark had many conversations with Gordon prior to the equipment being shipped. Gordon felt like we were in good hands and also felt like Mark was selling us quality products.

Wholesale Solar was initially reluctant to ship the supplies all the way to the Solomon Islands. They preferred to ship only domestically, but after I explained that the system was destined for a small hospital in the Solomon Islands, they agreed to coordinate the shipping all the way to Honiara.

Logistics support from Uepi needed to be ironed out. It was time to force the Kellys' hand on the solar issue. We needed their help, and up until this point, they had not offered to help. I knew I would have to pay for it, but we needed their boats and local labor to make the installation and medical mission a success.

I notified Gayle via e-mail that our solar power proposal had been accepted. I told her that this was going to happen and that we would need Uepi's help on logistics. She sent an e-mail to Grant mentioning sixty solar panels heading to Seghe, and I think that's when he felt it was in Uepi's best interest to get involved. After Gayle's e-mail, Grant began communicating directly with me. I may have forced his hand a little, but in the end, it was to improve the only health care facility in the Marovo Lagoon. The improvements would have positive future implications for the staff at Uepi and any resort guests who might need to use the hospital.

Grant immediately connected me with BJS Services in Honiara. They received and cleared all of Uepi's imported goods. Once the items were cleared through customs, BJS would deliver the goods to another company, Silentworld, for final delivery. Silentworld operated the interisland motorized barge service that serviced communities throughout the Solomon Islands. Along with consumer goods, Silentworld also shipped logging and mining equipment to the outer islands. Grant warned me that the shipping costs from Honiara to Seghe would be expensive, and I quickly learned that doing business in a remote part of the world wasn't going to come cheap.

CHAPTER

9

*T*he solar equipment was on a boat in the middle of the Pacific. I was rolling the dice with the timeline, but I hoped I had factored enough time for it to arrive prior to our arrival in the Solomon Islands. I sometimes had control-freak tendencies, and this was one of those times when I had to have faith that everything would go to plan. The items could not have been more out of my hands.

With three and a half months to go before our September departure, we were frantically busy. There were a lot of pre-trip planning items that needed attention. We knew there was great demand for a doctor in the lagoon, and we knew our group would be popular. Because we were advertising our arrival ahead of time, we had no way to estimate how many people would come looking for medical care. Preparing for as many medical contingencies as we could was taxing. We knew we wouldn't have all the answers or treatments for every patient, but we wanted to be as prepared as we could be.

The group had swelled to eighteen. The majority of the team was from Salt Lake City. We conducted a couple of pre-trip meetings at our house. The group was a nice blend of doctors, nurse practitioners, nurses, and non-medical helpers. Four of the participants were not from Utah. One of Suzanne's colleagues from her gastroenterology fellowship at University of Virginia, Dr. Jeff Tokar, was joining us. His friend, Dr. Danielle Shafer, a hematologist and oncologist from Chicago, had gone out on a limb and decided to join us based on Jeff's urging. The honeymooners, Kirk and Jenny Myers, were coming from Seattle. We were happy to have an infectious-disease doctor, Mark Oliver, on our team. He was looking forward to seeing diseases he had never seen but had learned about in training. Kathy Alderson, our neighbor and a recently retired neurologist, joined the group. She had been intrigued with my description of the upcoming trip that I had shared with her while paying her daughters for Girl Scout cookies. The last-minute addition, Dr. Kate Wilson, turned out to be superwoman. Not only was Kate an internal medicine doctor, but she had been a dentist for several years before becoming an internist. On this first group trip, she agreed to serve as our dentist, as there was no dentist available in the Marovo Lagoon. Our two nurse practitioners, Gwen Mitchell and Kaye Meidinger, were excited to embark on the adventure. Gwen had spent time in Africa, and Kaye had just received her nurse practitioner degree. Jeri Fowles was our only dedicated registered nurse.

Unfortunately, the full medical team would not be together for the entire trip. Three of the doctors from Salt Lake City couldn't leave with the group. Their plan was to come for the second week of the tour and stay an additional week after the main team departed. I wasn't sure how this would work, but we didn't have another option.

The volume of supplies we were gathering increased daily. It was imperative that group members share the burden in packing medicines and supplies. There was no other option for getting the medical supplies to Seghe Hospital in time. Regular air courier service to Honiara did not exist. Shipping something via UPS or FedEx was not an option. Compounding the problem was the fact that Solomon Airlines had considerable weight restrictions for baggage. The group was flying on Air Pacific through Nadi to get to Honiara. Solomon Airlines did not allow as much luggage as Air Pacific, so we had to follow Solomon Airlines' restrictions. The problem wasn't the jet service into Honiara but the small plane from Honiara to Seghe. The Twin Otter could only hold so much weight.

I was not sure I could cover all the contingencies we might run into, but I rented a satellite phone to at least have the option of communicating with the outside world. Traveling with a group of people to a wild third-world country enabled my mind to conjure crazy scenarios, and I wanted to have a communications capacity in the event that any of those scenarios came to fruition. Planning was my thing, sometimes to the point of squashing spontaneity. In this case, I didn't care because I had no idea of the situations that could arise with a group of eighteen people. Proper preparation would hopefully enable us to manage any crazy scenarios that may arise. Suzanne and I were about to get a crash course in what it was like to be tour guides. I didn't want to think about what additional responsibilities the role would include.

A month before our departure, I hadn't heard anything regarding the solar shipment. One person I had heard a lot from was the travel agent. Solomon Airlines had changed the schedule on us a couple of times prior to the departure. Of course I was nervous about this, but it was totally out of my hands. I was glad I had an agent working on it. Travel agents were becoming a dying breed, but in this case I was glad our agent was still in business.

Maybe I shouldn't put the airline's snafus on my shoulders, but that was my nature. I had assumed the role of travel agent along with managing all the logistics from the United States. Even though I wasn't booking the travel, I was the intermediary between the travel agent and all the participants. Whatever problems arose, I had to share them with the agent and/or the participants. It wasn't a place I liked to be. I was a good cheerleader and was able to rally the troops fairly well, but managing expectations and mitigating confrontations didn't appeal to me. I had no choice, however; Suzanne and I were taking eighteen people on a trip halfway around the world, and I had to lead the travel and logistical side of things while Suzanne led the medical aspects.

As the departure date neared, my nerves began to rattle. Two days before the team was to board the plane, I heard from Tony at BJS Services that the *MV Highland Chief* had been spotted off the port of Honiara. The vessel was carrying our solar power system. The timing was going to be tight ... really tight.

I expressed my concern to Tony regarding the timing of the ship's arrival. He explained that they would do their best to receive the goods and clear them through customs as quickly as possible. I didn't know Tony from the man on the moon; I had to trust that he was going to be on top of this and follow through. BJS was a family business and had been in Honiara for years. They were Australians and were known for running a quality business. For my nerves' sake, I hoped they lived up to their reputation.

We arrived at LAX, the worst airport in the world, in my opinion. For a town known for Hollywood, glitz, and glamour, why was the airport such a dump? To get from terminal to terminal, we had to breathe the worst air in the United States. All the vehicles driving around in circles on the lower level belched their exhaust into an area that had little air circulation. We should have had scuba tanks to get from terminal three to the Tom Bradley International Terminal. Noted.

Our group from Salt Lake found the Air Pacific check-in counter without incident. One by one, we deposited our bags and received boarding passes. Before long, we met up with Kirk and Jenny from Seattle. Then we noticed Jeff and Danielle were checking in while we sat at a restaurant above the check-in counter. With a couple of hours to spare, everyone met and got to know one another.

Four hours into the ten-hour nonstop flight to Nadi, Fiji, the pilot spoke over the intercom. He notified the passengers that the plane was making an unscheduled stop in Honolulu to take on more fuel. We didn't have a ton of time to waste in Nadi, so of course my hackles went up. We couldn't miss our connection to Honiara. Plus, why was a 747-400 stopping for fuel on a ten-hour flight? The aircraft was designed to fly sixteen hours or so without refueling. Could the winds have been that much against us, or had the political dictatorship in Fiji metaphorically agitated the winds enough to make it harder to get fuel in Fiji? Maybe the aircraft was topping off in Hawaii so it wouldn't require as much fuel on its next leg from Nadi back to LAX? I didn't know the answer. My tired, soon-to-be-jet-lagged brain threw out more answers than I wanted to contemplate.

Sleep eluded me while we sat on the tarmac in Honolulu. I was continually trying to determine how much time we had lost. After what seemed like two hours on the ground in Honolulu, we took off heading south to Fiji. The rest of the flight was fortunately a blur as my brain decided to unfurl the white flag. The two heavyweights, stress and sleep, duked it out, and fortunately for me, sleep was the victor.

We arrived late to Nadi, but thankfully not too late. We navigated the strange customs and gate-change situation. Once we passed the formalities, we had time to eat some droopy early morning French fries. I'm not sure when they had been cooked, but they took the hunger edge off a little. Even though the group was tired, everyone maintained feelings of excitement about the unprecedented medical and solar mission.

For some reason, I had in my mind that it was only going to take two to three hours to get to Honiara from Fiji. I was wrong yet again. It took two and a half hours to get to Port Vila, Vanuatu, for our only scheduled stop prior to Honiara. On our approach to Port Vila, the area looked a lot like what little we had seen of Fiji. It was very green and mainly devoid of trees. There were a lot of fields and a surprisingly large number of cattle.

As we taxied to a stop in front of the small terminal building, the flight attendant came over the intercom. "Ladies and gentlemen, everyone will need to disembark the aircraft and proceed to the transit lounge. It is important that you take your carry-on bags with you, although if you have any duty-free items, you should leave them on the aircraft or else they will be taken from you by customs officials."

I immediately thought that it was weird that everyone had to get off the plane. What type of a scheduled stop was this? We grabbed our bags and headed out. The entire medical team got off the plane before me. I was by myself toward the end of the line that stretched into the transit lounge. As I got inside, I was dumbfounded to see all the passengers going through a security check with metal detectors and x-ray machines. This still was not making sense to me.

As my turn to run the security gauntlet arrived, I could see the team sitting over in the transit lounge. I must say the word "lounge" conjures images of comfortable furniture and nice ambiance. Not here. Hard plastic chairs bolted to linoleum was as lounge-like as we were going to get.

I placed my backpack on the x-ray machine belt. I wanted to laugh because I really wasn't taking this seriously. Unfortunately, my American ego kicked in as well, and I felt as though these people were wasting my time.

"Sir, are these your batteries?" the screener asked.

"Yes, they're mine. Why?"

"You are only allowed to have eight batteries, and there are sixteen in your bag," the screener responded in total seriousness.

"What? … What do you mean, I have too many batteries? Those batteries are to be used in medical equipment during our medical mission in the Solomon Islands. There is nothing prohibiting me from taking sixteen batteries into the Solomon Islands," I said in a controlled rage.

"Sir, you are not in the Solomon Islands; you are in Vanuatu. You are only allowed to have eight batteries. We are confiscating eight of your batteries."

A thousand thoughts ran through my brain on how to respond without being taken away in handcuffs. I was not legally in Vanuatu. I had not gone through immigration proceedings, and they had not stamped my passport as having entered Vanuatu. They stole my batteries without any legal standing to do so, in my mind. I was furious, to say the least!

"Enjoy the batteries," I said to the guy as he took them from me. I knew I was potentially pushing some buttons by saying those words. I didn't have the luxury of staying around for another hour or two to demand to speak with the American consular agent about the incident. Granted, they were only batteries, but it was the principle that I'd had my property taken from me in a country where I had not been legally admitted. Also, we were going to an isolated part of the world that did not have a convenience store nearby to purchase more batteries from. I was so angry, it was all I could do to control myself from throwing a punch at that Vanuatu asshole behind the counter! I knew those batteries were going home with him or were going to be sold out on the street. This had been nothing more than a rip-off stop, and I was determined to tell the world about stopping in Vanuatu on Air Pacific, no doubt!

No wonder the cabin crew had told people not to take their duty-free items off the airplane. Those security guys probably loved the Air Pacific flight once a week. They were probably able to get all their household goods and booze just by making up phony rules to rip off passengers who weren't staying in Vanuatu for longer than forty-five minutes. It was bullshit! I don't ever need to go to Vanuatu again! Really, I shouldn't even say "again," because legally, I was never there! Back on the airplane, I stewed all the way to Honiara—and beyond, unfortunately. Letting go has never been one of my strong points.

As we approached Honiara, the day's travel got a little more interesting. The flight attendant announced that they would be fumigating the airplane prior to arrival in Honiara. I thought, *What the hell do you mean, fumigating the airplane? There are human beings on the airplane. You don't fumigate human beings!* Going through Australia for these trips to the Solomons was sounding better and better.

A few minutes later, a beautiful Fijian flight attendant strolled down the aisle with a plain white aerosol can in each hand. She walked up and down the aisle, spraying the cans over the passengers' heads until the cans were empty. Suzanne and I tucked our faces into our shirts, if for no other reason than to mentally feel better about the situation. That was bogus. What chemical had they sprayed on us? Why hadn't they opened all the overhead bins before they sprayed? I was completely aware of the terrible effects of the transportation of exotic invasive species, but what were they concerned with—head lice? Maybe they were just spraying aerosolized water, trying to put on a sophisticated first-world-like show for everyone. Maybe it was an aerosolized placebo so we could all feel good that we would be sterilized and clean upon disembarking at the very clean … Honiara airport. Who knew? One thing's for sure, it was not what I needed after being politely mugged by airport security in Vanuatu.

Once we landed, I had another worry to let go. We had to get the team and all the suitcases full of medicines through customs. Even though we had done this one time before, this time, the stakes were higher. I had no tolerance for losing any medicine like I had lost the batteries. The medicines were much more important than the batteries, and I wasn't about to let them go without a fight.

My instructions to the group were to wait at the baggage carousel until everyone had received their luggage. I planned to approach the customs officials as one group, and I would do the talking. I wanted to overwhelm them with a large group to show unity and to reduce the chances of them riffling through each bag. It didn't take long for the sweat to start flowing while we waited at the baggage carousel. The airport was not air-conditioned, and it wouldn't be too long before we all looked like weary, drowned rats.

One by one, all of the bags arrived. Whew, that was a relief. Bags full of drugs sitting in Fiji would not have been good. I notified the group to follow me and Suzanne to the counter. There were two lines: declare and nothing to declare. We chose the declare line, as everyone had checked the box on their customs forms to indicate they were carrying medicines.

Suzanne has mentioned more than once that I've said too much in certain official situations. I figured if I had nothing to hide, why not make honesty the best policy? She was of the mindset that there's no need to provide more information than is requested. I understood, but sometimes the little angel on my shoulder wants me to tell the whole, true story. Suzanne was probably right that I needed to keep my cards closer to my chest.

My plan of presenting the entire group to the customs officials worked. I had copies of their medical licenses in my hand as I explained that we all had medicines for Seghe Hospital. The customs agent looked somewhat like a deer in the headlights with the fifteen people standing in front of him. One by one, we walked through without our bags being searched. We didn't have anything prohibited, but customs officials have been known to make people's lives difficult, especially when trafficking too many AA batteries. (I just can't let that go.)

We exited the international terminal to the sea of cab drivers and other folks waiting to meet arriving passengers. We assembled toward the end of the terminal. From that point, we started the drowned-rat march to the domestic terminal. The sun was blazing, and the air was thick with moisture. The group started to lengthen as different folks lugged suitcases of differing shapes and sizes.

The domestic terminal was as dank and dark as on the previous two times Suzanne and I had visited. The good news was that we had cleared customs without incident, and the second batch of good news was about to hit us. The ticket agent was actually present upon our entrance, and he rattled off words that were music to my ears. The runway at Seghe was functional today. There would be no ninety-minute boat ride from Ramata to Uepi. What a relief after traveling nonstop from Salt Lake.

Suzanne and I had made this journey twice before, but flying over the Marovo Lagoon could never get old. The scenery was hard to beat. After fifty minutes in the air from Honiara to Seghe, the Twin Otter touched down and came to a stop in front of the airport terminal. Bringing a group of people to a place they have never been, enabled me to experience the unknown adventure again through watching their expressions and listening to their words.

A couple of boat drivers from Uepi greeted us as we deplaned. They helped carry our luggage a hundred yards to the small man-made harbor area carved out of the volcanic soils surrounding the airstrip.

After the luggage was loaded onto the two boats, everyone grabbed a seat and we were off to Uepi. The journey from Seghe to Uepi was a short twenty minutes. After twenty-some hours, the notion of almost being there, coupled with the beautiful scenery, seemed to stir new life into the group. Eyes lit up as we started to scoot along the water. The forested islands seemingly plopped down in an azure lagoon were idyllic, to say the least. The area engendered feelings of intrigue and discovery like nowhere else I had ever traveled. Passing villagers fishing from homemade dugout canoes solidified feelings that we were definitely in a remote and wild part of the world. It seemed like another planet from that to which we were accustomed.

Jill and Grant stood on the welcome jetty as our two boats approached. In my usual style, which left something to be desired, I didn't let one minute pass before I asked Grant about the solar power equipment. I think he sensed I was stressed over not knowing when the items would arrive. Unfortunately, he wasn't the bearer of good news. The items had not cleared customs. Because we were importing the goods duty- and tax-free, we had to have someone in the United Church sign off on the paperwork. Evidently, Tony was having a difficult time finding a church official in Honiara to fulfill this requirement. Grant's news didn't help my stress level. I had a team ready to go and no equipment to install. It was out of my hands, but that didn't calm my nerves.

While the welcome drinks were being enjoyed that evening, Jill gave the orientation speech. Next, she led the group down the path for a tour of the resort, which included finding our assigned cabins. As hard as it was for me not to give people too much information, Suzanne and I had purposefully shared little information about Uepi Island Resort. We loved it and we knew the food was off the charts, but we hadn't wanted to build up any expectations should others not enjoy it as much as we did.

Suzanne and I were in cabin one, the largest cabin. We didn't use executive privilege because we were the leaders but because our cabin served as the supply and pharmacy depot. It had a large front room with space for two cots and a couple of wooden shelving units.

That evening was long and tiring. Suzanne gave a short orientation and plan for the next day. People were nodding away during her talk, but we still needed to have all the medicines and supplies sorted, inventoried, and organized in cabin one. We needed an adequate amount of each medication repacked in a couple of suitcases to be taken to the village clinics each day. We put Kirk and Jenny in charge of the pharmacy. Not only were they on their honeymoon, but this would be their first experience serving as pharmacists. It was a joke that because they were on their honeymoon, we had purposefully put them in cabin six, situated at the end of the long path. … Maybe it wasn't a joke.

Prior to our arrival, Grant had been in contact with several villages to plan for visits from our medical team. Communication in the lagoon wasn't the easiest. Most villages had radios, but ensuring that the information was properly disseminated was a crap shoot. We had no idea whether the reception would be warm or cold, big or small, at the villages.

Our departure the next morning came way too soon. I think everyone could have slept a few more hours. We had to leave by 8:30 a.m. Grant mentioned that the church and hospital staff had prepared a welcome ceremony for the team. We were the VIP guests at the hospital, and we couldn't be late.

The arrival at the hospital was a delight. The nursing staff and folks from the United Church were on hand to present each of us with a lei as we entered the hospital. Chairs were arranged in the waiting area. Adjacent to the chairs was a large table covered with coconuts, sliced pineapple, and cookies. It was a delightful and welcoming spread. Smiling from ear to ear, Bishop Wilfred Kurepitu gave me a warm welcome. He was probably happy that we had actually returned like we'd said we would.

The welcome ceremony began shortly after the medical team sat in the chairs. The formality and order with which community gatherings and events were conducted quickly became evident. There was a master of ceremonies, who introduced the various speakers. Each speaker, representing part of the church, the hospital, or a local village, presented a thorough speech. After several speeches, the nursing staff sang a song that tugged on my heartstrings. I wasn't the only one in the group fighting back tears. The small gesture of a song meant a lot to us. They didn't need to give us anything, but a song was a fantastic start to the trip.

At the conclusion of the ceremony, some of the nursing staff took members of our group on a tour of the hospital. The place was still in terrible condition, but there had been a solid effort to clean the facility prior to our arrival. After the tour, I, along with Kirk, Gordon, and Terry, ventured out to put in a day's work. There was a lot to do prior to the arrival of the solar power equipment. The sun was so strong, I could feel my skin starting to blister. The heat was so great that our team of gringos had to take turns working out in the open.

Grant had provided a few workers from Uepi to help. More accurately, at this stage of the game, we were there to help the workers whom Grant had provided. Topher and Boyce were the carpenters and Sau was an electrician student. I found it ironic that there was an electrical training program in the Marovo located at Batuna. It was a school run by the Seventh-day Adventist Church and also included business and carpentry programs. There wasn't much electricity available for the students to actually see in action in the lagoon, and the school at Batuna had a large generator, but it didn't run all the time. The class had visited Uepi Island Resort on occasion to see electricity in action because the resort ran its generators twenty-four hours a day. I was hoping Seghe Hospital would become a field trip spot for future electrician classes from Batuna. Without solar power equipment, however, my dreams would need to be shelved.

Prior to our arrival, Grant had had some of his workers pour a concrete slab on the end of the maternity ward. The slab would serve as the foundation for the battery building. All the inner workings of the solar power system would be housed in the battery building. Our first task was to link the generator building to the battery building. The trenching that stood before us was not attractive. The weather conditions were brutal. Fortunately, we didn't have to trench too deeply, as the tools we had to use were not the best. The deep red soil was full of coral. I didn't mind digging, but add in the equatorial sun, and it was like working under the broiler in an oven. We took turns being out in the sweltering heat. We didn't want to overheat. I imagine the local guys were having a good laugh at the pale Americans digging for five minutes and then taking a break; this was just another day for them.

Architectural plans for the hospital were not available. The building had been built eight years prior to our arrival. No one currently at the hospital had had anything to do with its original construction. All we knew was that the bones of the facility were excellent. Unfortunately, the folks who had built the hospital had walked out the door the minute it was finished and hadn't left any long-term plan in place for how to maintain and care for the facility. It was a typical third-world aid project. There had likely been a lot of excitement when the project had been underway, and that excitement had probably carried forward for a couple years after the construction was finished. Had there been a long-term plan in place, however, the hospital probably wouldn't have now looked like it was built during WWII. Ah, the beauty of international aid projects.

We had to dig and try to piece the electrical connections together without knowing what was already buried. We could see a couple of septic tank lids buried away from the buildings, but we didn't know where the lines ran. Gingerly, we continued to dig. We found two pipes with the shovel; we hit one a little harder than the other. Fortunately, the pipe we partially broke was the existing conduit from the generator building to the main power panel in the hospital. The pipe we didn't break was the sewer line—wow! We weren't physically or mentally prepared to patch a broken sewer line.

While the digging was going on, the carpenters were busy framing the battery building. For the time being, it was nice not having the solar power equipment to lead us astray. There were more things to accomplish prior to unwrapping the first solar panel than I had been aware of.

Gordon and Terry went over the wiring plans multiple times to make sure we were trenching in the right place. We planned to bolt the power panel, containing the three inverters and charge controllers, to the wall of the maternity ward. The conduit running from the generator to the building would have to come up in the right spot because we didn't have unlimited amounts of cable. The thick cable was expensive, so we couldn't screw up.

Upon returning to Uepi that first evening after a full day of effort, most of the team changed into their bathing suits and donned snorkeling gear to explore Charapoana Passage. The intrinsic rewards received from working at the hospital on day one were bolstered by the extrinsic rewards offered by the stunningly beautiful and diverse marine life below the surface. A day full of serving people who have great need for health care and then finished off with looking at the most amazing coral reef in the world was a day full of nonstop highs, to my mind.

CHAPTER

10

*S*everal hot, sunny days had passed on this trip in the world's longest saltwater lagoon. The group was working well together. Everyone had undoubtedly experienced something new. The sights, sounds, and smells were all different from those of their lives in the States. The tropical climate and close proximity to both rainforests and coral reefs produced excitement at every turn. It was basically paradise ... without adequate health care. It was a huge problem for a country to not have adequate health care options for its citizens.

Working with the Solomon Islands nurses produced fruitful and thought-provoking interactions. Although our nurses had more comprehensive educational training, the Solomon Islands nurses dealt with a far greater range of issues and treatments daily than most nurses in the United States. The nurses in effect served as doctors at Seghe Hospital because no doctor had ever worked there permanently. Even though they addressed, and in most cases treated, every case that walked, crawled, or was carried into the facility, the nurses' hands were tied. Their RN training provided a broad range of skills, but they were only allowed to prescribe a certain number of medicines. Staffing issues, along with facility deficiencies, were the two main issues preventing Seghe Hospital from providing far more health care options for the people of the Marovo.

The majority of the team, minus the three doctors who were coming late, arrived at Seghe on a Monday. The other three doctors arrived on Friday of the first week. We worked Tuesday through Friday the first week and then Monday through Thursday the second week. The workdays consisted of a minimum of eight hours each, and some days stretched even longer. Our team had weekends off while in the Marovo. The first weekend couldn't have come soon enough. It had been a long week, and the team enjoyed two days of diving, snorkeling, and relaxing.

The second Monday morning arrived with good news. The solar power system had cleared customs. Unfortunately, my stress level remained high because the equipment had missed the scheduled barge to Seghe. The clock was ticking, and for us to get the project finished, we needed some serious progress with shipping. Grant worked every angle he could to kick-start some progress. He went the extra mile, and I appreciated his efforts. He and Jill had lived and worked in the Solomons for nearly fifteen years at this point. They dealt regularly with shipping and customs officials in Honiara, and they provided the companies in Honiara with a lot of business. My problem couldn't have been in better hands.

Leaving Uepi every day for eight hours was hard because I had no contact with Grant. I wanted information updates on the solar shipment, but I had to wait until we returned to Uepi. We had a satellite phone, but the rates were far too expensive to be using it for information updates. It wasn't until after the trip that I realized I hadn't even had Uepi's phone number if something crazy had happened. Brilliant.

One of the last villages the team visited was Tinge. It was on the "weather coast," on the southwest side of Vangunu Island. We had to go out beyond Seghe and then outside the calm waters of the Marovo to get to Tinge. Upon our approach to Tinge, the area was stunningly beautiful. The beaches were lined with coconut trees, and the forested mountains behind the village seemed to be endless. The village itself was well manicured, with beautiful flowers and gardens surrounding the houses. It had a small clinic, which wasn't large enough to allow all the members of the team to do their jobs, so some people had to stay outside. Specifically, Kate Wilson had to locate her dental shop out in a grassy open area. The first few dental patients she received were immediately assessed and given anesthetic so their teeth could be extracted. The medicine took time to work, so Kate was able to numb the school principal first, and then an eight-year-old boy. Kate said the boy's tooth really needed to come out, so she was glad to be there.

With the anesthetic having taken effect, Kate positioned the principal on a plastic lawn chair out in the open. Gordon's wife, Jann, assisted Kate with the dental instruments. As usual, when we started the clinics, people came out in droves, if not for treatment, to watch the team. A decent-sized crowd gathered to watch Kate pull teeth. The eight-year-old was in the on-deck circle, waiting for his turn. As Kate pulled the principal's tooth, he fainted in the chair. Kate carefully slid the principal to the ground and asked Jann to get a blood pressure cuff. The man came to quickly, and Kate had him lie there for a little while while she monitored him closely. After the dust settled, she looked around. Everyone was gone. All the spectators, including the boy who was already numb, had vanished. Not many medical teams, if any, had visited Tinge before. This incident may have derailed any dental business at Tinge for the foreseeable future.

When she was finished with the principal, Kate found the boy's mother, who said her son had run to their house to hide. He didn't want anything to do with getting his tooth pulled after watching what had happened to his principal. Kate went in the house and talked with the boy. He was miserable with the tooth; it needed to come out. There was no amount of persuasion possible to get the boy out of the house, however. The tooth would have to work its way out on its own. Watching the principal faint was an experience that neither Kate nor any of the others present would ever forget.

As the trip waned, so did my hope for finishing the solar power system. The team had treated 800 patients by the end of the trip. Gordon and I planned to stay several more days to tie up loose ends. The memories for the medical team would likely last a lifetime, but without a solar power system, I was trying to selectively erase memories from my mind.

The day before the majority of the team departed, we were asked to come to the hospital. We milled about the waiting area of the hospital, waiting for our next instructions. After an hour, one of the nurses summoned us to a school classroom building located behind the hospital. One by one, we entered the building to see an elaborate arrangement. The hospital staff and members of the church had gone all out to thank us for our service to the Marovo community. In the center of the room, a large table dominated the space. It was decoratively arranged with a massive quantity and variety of food. The village had come together with a lot of resources for the celebration. Bishop Kurepitu, hospital staff, and helpers from the United Church treated the team to a glorious farewell celebration. Two of the local police officers were there to show their support, as well.

Solomon Island customs were alive and well that afternoon. The master of ceremonies called community leaders to share speeches of thanksgiving for us. Many of the speeches emphasized the sacrifices that we had made to come treat the sick of the Marovo. The speeches wrapped up, and then the festivities began. Singing and music enveloped the room. The hospital staff stood at the front of the room. They danced and called names of our team members to come up to the front. One by one, we worked our way to the front. The hospital staff wrapped a sheet of cloth called a lava lava around each one of us, and we danced in circles and then slowly made our way back to our seats. It wasn't a conga line, but it started to morph in that direction.

Each lava lava was emblazoned with a map of the Solomon Islands and was full of eye-popping colors. Gifts were not necessary, but they didn't want us to leave without knowing how much they appreciated our service and care. I felt their thanksgiving through the smiles, food, speeches, and dance. However briefly, I forgot about the solar power system. The positive energy and excitement took me to a place I had desperately needed to go.

The next morning, I was greeted with a terrible feeling of anxiety. Those feelings could easily get the best of me if I wasn't careful. Suzanne and the rest of the team, except for three of the doctors, Gordon, and I, were leaving. Gordon and I had more work to do on the battery building in preparation for the hopeful arrival of the system.

Suzanne always said I was a pessimist, yet I contended to be a realist. On this occasion, she was right, hands down. Pessimism was winning. My intent to stay calm and let things happen had eroded completely. Remaining calm with a shred of optimism was really hard to do when we had personally invested thousands of dollars in the system and many other friends and family had donated thousands of dollars as well. I just couldn't get back on the plane without seeing the equipment land at Seghe.

On the day that the majority of the team departed, the Twin Otter buzzed around Seghe on its final approach. For building an airstrip in six or seven days during the Hem Big Fella Fight, the US Navy Seabees had done a pretty darn good job. Yeah, there was a spot that had settled, but my hat went off to that team for creating an airstrip that had lasted seventy-plus years.

The Solomon Airlines agent yelled at people to get off the runway. The strip was situated alongside several government buildings, homes, and a store. Folks had to cross the runway to get to the market, hospital, or seminary. I'm sure people knew they needed to get off the runway because the plane was coming, but they didn't seem to hurry. Ah, Solomon time.

I wasn't going to be alone, but my heart sank with feelings of anxiety as I said good-bye to Suzanne. There would be 8,000 miles between us when she got to Salt Lake. The stress of the solar power system not showing up didn't help my fragile mental state. I needed to calm down. Everything would be fine. It was times like this that I wanted my faith to kick in and to instill the soothing calm I craved.

Two hours after the majority of the team had left, Gordon and I were working in the battery building when Jimmy, the malaria technician, came running out to get me. "Allan, Grant Kelly from Uepi Island Resort is on the radio, and he needs to speak with you immediately."

I dropped the hammer and followed Jimmy back to the outpatient clinic. I sat down in front of the radio and clicked the button on the receiver. "Grant, what's going on?"

"Allan, the barge just left Uepi on its way to Seghe. The loadmaster on the boat told me that he did not have any record of your items on the boat. This guy didn't load the boat in Honiara. I just called and spoke with the loadmaster who actually loaded the boat in Honiara. He assured me your goods were on the boat."

"Okay, so when will the boat be here?"

"I told the loadmaster to make sure he stopped at the Seghe wharf so you could get on the boat. You have to do everything possible to make sure that boat stops at Seghe. Chase after it if you have to. You need to ask the loadmaster if you can search the vessel."

"What? Search the vessel?" I queried, getting nervous about what lay ahead.

"Yes, you need to ask to search the vessel to look for your goods. I was told they are on the boat."

"When should I look for the boat?"

"It's pretty slow—probably an hour or so. Good luck."

"Thanks, Grant. I'll let you know what happens."

Thoughts ran through my head like crazy. How would I stop this barge if the captain decided not to stop at Seghe? I was a white man in a very non-white country. I hadn't brought my US Coast Guard cap with me. My experience in redirecting maritime vessels was zero. My Pidgin English skills were next to nonexistent; I could somewhat understand it, but I couldn't speak it worth crap. Needless to say, my anxiety about Suzanne leaving had just walked out the door. My attention quickly turned to the fact that I was potentially going to play the main character in an international maritime incident. On top of that, I was in a country where my presence had little bearing on anything or anyone.

I walked back to the battery building, pensive, to say the least. I explained to Gordon that we had about forty-five minutes before we needed to head down to the wharf to flag the ship down. I don't know if it was his age or the fact that his bacon wasn't on the line here, but Gordon had a great knack for not getting too worked up over things. He was adept at pointing out to me that I was good at letting things get to me. I needed some serious help in that arena.

I silently prayed for God to make that boat stop at Seghe. There was an Uepi boat at Seghe somewhere, but I didn't want to have to chase after the barge. That would have looked like a fly trying to land on the rear end of a large steer. Flies get swatted when messing around the rear end of a steer.

On my third time walking out to the small knoll in front of the hospital, I could see the barge chugging our way. I walked through the hospital, looking for some hospital employees to follow me for help and support. Jimmy and a couple others were intrigued and followed us to the wharf.

The barge slowly passed Patutiva village, which was located across the channel from Seghe. Seghe was located on the southern most tip of New Georgia Island. The water between the two islands was full of swirling currents, sometimes presenting challenges to navigation. Fishermen in dugout canoes paddled casually to get out of the way of the vessel.

Closer and closer, the motorized barge came. I couldn't tell if it was going to turn toward the wharf or continue straight. The front of the boat looked and acted like a barge by carrying lots of various supplies on its open, flat deck. The back of the boat had an elevated bridge area from which the captain guided the vessel. The slow pace of the boat did not help to slow my heartbeat.

"Come on, you have to turn. Turn, turn, turn…" When the boat was nearly perpendicular to the wharf, the sound of the engine changed. Ever so slowly, the boat started to turn toward us. *Yes, sweet relief.* I could at least put away my make-believe Coast Guard cap. I'm not sure how the captain would have reacted to a crazy white man tailing his vessel while dramatically waving his arms and yelling for the barge to pull over.

Slowly, the barge approached the end of the wharf. Closer and closer it came. The large steel bow started to open downward toward the tip of the wharf. The massive door gently landed on the concrete with a screech as the boat continued to inch forward. A few seconds later, the deckhand motioned to the captain to stop. What a picture this was. The vessel was full to the brim with seemingly random items. Among the things were several salty-dog deckhands who did not have smiles on their faces. Amongst them was a gentleman dressed in nicer clothes and carrying a large bundle of papers in his hands. He walked off the end of the barge and called out, "Mr. Allan, I'm sorry, but my paperwork does not show any of your goods being on this vessel."

"Grant Kelly told me he spoke with someone in Honiara who said they saw the goods being loaded on the boat."

He rolled his eyes a little. Then he lifted the large stack of papers in a non-verbal response as if to show that if it was on the boat, it wasn't registered on his paperwork.

Okay, time for my courage to kick in here. "May I search this vessel, sir?" He looked at me funny but, thankfully, yielded. With a smile on his face, he waved me aboard. That was the first and maybe only time in my life when I felt like John Wayne.

The smell of oil and gasoline was strong. The ship was in good shape, but there was no mistaking that it was a boat built to do nothing other than haul freight. It was made of solid steel, and there was nothing soft about it. Where to start? I was looking at a boat that was probably thirty feet wide and eighty feet long. In front of me, in the center, were two trucks lined up. On either side of the trucks were pallets, some stacked two high. Behind the trucks, up against the bridge, were dozens and dozens of fuel barrels stacked nearly to the windows of the bridge. Pallets were stacked behind the trucks, as well.

Gordon had some minor back issues at the time, so he stayed on the periphery. All eyes were on me. Many of the pallets were draped in black plastic and had no identifying labels attached. I had not seen the solar equipment before it was shipped from the States, so I didn't know what to look for. My only option was to rip holes in the pallet covering to see their contents. Cereal was in this pallet and light fixtures in that pallet. Rice and other food staples were common. Industrial tools and other items likely heading to logging camps were strewn about. It took a while to make my way around the deck.

As I rounded the rear truck, I looked up to catch sight of the captain touching his watch as he looked down to the loadmaster. Shoot, this was taking too long and I wasn't finding my stuff. Stolid Solomon Island seamen glared at me. I ripped the plastic open on pallets and pushed items here and there to get a better glimpse at what was underneath and behind. *Come on,* I thought, *there has to be some solar equipment on this boat.* I figured thirty solar panels should make a sizeable pallet or box. Add a pallet of batteries and the power panel with the inverters and charge controllers, and it would all take up a fair amount of space.

I was three-quarters of the way around the vessel, and still nothing. I looked in the back of both trucks; those two pallets contained building materials but nothing solar power related. Halfway back to the bow on the opposite side from which I started, I knelt down to look at a small white tag that had some writing on it. There it was, the name of our nonprofit sponsor.

"I've got something here!" I shouted with elation and serious relief in my voice.

Gordon came aboard, and the loadmaster approached as well. I ripped open the plastic to find a large silver box—the power panel. The racking for the solar panels was in several long cardboard boxes. I also noticed a pallet that was about half full. Under the plastic were the sixteen batteries.

Before we could move any of the items off the boat, we had to move the first truck onto the wharf. The items were packed so tightly near the truck, it was impossible to move anything. Also, the batteries were not going to be fun to move, as they weighed 160 pounds each.

One of the salty deckhands jumped into the driver's seat of the truck. It was a large Toyota Landcruiser truck with a pallet of supplies in the bed. Over and over, he turned the key, but the truck wouldn't start. The loadmaster ordered several guys to push the truck. All the deckhands pushed, and it slowly started to move toward the front. At that point, it turned over and started purring like a Toyota should. I stood near the bow as the truck slowly drove down the bow landing deck. The driver obviously didn't see the massive hole at the bottom of the bow door; the left front tire went straight into it. At that very moment, the entire truck with the heavy pallet in the bed leaned precariously to the left. I grabbed my head, bracing for the truck to tip over on its side. It was going to roll off the wharf and into the water. Oh no, I didn't want to be responsible for this freak accident. I held my breath for a split second as the truck looked like it was at an angle beyond its ability to right itself. Miraculously, the truck didn't go over. It bounced back on all four tires violently and eventually stopped swinging back and forth. That was close!

There happened to be one truck in Seghe at the time, and it was down at the wharf. The vehicle may have been owned by the church, but I wasn't sure. The guys from the hospital came onboard and joined the deckhands in removing the batteries one by one. It took two guys to move one of the batteries. They didn't seem happy moving the batteries, and I couldn't blame them; the batteries were nothing more than giant bricks of lead. It took the guys about fifteen minutes to get all the batteries loaded on the truck. Then they drove the truck, which was obviously bearing a lot of weight, to the hospital and unloaded the batteries into the battery building.

In the meantime, the guys from the hospital and I took the racking and other components off the boat so the barge could continue on its way. One thing was missing. With the extra room available since the truck had been pulled off, I continued to look for the solar panels. *They have to be here*, I thought. There should have been one or two pallets stacked high with thirty panels. *Don't despair; just keep looking*, I told myself. A few more minutes passed, and I started rechecking pallets. Despair returned, looking uglier than ever! I was forced beyond my strongest sense of will to accept the fact that there were no solar panels on the boat.

Gordon was as dumbfounded as I was. Why, how, where, who? What the…? I rarely used curse words, but if there was ever a time to let go of a few bombs, this would have been it! I didn't explode, though. I had to compose myself and deal with the loadmaster. I immediately notified him of the shortage. He didn't know what to think of my claims, because he'd had no record of any of the things we'd pulled off the boat in the first place. I could have told him there should have been a bright red Ferrari on the boat, and he probably would have shrugged his shoulders just the same. He noted all the items that we had received and also noted that thirty solar panels were not on board.

No, no, no! This was not how this was supposed to have happened!

The loadmaster told me he would provide the information to his superiors when the boat returned to Honiara. There was nothing else he could do or offer me to make me feel better.

The deckhands drove the truck back on the boat, missing the hole this time. As I watched the boat leave, I couldn't help but think that the panels could still be on there. I knew I had looked at everything, but was there a slim chance I had missed thirty solar panels? It was hard to erase the shred of doubt that was lodged deep in my brain.

As the barge pulled away, several guys took the racking and other equipment to the battery building. I marched straight back to the radio. I tracked down Jimmy and asked him to call Uepi. A few minutes later, Margaret, who worked in the office at Uepi, answered the radio. I asked to speak with Grant, and several minutes later, he answered.

"Grant," I said, "I received half the equipment, but there were no solar panels. I repeat … there were no solar panels on the boat." Awkward silence.

"You must be joking."

"I wish I was. I checked the boat thoroughly, and everything but the solar panels was there."

"I'll notify Silentworld of the missing items and see if they are still at the warehouse in Honiara."

"Thanks for doing that. After we secure all the equipment, we'll head back."

My mood during the boat ride back to Uepi was cloudy, to say the least. Answers … I wanted answers … and I didn't have them. The equipment we had was fantastic, but it was completely useless without solar panels to collect the sun's energy and turn it into direct current. Gordon and I conversed on potential scenarios of where the panels could be. Maybe they had been stolen. It was 2008, and global demand for solar panels was taking off, after all.

I was tired of speculating, and extremely irritated! The twenty-minute boat ride to Uepi flew by. Once back on land, I went straight to my cabin and retrieved contact information for the shipping company, which I am referring to as Redtail Shipping. They were responsible for shipping the items from Los Angeles. I marched down to the end of the boat jetty and pulled out the satellite phone. Before long, I was connected to a customer service representative in LA. I calmly yet pointedly explained the problem, and the representative assured me that Redtail would look into the shortage and get back with me.

The next day was the final day for the three remaining doctors. Their day consisted of rounding on patients at the hospital and doing a little nursing education. The nurses at Seghe had soaked up information from all the docs throughout the trip. One of the docs, Dr. Mark Oliver, thoroughly enjoyed educating other medical personnel regarding infectious diseases, his specialty. Mark had been in the outpatient clinic, looking at a patient with one of the nurses, discussing various aspects of the patient's condition. It was an uneventful day. Around three o'clock, as we waited for the boat driver to come get us from the hospital, sitting in the open-air waiting room of the hospital, we heard a loud scream and an ensuing struggle. The loud rip of cloth was punctuated by another scream and then a scuffle. Shouting from a male voice started as the nurse whom Mark had been teaching ran out of the outpatient clinic, holding her ripped shirt. The other nurses came running to her aid.

The nurse's husband was the information officer for the hospital at the time. He came out of the clinic after her with rage in his eyes, his fists clenched. He threw another punch at her in front of all of us as two other nurses shielded his wife from the blow. "You bitch!" he yelled.

"Go, leave, leave!" one of the other nurses yelled.

One of the malaria technicians ran in and grabbed the husband and pushed him off of the hospital porch in an effort to control his rage. The husband walked away from the hospital. His wife was crying. This wasn't the first time he had beaten her. It came out later that he was jealous that she had been working with Mark during the day. She and Mark had had nothing but a completely professional exchange about patient care and the specific condition of a patient. There was nothing inappropriate, but her husband had viewed it in a different light and had taken his misguided perceptions out on his nurse wife.

This was a side of Solomon Island culture that Suzanne and I had not been privy to on our previous two visits. I felt terrible for the nurse. Thankfully, she wasn't badly hurt. Prior to witnessing the event, I had thought I was at a pretty low point because of not receiving the solar panels, but the terrible domestic abuse that occurred in front of our eyes certainly didn't help to soothe my downtrodden mental state.

CHAPTER

11

*A*fter twenty-two days in the Solomon Islands, Gordon and I were forced to return to the States without completing the job. Disbelief ate at my core. The mystery of where the solar panels were was almost too much for me to bear. There were a lot of gracious donations from many trusting individuals wrapped up in those panels.

Failure is never fun or easy to manage. Failing to complete a project that comprised a lot of other people's money contained a different set of emotions and responsibilities altogether for me. I had to go to church the next Sunday and tell people that the job wasn't finished. Even harder, I had to explain that the solar panels were missing, their whereabouts unknown. The news created many questions that I couldn't answer. I could only tell the story and let folks know that the company we had purchased the items from was diligently working on our behalf.

A couple of months of supposed investigations passed. Mark Coleman at Wholesale Solar obviously felt terrible because he had arranged the shipping. He was bending over backward, working with Redtail Shipping on our behalf. His dealings with them got more and more heated as the weeks turned into months. Redtail Shipping tried to claim that Mark had not purchased insurance on the shipment. Of course he had asked for insurance! Who in their right mind would not insure an international shipment worth nearly $50,000? That was absurd. He knew the fragility of the equipment; obviously, things could get damaged in transit. He also knew there was serious demand for solar panels in developing nations. These reasons, along with the fact that getting insurance was a good business practice, had Redtail's "no insurance" argument looking like Swiss cheese.

I didn't let Mark know I was working behind the scenes to try to get a resolution. Where were the panels? Where had they gone missing? An answer, that was all I wanted. Just give me an answer, damn it! Asking those questions to Redtail over and over did get me somewhere. The international shipping shell game had started.

"Sir, you are going to have to call the Sydney office because your shipment stopped at five ports in Papua New Guinea before it was scheduled to reach the Solomon Islands," the representative told me during one of my many phone calls. Conveniently for the Los Angeles office, Redtail also happened to have an office in Sydney, Australia. The people in the LA office were probably getting tired of the gnats buzzing in their ears and were likely delighted to be able to tell me to call Sydney. That was bullshit! We had paid a company in Los Angeles to ship our goods to the Solomon Islands. It was their responsibility to call Sydney, not mine! Talk about terrible customer service and shoddy business practices. The lack of utter responsibility boiled my blood. It was easy for them to pass me off to another country, and they did it without thinking twice.

The level of caring and love I tried to extend to fellow human beings was high. My Christian faith reinforced the need to treat others as I would like to be treated. It did open me up for a lot of disappointment, but I didn't want to act any other way. Unfortunately, a lot of people don't share this approach. Many, many businesses definitely don't share this approach. As the days and weeks went on, I learned firsthand that corporations are not designed to have hearts; they are designed for no other purpose than to make money.

Throughout this process, I just wanted these people to put on my shoes and to see what I was going through. I was trying to provide a free power source to a small rural hospital in the developing world. Couldn't they see this was a noble pursuit? Was no one at Redtail Shipping interested in getting to the bottom of where the panels had landed? I felt like I was dealing with animals who were trained to not dig deeply to find lost goods. Such digging would cost money, and corporations tried to spend as little as possible to make as much as possible. It made me cold to realize that no one at Redtail Shipping truly seemed to have one fiber of caring in their hearts.

As my search for the panels dragged on and on, it got to the point that people were obviously wondering if everything was on the up and up. A friend at church joked one Sunday, "Oh, maybe the Dalys needed a new boat." I chuckled for a minute, but the comment immediately put me on the defensive because I was putting every ounce of my being into this investigation and this project. I knew the comment was a joke, but Suzanne and I were financially secure, and doing something inappropriate with those donations was the farthest thing from my mind. It was a tough comment to digest.

Redtail Shipping from the outside looked to be designed to repel outsiders from gleaning too much information. I scoured its website, looking for names and contact information for people up the chain of command. The website was scrubbed clean of any sort of contact information other than the addresses and phone numbers of their various offices around the world. No names or titles were listed. Why was there so much to hide? Their perpetual response via e-mail or phone conversations was "We are looking into it." In my mind, those words were devoid of any action or sincerity.

The group coffers were not endless. I thought of ways to hold Redtail Shipping accountable without breaking the bank. The company was huge, with endless resources, and I was 5'10", with definite limits to my financial reach. I wrote a press release that I was going to send to local media outlets. Yes, I'd have the press hold them accountable! How could I smear them into finding the equipment? I dreamed of the coverage: "Big Business Screws Mom and Pop Charity … and Seems to Love Every Minute of It!" How flowery and sensational could I make it? I wasn't a fan of sensational media, or just media as it is today, but maybe I had to employ it to get results. I was reaching and desperate. Nothing seemed to be too farfetched for me to try.

We approached six months with no resolution. Six months from the time we had pulled the other equipment off the barge at Seghe, and still no answers. Six months of me and Wholesale Solar trying to get answers out of Redtail Shipping. Six months of being treated like a nuisance after we had paid more than $5,000 to this company to ship the solar materials to Seghe. Six months of trying to penetrate a company's façade to find one individual who had not been trained or brainwashed to not help customers who had goods go missing. Six months of questions from our gracious donors asking if I had found the solar panels yet. Six months of my stomach tied in knots of uncertainty about what I would do if the company never found the panels. Six months of despair with the real possibility that the company would choose not to refund our money. It was definitely this point in my life when gray hair infiltrated my scalp, no doubt.

One final option to try was to employ the pro bono services of my corporate attorney brother-in-law. He was aware of my troubles, but until this point, I had not asked him any legal questions. Doctors don't like medical questions outside of work, and I know it's the same for lawyers. I tried to respect and extend the same courtesy to him that I wanted extended to Suzanne. My strategy regarding holding Redtail Shipping accountable in the press raised red flags with my brother-in-law the attorney. He counseled me about using any disparaging remarks about a large company. Their attorneys would jump all over me, and then I'd have a potentially greater problem on my hands. That was not what I wanted to hear.

I asked him if he could write a nasty letter for me on his firm's letterhead. He was okay to do that but had to check with their conflict-of-interest computer program to see if his firm had ever dealt with Redtail Shipping. Just my luck, they had dealt in some way at some point with the company. My brother-in-law's hands were tied, and there was nothing else he could offer me, except deeper despair.

It was obvious to me that the company had no intention of upholding its contractual insurance obligation to pay us for the value of the solar panels. Without sinking thousands of dollars into paying an attorney to force Redtail's hand, I didn't know what else to do.

One evening as I settled in behind the computer, I thought to research the genesis of Redtail Shipping. There had to be a story behind when the company was started and by whom. Typing different sets of words into search engines produced fruit. The name of the company's founder came up. Then news stories about the guy popped up. He was a billionaire, no surprises there. Most of his time was supposedly spent on his yacht in Monaco. *How cliché*, I thought. Maybe I was dealing with Dr. Evil here. Then a link emerged that directed me to his family foundation based in the Caribbean. *Hmm, a family foundation based in the Caribbean, now that sounds one hundred percent legitimate.* My skepticism and sarcasm resulted from me being at the end of a very long rope.

Finally, I found an actual e-mail address associated with someone who likely had direct ties to this reclusive moneybags: the director of the family foundation. I immediately composed an e-mail to the woman. I poured out my heart and soul to her. I was figuratively on my knees, begging for a bone to be thrown in my direction. My pride and dignity were at the bottom of the Marovo Lagoon. This was my last and only real shot at getting some-one high up in the organization to look at my case.

Two days went by, and finally, I received an e-mail response from the direc-tor. My heart sank as I read the first line: "I'm sorry but I no longer work for his organization." Not only was the knife deep into my heart, but she was starting to twist the handle. But wait, there was a glimmer of hope here: "I am still in touch with him and I will forward your email to him. If he feels it is of merit, he will contact you." Thank you, thank you! This was a step in the right direction, at least. I just hoped I had adequately conveyed the amount of pain and desperation I had been through. In my response to her, I passionately explained that the nurses at Seghe Hospital were still forced to deliver babies by candlelight because we didn't have the solar pan-els. Come on! This guy had to have one tiny sliver of compassion in his body … although I knew a billion dollars could buy a pretty nice pair of blinders.

Several days later, my prayers were answered. My in-box had an e-mail from the billionaire himself. The hair went up on the back of my neck when I saw it. My nerves were paused on the precipice, ready to fall into elation or defeat. What would it be? I was somewhat scared to open the e-mail. What if he said, "Sorry, buddy, but we didn't do anything wrong"? I had no idea how I would react to that type of news after six months of beat-ing my head against the wall.

I clicked on the e-mail and … nothing. Where was the text? *There's no damn text in the e-mail! What the hell?* I scrolled up and down a couple of times. The only information in the e-mail was the owner's Blackberry number. That was weird. Something must have happened. Of all the e-mails in the world for the text to not show up in. … *Are you kidding me? Hmm?* Or was this the way billionaires communicated with other people? Maybe this was code, or maybe this was him wanting me to call him so he wouldn't be liable for anything he put in writing. He couldn't have been that chicken, could he?

Overcome with nervous fright and not knowing what to do with the phan-tom e-mail, I quickly responded: "Sir, I apologize for taking your time, but there was no text in your email. If you would be so kind as to resend it, I would greatly appreciate it." I hoped I hadn't somehow blown it with that e-mail. Hopefully, those two sentences wouldn't take him away from grapes and Dom Perignon being massaged down his throat by a team of beautiful personal body managers. Or maybe the team of massage therapists would have to take a break from working on his big hairy back. … Who knew? I just hoped he would take the time to resend the e-mail.

Suzanne was thrilled to hear the news that the mysterious billionaire had made contact. Sadly, by that evening, he had still not responded. I really needed to work on not jumping straight to the worst-case scenario. *Come on, have faith*, I told myself. I did have faith, but obviously, my faith needed to grow. Everyone who has faith is a work in progress, but I needed to rely on my faith in difficult situations and not jump straight to doom and gloom.

The next day, I received a present straight from heaven with a bow and beautiful silver lining! There were two e-mails in my inbox. The first was from the billionaire, and the second was from one of his henchmen. Actually, the other guy was the president of one of the billionaire's shipping companies. The first e-mail read, "William, will you please look into this." Bingo! I knew I had it solved at that point. Yes, yes, yes! After six months of sheer agony, I was about to fall into a soft, plush pile of success.

The second e-mail was from William. He explained that he was going to give me a guarantee that the situation would be resolved one way or another. They were going to accept responsibility for the lost solar panels if they could not find them. Oh, the sweet, sweet smell of answered prayers!

It took William a week of digging before he got back to me. I had a momentary relapse into doom and gloom during that week, but his e-mail quickly pulled me back to happy time. The solar panels had been located in a warehouse in Sydney. The Los Angeles office had determined that the Sydney office was responsible for the loss and had sent Sydney a bill for $30,000, the cost of the solar panels. I bet the supervisor who'd received the bill had said, "Hey, Herb, why don't you go out to the warehouse and see if there are some solar panels out there?" Sure enough, the panels had been sitting in a Sydney warehouse for six months. All that time, and no one had thought to contact me or the Los Angeles office about the wayward solar panels collecting dust in their warehouse.

What else was in that warehouse? How many other people, like me, were trying fruitlessly to find their missing goods? How long would the warehouse have kept the solar panels? How would they eventually have disposed of the solar panels or other "unclaimed" items? That was a real head-scratcher. It was nebulous and wrong on many levels. It sort of reminded me of the final scene in *Raiders of the Lost Ark* when the crate containing the ark is deposited in a warehouse, never to be seen again. My questions will probably never be answered.

In their embarrassment, Redtail Shipping put the thirty solar panels on a jet and flew them straight to Honiara. Now I was bouncing off the walls. We were going to celebrate at home and in church. I had visions of our stiff white Presbyterian church turning into a vibrant gospel choir on the day I broke the news. I could envision hearing loud amens from the congregation, with an immediate gospel response from the choir. Then I came back to reality, because that would never happen at a Presbyterian, "frozen chosen," church … unfortunately! Imagination is hard to beat!

After this was all over, I e-mailed the billionaire to thank him for his help. I also threw a bone out there to see if he would like to team up on a project with us in the Solomon Islands. To my utter shock and dismay, he did not respond to my proposition. Hmm.

Everyone was going to be happy about this news, I knew! The terrible eight-hundred-pound gorilla was finally off my back. I could concentrate on the next order of business. The second group medical trip was going to happen in a month's time. *Wait a minute. I just had a thought.* The thirty solar panels they were flying to Honiara were only half of the planned installation. This was the time to get the remaining panels to Seghe. I had to pull this off. A couple of major hurdles stood between us and an ultimately successful project. Number one was money. The additional thirty solar panels would cost nearly $30,000. There wasn't time to hold another fundraiser. Folks would have probably shown reluctance to donate more money after the six-month shipping saga, anyway.

I had no other alternative but to give Suzanne the sales pitch of my life. Fortunately, we had the money in our bank account, but I wasn't sure she would go for it. It was perfect timing, and it made so much sense to me to purchase the rest of the panels, but Suzanne was the one busting her butt, by scoping other people's butts, to give us the financial strength and freedom to be able to execute such a transaction. I was blessed beyond belief to be married to such an incredible and hardworking woman. After several minutes of intense thought and silence, she answered yes and was made even more incredible in my mind!

The ball was rolling and, I hoped, couldn't be stopped. There was a lot of logistical groundwork to do to get the new panels from the United States to Seghe before we arrived. Tony at BJS Services in Honiara worked his contacts like a master birder differentiates between a Hammond's Flycatcher and a Pacific-slope Flycatcher. He was on his game. He came through for us like I couldn't believe. Throughout the entire shipping thriller, Tony was on the sidelines. Working his business network, he was able to secure a fantastic rate on a FedEx aircraft to fly the panels from California to Australia. From there, another buddy of Tony's secured a beautiful rate on heavy lift into Honiara. Once in Honiara, it was smooth sailing for the panels via Silentworld's barge straight to Uepi Island Resort. Grant's e-mail notifying me that all the panels from both shipments had arrived at Uepi was maybe the best news I had ever received in my thirty-seven years of life.

Adding to the good news regarding the solar panels, I didn't have any problems getting enough people to join us on the trip. We had a few nurses and several docs, along with a few nonmedical helpers. Gordon planned to finish coordinating the solar power installation. Another friend, David Houghton, came along to provide additional know-how and muscle to the endeavor. It was going to happen this time.

CHAPTER

12

*T*he second group trip, in May 2009, got off to a great start. Walking into the locked storage building at Uepi was surreal. Those sixty sheets of polysilicon covered in glass and wrapped in aluminum had been elusive for six months. They were sitting before me as if I had just discovered the greatest treasure ever unearthed. My smile was one of pure victory. "Thank you, Lord!" I said quietly. My brain couldn't have dreamed a roller coaster ride like that, nor would I have wanted it to. I hoped future shipping transactions would not be as eventful, to say the least.

Unfortunately, two of the panels had been broken in transit. That meant we had to leave three panels out of the planned sixty-panel array, as the panels were wired in series of three. We had to make due with 525 fewer watts being produced. There would still be 10,000 watts coming off the roof; that would be plenty for current and future energy needs at the hospital.

The solar panels took up a lot of space. Fifty-seven panels would have required two of the dive boats to transport them to Seghe. Jill and Grant's son, Jason, allowed us to use his small barge to transfer the panels to the hospital. Jason had moved back to Uepi within the past six months, after finishing his college degree from Griffith University in Brisbane. His degree in international business would suit him well as he began establishing his own sustainable timber business in the lagoon. Jason's barge was primarily for transporting timber, but we were grateful he had made it available to us this day.

Transporting the panels by barge from Uepi would take a few hours, so while they were traveling, David Houghton and I spent some time in the pharmacy. David was on the trip to help out however he could. His wife,

Julie, was a nurse from St. Mark's Hospital in Salt Lake and was also on the trip.

The Solomon Island pharmacist in training was not at Seghe because of some health issues. She was expected back soon, but no one knew the exact day. She had been gone for a while, and the area had become so cluttered with trash and unorganized items, it was effectively unusable as a pharmacy. The two rooms that housed all the medicines were in shambles, so David and I figured we could help out by cleaning up some of the mess. There were miscellaneous papers strewn about, many of which were several years old. Unopened boxes were buried by partially opened boxes. The floor couldn't be seen throughout most of the room.

We found a large box and started to fill it with items that we deemed to be trash. Before long, the place was starting to look better. We found five boxes that contained brand-new IV poles. The poles came with nice bases that had quality plastic wheels on them. We assembled all the poles and rolled them out into the main ward. One of the nurses didn't seem very happy with us. We explained that the poles could be moved from bed to bed to hang IV bags. She didn't want to have anything to do with them. She preferred to use the sticks or metal rods attached to the beds. It was a head-scratcher for us. We would have to have the doctors tell the nurses that the poles were necessary and should be used.

Later that day, we were caught off guard as the pharmacist in training returned to the hospital. She walked into the pharmacy and immediately turned pale. Oh no, what had we done? We had simply been trying to help by straightening the room, but we had overstepped our bounds big time. It wasn't our room to straighten in the first place. She walked away in disgust, and I promptly followed and offered a warm and sincere apology. I explained that we had been trying to help because we knew she had been away and not feeling well.

Before long, I felt the ice had been broken and we were back on good terms. It was my first cultural dustup, and I felt really bad about hurting her feelings. After that incident, I never forgot that we were simply visitors, there to help, not to take control. That pharmacy had just been screaming for a thorough cleaning, though.

Gordon, David, and a crew from Uepi served as the main installers of the power system. There was a lot to accomplish in the two weeks of the trip.

All the racking had to be fastened to the corrugated iron roof before the panels could be installed. As each panel was installed, it had to be connected to the other two panels in the series. Next, a longer cable connected the panels to the combiner box that was bolted under the eave, above the battery building. From the combiner box, the wires went down to the charge controllers. The controllers were responsible for putting DC current into the batteries and for managing electricity flow between the batteries and the inverters. The inverters converted the DC into AC and sent the AC power into the hospital to be used by the lights and any appliances that needed electricity.

There was no grid to tie into, so the solar power system for the hospital would be a stand-alone off-grid power plant. It would have its limits; thus, a fair amount of education would have to take place before we turned it over to the hospital staff. The batteries needed to be treated with respect to maximize their useful life. The hospital staff being properly trained on what appliances could and couldn't be used during different times of the day could be the difference between the batteries lasting more than seven years or fewer than seven years.

For the first few days of the trip, Gordon, David, and the local helpers installed the racking and panels. The weather was not our friend that week. It was blazing hot … so hot that the Solomon Islanders were sweating while on the roof. Solomon Islanders don't drink a lot of water, so when they're sweating, the heat is definitely unbearable for the pale-skinned foreigners. David did a great job coordinating the activities on the roof of the maternity ward, but he had to make frequent trips into the shade for relief and hydration. Gordon spent a lot of his time wiring the connections in the power panel and making sure the roof connections were going to plan. One of the workers from Uepi was training to be an electrician and was a fantastic help with the wiring. We used pieces of cardboard from the panel packaging to cover the panels once they were fastened to the racks. Not only did the panels get very hot, but they were also live with the sun shining on them. The guys had to be careful plugging the various wires in because power was coming through to the combiner box whether they liked it or not.

The solar power system was finished on the first Friday of the two-week trip. It was a pleasure to see how quickly the power plant had become operational. Turning the breakers on and seeing the lights illuminate the hospital produced a tremendous feeling of accomplishment in all of us. Even though the system was operational, before we left that Friday afternoon to head back to Uepi, Gordon shut the entire system down for the weekend because there was plenty of work yet to be finished on the battery building. Electrical usage policies and guidelines needed to be created and then discussed with the hospital staff before the power could be turned on indefinitely. Too much money, stress, and time had been involved in the project for us to not ensure that it would be cared for properly.

David, Gordon, and I returned to Uepi in one of the smaller boats. After showering and changing clothes, I heard the medical team return. They had traveled northwest forty minutes to the Eucalyptus School located on New Georgia Island. The school belonged to the Christian Fellowship Church (CFC), which had been founded many years earlier by a man who claimed to have been visited by God and then gathered converts who believed his story. After living in Salt Lake City for so long, I was very familiar with this type of story and the socially controlling church structure that ensued.

The CFC owned a lot of land from Vakabo all the way to Kolombangara Island. They had sold most of the timber on their land and as a result had amassed quite a fortune. Schooling was provided to the children of CFC members for free. Eucalyptus School was a CFC boarding school. The authoritarian rule of the church leader permeated many aspects of the members' lives. This funneled into health care, as well. We weren't sure if people were supposed to receive medical care from only the leader of the church.

Regardless, not many people had shown up to the clinic at Eucalyptus that day. It was so slow that one of the nurses had suggested that the team leave early. The decision was made to stick to the schedule and stay a couple more hours, however. As the team sat in the small clinic building, a man and a woman walked to the triage station. The man carried a piece of paper and described their problem. The woman with him was twenty-three years old and walked into the clinic under her own power. Her companion explained that she had been viciously attacked by a crocodile eight days before.

Without any delay, members of the team took her back to a private room to assess her wounds. The woman not only had survived the crocodile attack but was also a recent survivor of cerebral malaria. She had contracted Plasmodium falciparum from a mosquito the year before. Fortunately, she had survived the disease, but unfortunately, her mental state had been completely altered. She would never again be the person she had been prior to the bout of malaria.

The man traveling with her was the local nurse from Keru Clinic, another forty minutes by boat to the northwest. Keru was located on an island adjacent to the landing strip at Ramata. The nurse had seen our schedule and felt he needed to take the patient to see the doctors. He was out of medicines and supplies to continue treating her.

As the nurses and docs had the woman undress, they were horrified at what they saw. After removing her lava lava, they couldn't believe the damage the crocodile had done to her hip, legs, and vaginal area. She had been kneeling in the water when the crocodile had attacked her in the crotch. The massive chunk removed from her hip was likely from the croc's teeth. She had sustained three massive lacerations adjacent to her labia and anus and one four-inch long gash at the bottom of a buttock. The scene was brutal, to say the least.

The nurse had done the best he could in suturing the wounds closed. We thought, but weren't sure, that he'd used lidocaine to numb the wounds before he had sutured and, in some instances, double sutured. He did tell us that he didn't have any paracetamol, which is the same as acetaminophen, for her. The wounds were massive, and I couldn't imagine not having any pain medicine whatsoever for the eight days since the attack. That was inconceivable. How was this woman able to go to the bathroom or sit down without being in excruciating pain? How was she able to clean herself after going to the bathroom?

The woman's vital signs were going downhill. Her blood pressure was falling and her heart rate increasing. She was becoming septic as a result of the infection brewing in her system. All the sutures had dehisced, or blown open, that day. That was the only thing going in her favor, because it allowed the infection to drain out of the wounds.

Our team's nurses started an IV immediately to get fluids and antibiotics flowing. They threw every antibiotic they had into her in a last-ditch effort to try to prevent her dying from sepsis. The nurse had not had the appropriate antibiotics to combat the bugs present in a crocodile's mouth and so had not been able to control the infection. The team had the proper drugs, but they didn't know if they were treating her in time.

The nurse who had brought the woman provided Suzanne with a comprehensive two-page history that he had meticulously kept for the past eight days. He asked Suzanne for medicines and supplies so he could continue to care for the woman. Suzanne looked him in the eye and told him that he had done a great job but she had to take the patient. The nurse burst into tears right there because he had given the woman every ounce of his care and devotion over the past eight days to get her to this point. He was obviously physically and emotionally drained. It must have been a relief to him that someone else was going to continue providing her care and that she would get the care she needed to give her the best chance of survival.

Suzanne made the call to put the patient and her mother, who had come to the village with her daughter on the boat back to Uepi. The boats belonged to Uepi, not to Suzanne, so her decision left her a little uneasy, as she was making an executive decision without discussing it with Grant. She didn't have a way to contact Grant in advance, so she went with her gut. We had the money to pay for the transport. This was the reason we were there, to treat people who needed medical care. Fuel would be required to get the woman to a surgeon in Munda, Gizo, or Honiara. There was no question that we would take care of all the expenses for her.

Suzanne knew the woman needed surgical care. We didn't have the personnel or facilities to conduct this type of surgical intervention. Upon arriving back at Uepi, Suzanne discussed with Grant the need to get the woman to Seghe and then have her transferred to another facility that had a surgeon.

It was at this point that I emerged from cabin one and noticed there was a substantial amount of buzz occurring out at the boat jetty. Approaching one of the dive boats, I could see the woman lying in her mother's arms. There was an IV bag hanging from the boat canopy. They were sitting there calmly, as most Solomon Islanders seemed to do regardless of the situation.

I heard Grant say, "I think there's a surgeon at Munda."

"Is there any way to contact them?" Suzanne questioned.

"We can call on the satellite phone, but no guarantees they will answer."

In the United States, it would have been a terrible time to get a doctor on the phone: five p.m. on a Friday afternoon. Incredibly, Dr. Dina answered the phone. Suzanne reported that she was thrilled to hear Dr. Dina speaking her language, medically. He mentioned that the patient probably needed surgical debridement and that he would be available whenever she arrived. This was music to Suzanne's ears. She thought if they could get the infection under control, there might be a chance to get the wounds properly closed and possibly have the woman pull through.

There was some prep work to do before the woman could be transferred to Munda. It was too late in the evening to do the transport, because there were some very narrow, potentially treacherous passageways to navigate that should not be done at night. The plan was to transport the patient to Seghe that night and clean the wounds prior to an early morning transfer to Munda.

While standing on the boat jetty, I reassured Grant that we would gladly pay for the fuel for the transfers to Seghe and Munda. He didn't seem too concerned, as this was a serious emergency, but I wanted him to know that this was the business that we had come to do and we would meet all of our obligations.

When Suzanne arrived at Seghe Hospital with the patient, the newly installed solar power system was of no use to her and the nurses because we had shut the system down. Fortunately, Suzanne didn't know the power had been on earlier in the day; it had been such a whirlwind when they had arrived at Uepi that I hadn't had the chance to share the good news. I didn't even think about sending Gordon over to turn the system on so they could have light. My mind had gotten a little sidetracked when I'd heard the words "crocodile attack."

It was a crash course in flashlight medicine techniques, and Suzanne quickly learned how challenging the Seghe nurses had had it in the past several years, delivering babies and dressing wounds by candlelight or flashlight. Every time the nurse with the headlamp looked away, the field would go black. They were also sweating because of the heat and humidity, and the delicate situation in front of them.

Suzanne and the nurse had to attend to the mother briefly because she almost fainted when she saw the extent of her daughter's wounds. "I … I didn't know how bad it was," she said of her daughter's wounds as they got her to a seat. It was really bad, and Suzanne hoped it was going to get better, but there were no guarantees. They started to remove the old suture, which at this point had turned into a foreign body. The suture needed to come out because it was dirty and likely complicating the infection. Once the suture had been removed, they cleaned and dressed the wounds more than adequately to make it another twelve plus hours to get to Munda.

Eight days since the brutal attack, the young woman finally received her first Tylenol. Remarkably, it actually made her a little sleepy. That she had endured that much trauma and infection was amazing. Adding it all to an area of the body that can be hard to keep clean normally without the addition of several large lacerations was difficult to even comprehend. The young lady was a fighter, and a lot of people in the developed world could learn a lot from the courage and pain tolerance she exhibited.

On the way back from Seghe, Suzanne received her reward. The boat driver stopped the boat in the middle of the widest section of the Marovo Lagoon and turned off the motor. The stars couldn't have been brighter anywhere else on the face of the earth. There was no light pollution for hundreds, if not thousands, of miles. The southern sky and constellations were brimming over with the brilliance of billions of shiny diamonds randomly hung in the sky for their enjoyment. It gave them a chance to unwind after dealing with the day's emergency. Their day had begun with horror and urgency and ended with pure peace and God-given rewards.

13

*T*wo of our friends on the trip, Mike and Andrea Heidinger, worked for a green building material company. They had some interesting conversations with Jason regarding the timber-harvesting situation in the area. The stories were not pleasing to the ear; nevertheless, they needed to be heard. The country was quickly running out of economically viable timber. Even though the timber situation in the greater Solomon Islands was bleak, however, some villages in the Lagoon actually had a bright future, thanks to Jason's new business.

The logging scene throughout most of the Solomon Islands was disgusting. The destruction caused by unregulated logging, coupled with the terrible business practices that the Malaysian logging companies employed, left me shaking my head in sadness and anger. We in the developed world can get nice furniture for a really cheap price; I saw firsthand who really pays the remainder of the cost. These villagers were taking the brunt of the profits in the ass. Their forests and villages were being destroyed so I could go down to any of the big-box stores in the United States and buy a cheap piece of furniture. The stores make the furniture feel very warm and cozy, and it's very easy to buy the furniture when you don't have a clue where the wood came from.

The logging companies would come in and set up a contract on a single corrupt signature. The contract would often spell out prices for A-, B-, and C-grade logs. The loggers would then take every tree in the given area, dragging them out with chains and bulldozers. When it was all finished, they would come back to the village elders and say, "Oh, there wasn't much A-grade timber" (a blatant lie) and then would pay less based on B- and C-grade logs. After the loggers completely denude the hillsides, the rains continue to come. The thin dark-red topsoil rushes down the hill and runs into the lagoon. The once pristine coral reef in front of the village starts to become covered with red sediment. Coral will not thrive when covered in sediment. When the coral dies, the fish either die or move elsewhere. Then the villagers, who used to rely on their own coral reefs, have to paddle much farther to fish, have to buy fish from other villages, or have to buy canned fish. Their forest resources, including topsoil, are gone. Their coral reefs and fish resources are destroyed. Their lives are changed forever.

Jason's company aimed to break this terrible cycle and to give the villagers of the Marovo Lagoon an alternative for managing their forests. He started to lock up timber rights through written contracts with villages around the Marovo, establishing village-run harvesting operations that managed and harvested their own forests instead of handing the forests over to unethical foreign companies. Jason planned to use the latest research about sustainable timber harvesting to provide the villages with the maximum amount of financial return for their forests while harvesting only two to three trees per hectare every three to five years, or less, depending on what the forest would sustainably replenish, which sometimes would be less than one tree per hectare every three to five years. Looking at Jason's community-managed forests from a distance, you'd never know there was an active timber-harvest program in place there.

The villages participating in Jason's method were earning the same amount per hectare as the Malaysian loggers paid, but they were making this amount every three years, not just one time! The forests were left in natural equilibrium, unlike the areas harvested by the Malaysians, who didn't leave any trees behind on their parcels. This seemed like it would be a no-brainer. Village elders unfortunately continued to be swayed by slick-talking, cigarette-smoking, big cash wad-carrying, unscrupulous Malaysian loggers, however. I could understand the temptation, because if someone dangled keys to a brand-new Ferrari in my face, I would likely get excited and take the deal. Unfortunately, the devil was in the details. In this case, nothing was left but scarred red earth and broken lives wherever the clear-cut devils were allowed to ply their evil trade.

Throughout the second week of the trip, the medical team continued visiting villages, passing logging eyesores along the way. Gordon and some workers from Uepi toiled more on the solar power system and battery building. The trip was going really well. We had visited new villages on this tour, Telina among them.

Telina was forty minutes to the southeast of Uepi. The village was located on a small island and had a couple of neighboring villages adjacent, on neighboring Vangunu Island. As we pulled up to the small rock jetty at Telina, the sky opened up on us and poured rain. Starting off the day wet was never fun in my mind, and it was a challenge getting up the steep, muddy hill to the church. Fortunately, several local guys came to help carry the bags of medicines and supplies.

When we reached the top of the hill, the village spokesman, John Wayne, told us they were not ready for us to enter the church. They had prepared a welcome ceremony for us, and we needed to wait a few minutes. It was raining at a good clip, so we headed for shelter underneath a house. We joked with one another while standing in soaking ponchos, hair dripping wet.

Incredibly, ten minutes later, the clouds parted and the sun came out. John Wayne told us to come out into the open field and wait. A group of young warriors emerged from behind the church. They came running with spears and hatchets at the ready. Their bodies and faces were painted with white, and their clothes were covered in grasses and burlap. They yelled at us in their native Marovan language as they taunted us with their weapons. Some played serious, and some couldn't resist smiling and laughing. At that moment, I was again relieved that headhunting had been left behind in 1911 when Christian missionaries had set up shop in the lagoon.

After the warriors were quelled, another group gathered in front of the church. There were many young children and adults standing together. Two men held guitars, ready to start a tune. In an instant, a melodious chorus came forth from the small crowd. The voices were light and soothing as they sang, "It's a welcoming, a welcoming, a Christian welcoming." What a joyous way to start the day. John Wayne provided a further, touching welcome speech, and then they invited us to enter the church.

It was a big, unfinished building. The concrete floor was solid, yet not covered with wood or tile. The open rafters had electrical lines hanging, but they were not connected to any fixtures. Welcome swallows flew around the inside of the building, tending the two mud-cup nests they had secured to the walls. Rudimentary wooden benches lined the inside of the church. We started to assemble them in areas that would be used for triage, pharmacy, testing, etc. There were a couple of private rooms behind the altar where the doctors would set up shop. Kate, the dentist, was going to a larger room behind the altar. She needed access to a window so the patients could spit out blood and saliva during the extractions.

David and I had left Gordon for the day to help with the clinic because we had been told that Telina would likely have a big group. It did. The back of the church quickly filled with prospective patients. The clinic seemed to run rather smoothly. I helped Mike and Andrea in the pharmacy while David fit people with reading glasses.

Toward the end of the day, David approached me in the middle of the church. "You know this is about the coolest thing one could ever do. …" He looked at me and looked away and then looked at me, and I agreed. We both realized that there was a touch of emotion working its way to the surface, and we walked away from one another. It was typical of two guys having an emotional experience and wanting to share it but not wanting to show it. I was thrilled that he was enjoying himself and reaping the personal rewards that come with selflessly helping those in need. That feeling had no equal, in my mind.

We made it through our last clinic day on Friday. The weekend was upon us. The only thing to do was relax and enjoy some diving and snorkeling. After dinner, Grant explained to everyone about the opportunity to take a full day dive/snorkel trip away from Uepi. The trip would take us in the direction of Tetepare Island, the largest uninhabited island remaining in the South Pacific.

First, we would dive on a sunken tuna boat. On the maiden voyage of the boat about five years earlier, it had slammed into the reef at night. No lives had been lost in the accident, but the boat had been stuck until a salvage team had arrived to pull it off the reef. As it had been dislodged, the vessel had immediately taken on large volumes of water. The salvage team had cut the line and the boat had sunk, stern first. The stern had lodged perfectly in a cradle approximately 115 feet below the surface. The water was as deep as the boat was long, so Grant said we would likely see the tip of the bow poking out through the waves upon our arrival.

The second dive spot for the day was scheduled for Penguin Reef. Grant explained that the reef had been discovered by a ship called the *HMS Penguin*. The reef was definitely too far north for there to be actual penguins anywhere near by. Grant described a reef in almost pristine condition. We would descend to about thirty feet and then slowly swim around the island until we were relatively low on air. That would be the end of our first tank. Each diver had two tanks for the day's four dives.

Lunch would be served on a beach overlooking a small lagoon and massive limestone cliff face. This lunch break would also serve as our surface interval to help decrease the amount of nitrogen in our bodies before we dove again. At the bottom of the cliff was a sinkhole in the Bapata passage. The passage served as a shortcut for people going from the Seghe area to Viru Harbor or Munda. Part of the passage had been bombed by the New Zealand Navy to create this shorter route.

Grant warned us that the sinkhole wasn't the best for people who were still working on their buoyancy or who were claustrophobic. He described a vertical shaft that was about eighty-five feet deep and about as big around as an elevator shaft. The dive would start in brackish water, and then at the bottom, the divers would go partly under the cliff and come out in a striking canyon that emptied into the ocean. Toward the bottom of the canyon lay the remains of a sunken Japanese barge from WWII. He warned us not to try to get to the barge because it was deceivingly deep, at around 130 feet. He told us to keep our eyes open and look for flashing scallops on the walls during the descent.

After the dive at the sinkhole, the boats would stop at the end of the Seghe airstrip for us to dive on one of two aircraft in the water. The first option was a Dauntless dive bomber from WWII that had crashed and was located nearly fifty feet below the surface. It reportedly had a torpedo still fastened to the fuselage. The other option was closer to the runway and in only twenty feet of water. It was one of the most rare of WWII aircraft to be seen today. The P-38 Lightning hadn't actually crashed but had been pushed off the runway so another aircraft, low on fuel, could land. Grant said the plane would be visible to snorkelers and could even be reached by someone who could dive down to twenty feet while holding their breath. This was the plane I was looking forward to seeing. I had seen it before on a previous trip, but the beautiful purple soft corals stuck to the undersides of the wings, and the myriad other sea life, never got tiring. The bullets were still visible in the gun magazine, and a stunning anemone fish had claimed the cockpit as his or her home.

Almost all the hands went up when Grant asked who wanted to go on the trip. We received further instructions for the next morning. We needed to arrange all of our gear well before breakfast and to be ready to leave immediately after we finished eating.

After two weeks of clinics and a major solar power installation, no one stayed up late. The next day's activities would require a fair amount of energy, so bedtime it was.

The next day went to plan. The morning dives were incredible. Penguin Reef contained so many fish and coral species, it was nearly a mind scramble. The tuna boat was cool, but wreck diving didn't do much for me. The dive instructor decided to change the lunch spot to a different island, so the beautiful limestone cliff in the Bapata passage would have to wait until the sinkhole dive. The sinkhole was located at the base of the limestone cliff.

The beach where we had lunch was as an idyllic South Pacific paradise as you could ever find. The spot could have adorned any travel magazine cover in the world. The only concern on a deserted tropical beach was to not sit under a coconut tree. A falling coconut could kill a human; by the time you realized a coconut was falling, it might be too late to react. Our lunch of roasted local chicken was delicious. We ate it with fresh salad and homemade cookies to finish.

Toward the end of lunch, the serenity of the break was interrupted by a lot of noise coming from one of the boat radios. It sounded like someone screaming at the top of their lungs.

Jason had three friends visiting. They had been off camping and surfing at their secret spot, only a half hour away from where we were eating lunch. We hadn't seen them or spent much time with them during the trip, and I actually had sort of forgotten that they were there.

One of the Uepi staff swam out to the boat to check the radio. The screams issuing from the radio were coming from Jason. He was demanding that we meet him ASAP, as they had a medical emergency. His friend Drew was seriously injured, but we didn't know how bad it was until we met the boat.

Jason and his friends had been surfing out near Tetepare Island when disaster had struck. The geologic and hydrographic makeup of the place had allowed for a freak wave to close the normally passable passage. Drew had been in the front of the boat as Jason had been forced to accelerate through the cresting wave. Something hadn't gone to plan. Drew had been launched into the air and had come down next to the large D ring on the bow of the boat that held the bowline. Fortunately, his eye had missed the steel ring, but his face had plowed into the fiberglass next to the ring. Drew had immediately gone limp and seemingly lifeless for a time. Blood had started to gush from around Drew's eye, all over the light gray fiberglass. Once the boat was beyond the breakers, the other guys in the boat attended to Drew. He came to very slowly.

Upon meeting Jason's boat, Suzanne, Kate, and two of the nurses jumped in to attend to Drew. We passed over the first aid kit. Jason was visibly upset. The nurses provided Jason with comforting words, and then their boat was off, speeding toward Uepi as fast as possible.

The emergency, along with a massive thunderstorm, killed our desire to continue diving that afternoon. I had never experienced rain like that before. Several of us huddled in the back of the boat with umbrellas stretched out in front, serving as makeshift shields against the pummeling rain. I don't know how the driver could keep his eyes open during the deluge. That was the best example I had ever seen of how quickly the water cycle can work, from evaporation to condensation, and then to downright open floodgates from above.

Upon their arrival to Uepi, Suzanne and Kate made a makeshift surgical suite in Jason's house. Not only were both of Drew's eyes starting to turn black and blue, but the one eyelid was filleted open like a fine slice of Chateaubriand. The cut was so deep and all the way across his upper eye that the skin folded over to make a second eyelid.

Kate started sewing the wound but was having a hard time seeing the fine suture, as they were using the smallest stuff they had to prevent scarring as much as possible. Suzanne took over the job and finished suturing the laceration, which was more than an inch long. It had been a long time since she had actually sutured human skin. She had been a gastroenterologist for several years, so suturing hadn't been part of her daily routine since her residency. Fortunately, she had spent a little time with a general surgeon friend in Salt Lake City prior to the trip to refresh her skills.

On the other side of Drew's nose was a nice dog-ear flap that also required sutures. With all the bloody openings sewed shut, Drew was only partially in the clear. He had sustained serious head trauma. We were nowhere near an MRI machine. There wasn't an MRI in the Solomon Islands, and I

116

wasn't even sure whether there was enough electricity being generated in the Solomon Islands to power up an MRI.

Drew was responding, but he was definitely out of it. Was there bleeding in his brain? Had he received a severe enough concussion to cause swelling of his brain? These questions were not easy and maybe not possible to positively answer without proper imaging, but after a few hours of intense observation, Kate and Suzanne made the decision not to evacuate Drew. His vital signs and brain functions seemed to be heading in the right direction. A few members of the medical team took turns looking after him throughout the night to monitor his status.

A couple of days later, Drew showed strong signs of recovery. He showed up to breakfast wearing big sunglasses, which did a good job of hiding the sutures and dark color scheme adorning his eyes. The timing of the accident couldn't have been better for Drew. Two days after the injury, the team, except for Gordon and me, departed for home. At the time of their departure, Suzanne and Kate were confident that Drew was out of the woods with regard to any potential brain injuries from the accident.

This experience with Drew seemed to strike a great deal of interest and curiosity in Jason toward medicine. It was as if a major light bulb had been turned on within him. After the incident, Jason gravitated closer to our team and expressed interest in joining us on the next medical tour. I was certainly all for having another member of the Kelly family jump on board the project.

14

*P*lanning extra time to stay at the end of the medical trip had been good forethought. As on the first group trip, everyone went home except Gordon and me. There were last-minute items that needed to be addressed. I needed to feel good leaving the solar power system in the hands of the hospital staff.

We gave explicit instructions regarding usage of the air conditioners. Five air conditioners were located in various rooms of the hospital. The two that we figured would get the most use were in the pharmacy and in the malaria lab. The pharmacy was a no-brainer because the room had no windows and it was preferential for the medicines to be kept cool. The malaria lab and other offices were less vital for cooling, but we had a feeling the workers would want to use the units because they had already been installed when the hospital had been built in 2000. Gordon and I questioned whether we should have even allowed the air conditioners to be used on the solar power system, but we decided with rules in place, they could be used on a limited basis.

One final item that needed to be buttoned up was with the battery building. It was a must to install hardware cloth over the four vents to prevent rodents and snakes from gaining access. The hospital hosted some rather large, fast spiders. I didn't know what they were or if they were dangerous. They had moved into the battery building, so we did our best to dispatch them when they made an appearance. Ants were also coming in and checking out the new digs. Keeping the building clean and free of critters would take some work, but it was possible with regular inspections.

While nailing some hardware cloth to one of the vents, I heard someone calling my name. It was one of the nurses. I walked out and asked, "Yeah?"

"Allan, how do you spell your name?" she asked.

"A-L-L-A-N."

Pause. … "Okay, how do you spell your last name?"

That question made me wonder what was happening. "Why?" I asked as I grabbed my backpack and headed out to meet her.

"There was a baby born last night. It was the first baby born under the solar," she said with a thick Solomon Islands accent.

"Really? What time?"

"I think 9:24 last night. The mother wanted an honorable name to name her baby boy. She wants to name her boy after you."

"What? Are you serious? The first baby born … named after me?" I asked, totally flustered. I didn't have any children, and this caught me off guard, to say the least. Overwhelmed by the news, I pulled out my camera and followed the nurse into the maternity ward. There, I found the mom, named Sandra, sitting on an adjacent bed to the bed that little Allan was lying on. There was a light blue mosquito net draped over the bed. He was gorgeous, lying there asleep. Sandra was obviously spent after giving birth about twelve hours before.

The three of us spoke softly. The nurse helped interpret, as Sandra's English was a little rusty. She was twenty-three years old, and little Allan was her first child. She was a single mother and had come to Seghe, accompanied by a girlfriend, to have her baby.

The nurse filled out little Allan's birth book. His first name was Allan Daly. It was wild, looking at the book and seeing my name with a couple names following it. I didn't know what social protocol was for this type of an event. Jill and Grant would have to provide some guidance on whether I should buy little Allan some baby clothes or what. I didn't know, but I figured I needed to do something. Sandra wasn't naming the child after me to try to receive gifts, but I had so much compared to her, and my giving nature made it a foregone conclusion that some sort of gift would be in order. I took some video of Sandra and Allan and told her that I would be back to see her the next day.

Gordon was impressed to hear about all this. This was a big deal for me. It left me out of sorts. I couldn't wait to report back to Suzanne and the rest of the team who had already left. My concentration for the rest of the day was not at its peak. This event was monumental. I needed to report to Suzanne and the others that there would be an Allan Daly running around the Marovo Lagoon for some time to come.

Gordon, myself, and the local workers finished working for the day and loaded all the tools back in the boat. I didn't like where we had been parking the boat. It was mosquito central. They always gravitated toward me when they had a choice in blood types. That's not a time you want to be viewed as being sweet.

Topher, the head carpenter from Uepi, pulled the boat out of the spot and turned it toward the tip of Patutiva village, the first land marker we had to pass while heading back to Uepi. As we passed Patutiva village, the emotion hit me like a freight train. The past year had been full of roller coaster-like highs and lows. After being at the bottom of a pit for six months with no resolution in sight over the lost solar panels, I found myself at the top of the highest coaster on Earth. The project had been difficult to put together and endure, but all the pain faded. As a result of all that mental anguish, the nurses at Seghe Hopsital had for the first time delivered a beautiful baby boy under the bright lights powered by our solar power system. This was a game changer for this community. It was a game changer for me as well.

I dropped my head in my hands and let the tears of joy flow without the others in the boat knowing. I was crying, probably much softer than little Allan had the night before. He had entered the world under bright lights that burned bright as a result of a lot of blessings, scrappy perseverance, and excellent teamwork. To date, this was the greatest achievement of my life. I wasn't quite sure how to top that experience, but there would be plenty of time to ponder the future.

At dinner, Jill and Grant were surprised and thrilled to hear that a baby had been named after me. They said there had only been a few babies ever named after white people in the lagoon. Two of them were named Grant Kelly. My desire to purchase baby clothes or towels were met with agreement from Jill and Grant. They told me not to go overboard but to stop at the local store at Seghe and pick up some items.

The next morning, our crew dropped all the tools off at the battery building. I walked down to and across the airstrip to the store, which was a few doors down from the light blue police station. I didn't have an endless amount of cash with me, and I remembered Jill's words of guidance to not go overboard. It was hard for me not to buy Sandra and little Allan everything in the store. I had a baby named after me, and I wanted him and his mother to be well taken care of. I even wanted to grab some cigars and start passing them out, although I must say the child did not look anything like me. Also, I had no idea if Solomon Islanders were aware of that old practice of the father passing out cigars when he had a new baby. Smoking wasn't my thing, anyway, but all those thoughts of celebrating this new life flooded my brain, and I just wanted to celebrate however I could. The storeowners probably liked my visit, as I purchased a couple of baby outfits and a few towels. I didn't break the bank, but by Solomon Islands standards, it was considered a nice gift.

With purpose in my stride, I hastily made my way back to see "my boy." I had the nurse check that it was okay for me to enter, and I walked in with a couple of bundles of newspaper-wrapped gifts. Sandra's face lit up with a beautiful smile as I presented her with the gifts. She was surprised and very appreciative to have the new clothes and towels. We took some photos together, and I walked out of there without actually touching the ground— or so it seemed. Giving produced the greatest feelings in me. Sharing my blessings with those less fortunate was my ultimate drug, and I wasn't about to stop enjoying it.

Before long, another trip had come to an end for Gordon and me. It was time to return to the States and to rejoin our wives. Sandra and little Allan Daly had left Seghe and headed back to their village near Batuna. I was already looking forward to the next trip. Hopefully, she would bring him to the clinic so the group could meet him.

Back on planet Utah a few days later, I hadn't gotten tired of sharing the story. People must have thought it was my child, with the way I was talking about the experience with such pride and exuberance. People at church loved the story, and regardless of whom I told, it seemed to produce a warm smile.

Two weeks after returning home, I received an e-mail from Jason. This was the first time we had e-mailed one another. We were still not very familiar with one another, but this communication greased the skids toward creating a closer friendship. He explained that Uepi had received communication over the radio from a group of Australians doing some work at the hospital. Their plan was to unload new hospital beds and to do some planned renovations of the doctor's house. A house had been built for a doctor several years before, but because a doctor had never been posted to the hospital, the house had fallen into disrepair. There were also a couple of nurses in the ragtag group who were there to support the Seghe nurses. I had left the Solomons on the top of the highest roller coaster in the world, but as I read through the e-mail, the coaster eased down a precipitously steep hill.

Evidently, the group had brought several power tools with them for the renovations. One of the malaria techs had tried to explain to them that they couldn't use all the power tools because of the solar power system. In typical "white man" fashion, however, the Australians had peacefully overpowered the Solomon Islander and chosen to use the power tools however they saw fit. One of the Aussies had told the malaria tech that a couple of the team members had solar power systems at their homes so there was nothing to worry about.

As they had plugged in multiple power tools and started their work, they had obviously overloaded the 10 KW system and something in the battery building had blown. The entire system had shut down. The hospital had no electricity and was back to square one. The battery building was purposefully locked and secured so no one messed around with the system or stole any of the batteries. It was also a potentially dangerous place to be because the amount of power flowing through the batteries could kill someone.

Grant Kelly at Uepi Island Resort was the keeper of the key to the battery building. The malaria tech had explained this to the Aussies, and thus, they'd contacted Uepi on the radio. They had explained that they were having troubles with the solar power system and wanted to have the key to check on some things in the battery building. Grant knew about all the resources, time, and effort that had gone into installing the system, as he had been involved from the get-go. He didn't know these people and had thus denied their request, and rightfully so.

The group of Aussies working at the hospital was governed by a different set of principles and didn't like that the request for access to the battery building was denied. Finding Grant's response unacceptable, they took matters into their own hands and broke into the building. They were obviously greeted by a solar power system the likes of which none of them had ever encountered. Saying a couple of them had solar power systems on their houses likely meant that they had grid-tied systems, not stand-alone off-grid systems. They didn't even know what they were looking for, or at, for that matter. They had screwed up big time, and now they didn't have any electricity to continue their work.

A couple of days later, Jason and Grant had gone over to the hospital to check on the solar situation. The malaria tech was very worried and very sorry for what had happened. He had explained to Jason that he had tried to stop the Australians but they wouldn't listen to him.

After studying the inverters for a little while, Jason and Grant had started throwing breaker switches, and the power had come back on. They didn't know how to assess if great damage had been caused to the batteries or inverters. That would have to wait until Gordon's next visit, and I wasn't sure when that would be.

After reading the e-mail from Jason, I came unglued. Australians were our allies, but I was ready to find this bunch of rebels and wage war. We had just installed the solar power system—brand new! Two weeks later, a bunch of thugs, who had initially meant well, had come in and potentially caused irreversible harm to the $85,000 system. I had been to the lowest depths of the human psyche trying to figure out where those panels were for six months. These people, in one afternoon, may have compounded all that stress and undone all the subsequent success. The words that were coursing through my brain were unspeakable. The rage that was pulsating through my veins was barely controllable. Get me on a flight to Oz, because I have some folks to see!

I sent an e-mail to Jason telling him that I wanted the Australians' heads on a platter—metaphorically speaking. He responded that he was taking care of it and that we shouldn't make too big of a stink. Evidently, the Australians were guests of a village in the lagoon and had come with good intentions. I was with that reasoning for about five minutes, and then the war drums started to beat in my head again. Forgiveness takes center stage in my faith, and it is very important in letting go and releasing the wrongs that people commit against us. I knew that, and I would get to that point ... eventually. My personal being would not let this go without an e-mail response to the perpetrators, however.

The first salvo was a crushing volley of "how dare you" and "who do you think you are to destroy the solar power system that we just finished installing two weeks before you arrived?!" Did they have no respect for anyone else's work or contribution to the hospital? Maybe they thought because they were bringing new hospital beds, that entitled them to the title of Saviors of Seghe. Assholes! I paced back and forth in our office. Rage was about to flow from my fingertips. I didn't like anger, and I was not a fan of confrontation, but eight thousand miles of ocean standing between me and the ragtag bunch of solar expert wannabes emboldened me to let them have it.

Yes, yes, yes, they had meant well. I was not belittling that point. Our group did not own the system, either. We had given it to the hospital as a gift. Believe me, the hospital did not have the money to fix the system after someone potentially did irreversible harm to it. I wanted to yell at the Aussies, "Think, just think for one minute before you plug all the power tools in the world into the socket and go nuts! You aren't in Australia." Had they noticed that they had traveled to a third-world country where things were different—very different—from Australia? Where did they think all the power was coming from, a nuclear power plant in the Solomon Islands? Please!

Our team was committed to this facility, and we would be back. Were these people committed? I had no idea. I didn't even know what group they were representing. That was probably a good thing.

A couple of days later, I received a scathing response back from one of the rapscallions. "How insensitive could you be," he retorted. "You don't have a shred of decency," and blah blah blah. Well, at that moment, he was correct. In my mind, for how reckless they had been, they didn't deserve a shred of decency from me. They were clueless as to what we had gone through to get that system there and running. He had offered no apologies. He had not admitted to doing anything wrong. I've got one for them—it's called "breaking and entering." That's a crime in the United States. Oh, the arrogance! Speaking of arrogance, that trait is normally reserved for Americans on the world stage. *Thank you for the hospital beds, and good riddance!*

I'm not good at keeping things from people. Eventually, Jason found out that I had written a nasty rebuke to the Australians. Understandably, he was not pleased with me. We didn't know one another very well. He didn't want to alienate a group who was coming to provide assistance to the local hospital. I understood his thoughts, but I wouldn't have been able to sleep if I hadn't vented my feelings to those people.

CHAPTER

15

I knew I eventually had to move on from the Aussie solar debacle. Suzanne and I planned to coordinate the provision of health care to the people of the Marovo every six months. We were not going to be a one-and-done medical team. Dropping in and dispersing supplies and never returning was not how we planned to take care of business. This was going to be a success, and a long-term success at that. In our minds, short-term medical missions were not nearly as successful as they could be with long-term commitments. I was learning that the one-and-done medical trips were basically a waste of time and effort. Yes, some people would receive relief for their ailments, but when the shotgun medical team left, the people would be no better off than before the team had arrived.

Coordinating the trip every six months didn't leave a lot of time for me to smell the roses. Upon returning to the States, I immediately worked to get more participants for the next trip. Raising money was a challenge, but finding participants was equally as challenging. The trip was expensive, no doubt about it. There were tax incentives for going on the trip, but still, having to fork out $5,000 dollars to volunteer for two weeks was a tough sell for many people. I needed all sorts of people, including docs, mid-levels, nurses, dentists, and nonmedical folks. Our recruitment net was cast wide, and I couldn't afford to be too picky. The folks who were interested seemed to be genuinely invested in furthering our goals of providing quality medical care to the people of the Marovo Lagoon. Thankfully, the first two trips had been free of any personnel dramas.

The third trip yielded a great crop of docs. We had a married couple, both of whom were ER physicians. In my initial conversations with them, one of the trip's selling points, albeit morbid, was the crocodile attack. Of course, ER docs have typically seen it all, but one thing that most ER docs in the

United States have not seen is the victim of a crocodile attack. It was an odd selling point, but it helped to get them there, and I was pleased with the outcome.

Even more exciting than the great crop of docs was the fact that Jason would be coordinating the events on the ground for the entire trip. He was keen to get more involved and to learn about medicine in the process. Suzanne and I knew his language skills would be a major asset to the tour. He was a twenty-three-year-old who had a brain that was still as absorbent as a sponge. His eagerness to be involved was welcome and uplifting.

Arriving at Seghe Hospital for the third trip's welcoming ceremony in November 2009 was a mixed bag for me. It was great to be back, and I enjoyed getting to know Bishop Kurepitu better. He was a class act, and I think he was genuine in his faith and dealings with the church. I was thrilled to hear him say that the solar power system had changed the facility, staff, and entire community. He said the hospital was a different place. People far and wide were commenting about the lights being on all night long without any noise from a loud generator. Ah, music to my ears!

During the welcome ceremony, the bishop started his speech with a prayer. After the prayer, he said, "God said let there be light!" At that moment, one of the hospital staff turned on the light switch. The fluorescent tubes sputtered on, and everyone clapped and cheered. I'd had a feeling he was going to use that. … Well played, Bishop.

Before the first day's clinic started, I walked around the hospital and noticed the plaque in front commemorating the construction of the hospital in 2000. Anxious feelings invaded my brain. The place was a dump. I had gone to hell and back to bolt $85,000 in equipment to the roof of a dump. The facility was not being maintained. No one was being paid to clean the hospital regularly, and it showed. Change needed to happen, because I was getting nervous.

Throughout the next week, I discussed my concerns with Suzanne and the Kellys. They were in agreement that things needed to change at the hospital. Jill explained that she had served on the hospital board but resigned after a while because it was completely ineffective. It had been a waste of her time. That type of ineffective system couldn't continue, or else the hospital would fall apart.

I had to present my concerns and thoughts to the bishop. I wrote a letter, the bulk of it stating that I had the power to turn Seghe Hospital into the flagship hospital for the Solomon Islands. I would go to the end of the earth for this facility, but I wasn't going to clean it. That was where I drew the line. I had busted my butt getting the solar power system installed. The church and local community needed to take care of some of the responsibility for the facility. After all, the hospital belonged to the community. Paying someone to clean it and keep it in good shape was not a huge deal in my mind.

I wasn't clear on the bishop's true responsibilities with regard to the hospital. I knew the building sat on church-owned land, but I didn't know if the bishop was truly the boss of the facility or if that fell on someone else's shoulders. A hospital board was in place, but as Jill had told us, it was ineffective. Changes needed to be made fast before my feet got cold over the entire project. The facility had been forgotten and basically discarded since it was built. Now that our group was involved, those days were over. If the church and local community didn't want to take responsibility, then I was going to pull out all of our future support for the facility. The bishop would know I was true to my word because I had followed through with the solar power system.

We delivered the letter to the bishop. Obviously, my concerns raised his concern. He invited Suzanne, myself, and the Kellys to a meeting with the hospital board during the final weekend of the trip. It would be a great opportunity to discuss these issues with all stakeholders. Hopefully, we could figure out a way to move forward and ensure proper management and maintenance of the facility for the near future.

Toward the end of the first week of the trip, chinks in the personnel armor began to form. Our nursing team was fracturing, and one individual seemed to be causing the pain. I saw the personnel issues firsthand on our visit to Eucalyptus School. This was where the crocodile attack victim had shown up on the previous trip. A lot had taken place at Eucalyptus since we had been there last. When we pulled up to the wharf, it was obvious that a large building had been constructed close to the water's edge. It was a thatched-roof building that was very long, much like a long barn at a fair ground in the United States.

Everyone grabbed the medicines and supplies, and we walked toward the school. As we approached the large building, a couple of people were coming out. The scene was strange. A younger man was helping an older man walk out of the building. A few younger people were standing nearby, looking frightened, and didn't make a sound. Kate Wilson immediately reached for her camera. She was not only a doctor and dentist but was unofficially the trip shutterbug as well. She pointed her camera at the two men, and before Jason could tell her not to take photos, I heard the sound of the shutter opening and closing quietly.

I knew whom we were looking at, although I had never seen him before. Jason's reaction, along with the scared locals, clued me in to the fact that this was the head of the Christian Fellowship Church. It was this man's father who had had the initial "visitation" and subsequent "revelation" about starting his own church. After his father had died, the man we were looking at had assumed control of the church.

This man was not well. He emerged from the building guided by one arm, with a walking stick firmly attached to his other hand. His head was covered with wild, long gray hair. His clothes were tattered and barely hanging on his body. The image that I won't forget is how he wore a pair of bright yellow-framed sunglasses with one of the lenses diagonal up above one eye. They almost seemed like children's sunglasses. It didn't match the picture I had in my mind of a charismatic man who commanded the allegiance of thousands and controlled the purse strings of millions of dollars. With the way he looked, I had a hard time seeing a charismatic leader, but leaders of Christian cults throughout the years have all had distinguishing characteristics or leadership qualities that have caused people to follow them.

The man spoke to his minder, and Jason approached and introduced himself, then me and Suzanne. The church leader shook our hands. He mumbled a few words to us that were not comprehensible. His minder said a few more words to Jason that pertained to the new building, and then the leader and his minder slowly went on their way to the wharf, where they climbed aboard a waiting boat.

It was a strange encounter, but it definitely fit the bill for what I had heard about the gentleman and how his followers were petrified of him. Jason explained to us that the building had been built for his birthday celebration and that we were not to use his private bathroom, which was located outside the far end of the structure. Many of us commented on how it seemed a rather lavish amount of effort put forth in such a poor place, all for one person's birthday.

As had been the case when we had last visited Eucalyptus, the turnout was minimal. Some students from the school came down to see the docs, but there wasn't much to do. Because the clinic wasn't busy, Kate showed a couple of the docs the finer points of pulling teeth.

Halfway through the day, one of the nurses, Char, came to me and described a terrible, disgusting scene inside the church leader's private bathroom. My "irate-ometer" went from zero to sixty in nothing flat! She had a very strong, often too strong, personality. People frequently felt bowled over in her wake. I expressed my displeasure with her supposed voyeurism into the forbidden toilet but didn't linger long enough for a confrontation.

I wasn't abrasive in my dealings with others, but unfortunately, there were people on the trip who chose to be abrasive to others. I stewed over the incident for the rest of the day. It wasn't until sometime over the weekend that someone told me Char had been playing a joke and hadn't actually gone into the private bathroom. If it was a joke, I wanted to say, tell me a little sooner after the punch line. Don't let me stew on it and get more and more angry. That incident didn't help Char's standing with me over the next several days.

At Batuna Clinic, there were no buildings close by. Upon our arrival, we asked the clinic nurses to find tables for the triage station and pharmacy. As I've mentioned, things move on a different schedule in the Solomon Islands. There weren't any trucks to quickly transport the tables. Ten, then fifteen, minutes passed. Then I heard a loud voice yell, *"I need tables!"* I quickly turned around to see people looking in trepidation at Char. First of all, we were guests in this community. Second, Solomon Islanders are quiet and reserved people. They already referred to Americans as loud. Now that label was permanently affixed to our team. My patience with Char was growing thin. I needed team players; anything less was unacceptable in my mind.

It was so hot in the Batuna Clinic that day that Kate referred to the dental room as the incubator. One of the ER docs sweated so much, his scrubs dripped a puddle on the floor in his exam room. We were slowly basting in our own fluids.

Finally, the beautiful and bright spot of the clinic arrived. Sandra, little Allan Daly, and Allan's grandfather came to see us. Both Sandra and little

Allan looked great. He was asleep, and I actually got to hold him for a little bit. I paraded him around like a proud father, even though none of my DNA was in the child. Suzanne and some of the nurses came out to take pictures.

The grandfather did most of the talking, but that was probably customary. He was slick and persistent. He looked familiar to me. I had probably seen him at Uepi during one of the carvers' days, when local craftsmen showed their wares at the resort. He began to talk to me about options for us in relation to little Allan and Sandra. At first I didn't quite get what he was talking about. Then I began to figure out that he was talking about some sort of entitlement that seemed to be owed to them for naming the child after me. He didn't come out and say that we needed to do anything for the child, but he was encouraging Suzanne and me to be involved with little Allan. I preferred encouragement over entitlement.

I about fell over when he presented his grand plan. He offered for Sandra and little Allan to visit us in the United States and then just Sandra would come back. Wait, I … what? I immediately got hot, and my face turned red. What the … ? I had never thought kids were in my future. While my facial expression was probably one of horror, Suzanne was smiling from ear to ear. Oh boy, no, no, no. I didn't know how we could continue focusing so much energy on the Solomon Islands and providing care for so many babies if we were to do that because I would then have to focus all my energy on one baby. I also freaked out because I would be the caregiver for the child. Although I was mature, I didn't consider myself mature enough to take care of a baby. Suzanne seemed much more ready for the venture than I did. People have to have babies, I know. I'm very thankful my parents decided to have me. More and more, I had been seeing friends who'd had babies, and they had been forced to become very focused on their children, which they should, but other activities and interests had suffered because of that necessary parental focus. I was committed to the Solomons, and I didn't want that to be derailed.

Little Allan had a mother. Sandra was not married, but I didn't know if she didn't want to raise Allan or if her father didn't think she could raise him by herself. I think Sandra's dad wanted her to continue her education and thought maybe having the baby would make that harder. Not wanting to pry, I failed to ask what the situation was with little Allan's father.

After Sandra's father saw my reaction regarding keeping the baby in the United States, he threw me a bone. He asked if we would send Sandra to school. My heart was open and willing to help this single mother. Throwing college into the conversation did make me pause for a second, though. I wasn't sure to which college he was referring. There were other things that went along with it, like tuition and frat parties. Through a muddled conversation, I learned there was a two-year business program at the Batuna school located on the hill behind the clinic. I told him that Suzanne and I needed to talk about these things and we would get back to him via Jill and Grant. He was fine with that arrangement.

Suzanne and I enjoyed a few more minutes with Sandra and Allan, and then we had to get back to work. The patients were stacking up, as Batuna was one of our heaviest clinic days.

Suzanne and I later discussed the Sandra situation at length. After consulting with Jill at Uepi, we learned that adoptions from the Solomon Islands were not legal. My immature side didn't need to hear anything else; Jill had spoken, and it wasn't legal to adopt the baby. That was the story, and I was sticking to it! Suzanne and I decided to send Sandra to the local two-year business school. We felt it would be best if she were able to care for little Allan, and giving her a higher education was the best way to make that a reality. Money wasn't a deal breaker, but fortunately, the business degree wouldn't cost nearly what it would cost in the States.

Before we left Batuna, one of our docs and his children pulled out a gift for the community. He was an ophthalmologist and had brought his entire family on the trip. I had been unable to fill the rest of the rooms at Uepi, so there had been space for his wife and three children. His wife was an RN and during the medical tour worked in triage, and his kids helped him in the eye clinic. He had rallied his church and received donations of newborn baby kits, hygiene kits, and close to one hundred soccer balls. At each village, his kids had been pulling out a dozen soccer balls and pumped them up. The local children were thrilled to see the balls. Laughter and play broke out throughout each village as the soccer balls were given out. Soccer was a big deal in the Solomon Islands. The gift was a big hit, and we were glad he had gone to all the trouble to bring the soccer balls.

After Thursday's clinic at Batuna, we visited Vakabo on Friday and then enjoyed the weekend. Monday's clinic was at Telina, and as always, the village welcomed us with a beautiful welcome ceremony capped off with song and speeches. After returning from Telina, one of the nurses came to me at our cabin and spoke nervously about how she didn't like the treatment she was receiving from Char. She grabbed my arm, shaking as she said, "I think I need to confront her. She can't keep treating the other nurses like this. She's been bossing us around the entire trip as if we don't know what we're doing."

What the hell was happening here? We had all paid the same amount of money to fly twenty-five hours to donate our time and take care of people. No one deserved anything more than anyone else. Everyone did deserve to be treated like human beings. I told the nurse that I would take care of the situation for her. As the trip coleader, it was my responsibility to deal with something like this. Why was I having to even stress over this? Hostile work environments can be toxic and very hard places to be in. I didn't like the fact that our trip was turning into a hostile work environment for some members of our team. Why was it so hard to treat people—colleagues, even—with respect? We're all different; this I know, but can't we all just put aside whatever demons may be inside our brains for two weeks? The morale, cohesiveness, and effectiveness of the group depended on people working together as a team.

Confrontation was not my strong suit. Drama was not my friend. The entire situation going on before us was the definition of drama. As a child, I had learned early that it was easier for me to take a passive stance when it came to confrontation. If passivity was not an option, then my response had the potential to be overly aggressive.

Soon after I spoke with the concerned nurse, Char and another nurse came up to the deck of our cabin. Suzanne and I were trying to unwind because we had just come back from a clinic. Josh, the assistant manager of Uepi, had a skin infection that we were going to treat with antibiotics. The medicines were located in our cabin, of course. Upon walking up the steps of our deck, Char called out, "Suzanne, I'd like to get the medicine to give to Josh."

Suzanne replied, "I am going to give it to him in a little bit."

"I'd really like the medicine now to take down to him," Char insisted.

Snap! The boat to passive town had just left the marina, and I was not on it. My knee jerked, and I let out the loud, stern command: "Suzanne will take Josh the medicine, and you can like it!" Silence … and more silence.

My heart was racing, and my blood pressure was on the rise. Silence. I watched through the screen as Char and the other nurse slowly walked off the deck and walked away. I could hear words being muttered but could not decipher them. I imagined I would be hearing more about this, but that was okay, because the confrontation needed to start.

That night at dinner, my passive tendencies were back. Of course, I was trying to avoid further confrontation. I walked to the bathroom, which was at least thirty feet away from the dining room area. As I came out of the bathroom, Char confronted me. "Allan, you were very disrespectful to me earlier, and I want you to apologize."

The boat to passive town quickly departed again as I waved good-bye to it. "I was disrespectful to you? You have been completely and unacceptably disrespectful to several people on this trip from day one."

She responded, while in my face, "This isn't about me."

"Yes, it is about you, and I'm done with you!" I said. I walked past her and sat down at the table. Good thing I had ordered a gin and tonic earlier, because I needed a stiff drink after the brief yet tense encounter.

I lay in bed with Suzanne that night, reflecting. For the first time in three medical tours, I was having a terrible experience and I wanted it to end. It was absolutely crazy that this was even happening. Lying in bed, Suzanne was stunned when I told her how one nurse had come to me like a nervous wreck because she felt like she needed to confront Char. We were stuck in the Solomons with this group for another week; the situation wasn't going to change, so we just had to deal with the cards we had been dealt. I felt bad for the team members who weren't having the experience they should have had, as a result of the conflict.

We made it to the final weekend of the trip—barely. Jason, Grant, Suzanne, and I went to the hospital to meet with the bishop and hospital board. Expectations weren't high from anyone in our party after hearing stories from Jill regarding past hospital board meetings. I hoped this one was going to be different, however. The bishop was aware that we weren't happy with the current state of the hospital and that we wanted change. We didn't have to have change, but if they wanted us to continue to provide improvements to the hospital, change wasn't optional.

The meeting was held on the deck of the doctor's house. It's funny that we called it the doctor's house because it had initially been built to attract a doctor to Seghe, but there had never been a doctor in residence. The building had been built with cheap materials. The termites, or white ants, found the walls very tasty. The Aussie wrecking crew that had come in six months prior had done some things to make it better, but it really needed to be completely gutted. Concrete wall sheeting was the only wall material the termites weren't eating. The deck overlooked the main entrance to the hospital and had several eggplant shrubs and pole bean plants around the perimeter. It blew my mind that the eggplants never died back.

The deck looked over a house in front of the lagoon. That house needed to be razed; I considered it to be unlivable. Unfortunately, however, one of the hospital's nurses and his family had no other option but to live in that house.

As I looked over that house, I thought about my relationship with the bishop, which was good, yet in its infancy. This was the first formal meeting in the Solomon Islands that Suzanne and I had attended. I hoped Grant was going to take the lead when it was our time to speak.

The bishop started off by acknowledging the letter I had sent him and then offered his support of the principles I had outlined in the letter. He was on board and in agreement that the changes needed to occur. He also agreed that a full-time hospital administrator must be hired to manage the day-to-day activities at the hospital. We talked about how various groups had shown up with good intentions but without the knowledge and guidance of the hospital staff at times. The activities of all well-intentioned groups needed to be encouraged, but only after they were channeled through a central person responsible for making sure efforts were appropriate and not duplicated. There was unanimous consensus among the meeting participants that these items were important. We knew follow-through was imperative.

Grant took the floor and shared the Kellys' history with the hospital. He mentioned Jill's involvement on past medical boards and how frustrating it was that nothing had ever been accomplished. He implored the board to get involved and to work for the betterment of the hospital. After all, the hospital belonged to the people of the Marovo Lagoon. His statements reaffirmed their continued support, but also their reluctance to support a hospital facility that the locals wouldn't also support. The Kellys would not and could not be our group's only other partners in this push to create a long-term administrator position and long-term cleaning and maintenance positions.

During the meeting, the bishop made a joke, nominating Jason as the new hospital administrator. We all laughed and said yes, that would be a great idea. Jason chuckled and respectfully declined because he had enough on his plate with starting his timber business.

The meeting ended with a commitment from the board to find a full-time hospital administrator. The specifics of this objective had not been ironed out, but the bishop and other members of the board knew progress was needed to ensure the future participation of our medical group. I left the meeting with a sense of calm and felt reassured that the church and the medical board were going to step up to the plate and provide more care for the hospital. It was an excellent way to wrap up an otherwise dreadful trip.

CHAPTER

16

*B*ack in Salt Lake, I wrestled with how to fill the hospital administrator and janitorial positions. We needed a central point person to coordinate all the happenings with the facility. The bishop didn't have the time to manage the hospital. I thought it was important that the person not be church related. The facility was situated on United Church property, and the church already had influence and oversight on the building.

Speaking of non-church-related individuals, I received an e-mail from Jason two weeks after we returned. I couldn't believe my eyes. He had stepped up to the plate in a huge way. The e-mail said that he had volunteered to serve as the interim Seghe Hospital administrator. Awesome news! It was obvious that Jason enjoyed a test, and there was no doubt this role would provide plenty of challenges. Jason had lifted a huge weight off my shoulders. I somewhat let my guard down now that there was a point person responsible for looking after the facility and the solar power system. Jason was local, talented, energetic, and had a vision of what would be beneficial for the local community. His abilities to navigate the culture and to get things done would be crucial to the continued development of the facility. We were off and running!

Time between trips seemed to fly. With continual logistical items to manage and participants to round up, the next departure came quickly. The month prior to departure contained the usual craziness that happens before every medical tour. Medicines needed to be gathered, supply inventories combed, and gaps filled. Doctor licenses had to be e-mailed to the Ministry of Health for medical privilege clearance. Jason, Suzanne, and I solidified the village clinic schedule so he could distribute it throughout the lagoon.

I was doing my fair share of coaxing people to join us on an incredible adventure 8,000 miles from the United States. Maybe I needed to change careers and be a travel agent. While trying my best to coax others to join us, I was approached by another group who wanted me to join them in the Solomon Islands for a medical tour.

The organization was based in the States and had been doing medical work in Fiji for several years and for some reason wanted a change in venue. The woman who contacted me told me of their plans to take a team of roughly twenty people, the same size of our teams, to charter the Bilikiki dive boat to tour the country, providing medical care. She mentioned that they were avid divers and there would be plenty of time to dive. She had gotten my e-mail address from Uepi, and we had eventually connected on the phone. Her invitation was for me to join them on their tour, scheduled to be a month or two prior to our trip. She asked me a lot of questions about who I used for customs clearance and made it well known to me that they were shipping one million dollars worth of medical supplies to Honiara. It sounded like they knew what they were doing. I wasn't quite sure what I could offer.

Surprisingly, the group planned to visit Seghe Hospital. I thought it was a great idea because Seghe didn't have a doctor, and any chance for the locals to see a doctor was a good thing. The timing of their trip didn't work out for me; thus, I was forced to decline the offer. My time needed to stay focused on our endeavors at Seghe. I was eager to leave our last trip behind me. There were people scheduled on the fourth trip whom I didn't know, and I hoped they weren't drama queens or kings.

We arrived at Seghe to an incredible surprise. Jason's first major undertaking as the interim hospital administrator had been to build a medical waste incinerator. The medical waste pile that had been such a terrible scene was gone. Jason had used a World Health Organization incinerator design, and it had turned out wonderfully. He explained that the nurses from the hospital had picked through the entire medical waste pile by hand and removed all the sharps and incinerated them. What an incredible feat! The hospital was much more attractive as a result of this one improvement. What a way to start the trip.

That afternoon, after we had arrived at Uepi, I walked past the dive shop and caught the eye of one of the dive masters. He approached me and spoke about the American team that had just visited Seghe. He was visibly angry as he explained what had happened during their visit. Like our team, the team that had rented the dive boat had put out a schedule of where they would be on certain days. They hadn't stayed just in the Marovo Lagoon. They had traveled all over the country for two weeks. It was quite ambitious, in my mind. The dive master continued to share a story of how they had told the local people they would be at Seghe for two days of clinic. Many patients from the first day who could not be seen had returned the second day. He was furious as he told me that the medical group had left the next morning without adhering to their schedule. When the team left well before their scheduled departure, it caused a local uproar. Locals were very angry that they had been told the team would be there both days and then had not followed through. Some people had paddled from far away, and others had spent money on fuel to get to Seghe to see the doctors. It was a bad scene.

I couldn't apologize for that group just because they were American like me. Obviously, the person who had made the decision to leave early hadn't been thinking clearly. Their reputation was tarnished for good. I hoped this careless act wasn't going to reflect negatively on our efforts in the Marovo. I assured him that we would continue to stick to our schedules and that type of thing would never happen from our group. Yikes.

A few days later, we visited a different clinic for the first time. Cheara Clinic was strategically built near Patukae School, Chubikopi village, and Chea village. There were several hundred people between those three places to keep the clinic busy. Jason notified us that we needed to make room in the boats for furniture. The clinic was relatively new, but it did not have any furniture. He explained that the clinic was a project managed by the Australian aid organization AusAid. The project had been so poorly managed that the managers had spent so much money on flying the head honchos in for the opening ceremony that they had blown through their budget; hence the reason we had to bring our own furniture with us. There had been no money left for furniture. Hello! That was ridiculous. It was another international-aid project failure. Jason said he could have gone on and on about other projects that had since crumbled.

Arriving at Cheara was no picnic. The boats pulled up to a swamp with some round logs randomly placed on the ground to serve as a makeshift walkway. Hauling the furniture up to the building was challenging, but some locals helped, as they usually did.

The building looked nice from the outside. As with most buildings in the Marovo Lagoon, it didn't have a bathroom. The ladies in our group were not fans of this one bit. The clinic sat at the bottom of a steep hill. On the hill above the clinic sat a couple of homes. There was nowhere to go to the bathroom except out in front of the clinic in a tall grassy area. People on the hill could look down on folks trying to go to the bathroom. Personally, I didn't like having to walk into the swampy grass to pee. I didn't know what I was stepping on. It could have been mud or it could have been feces; I couldn't tell. I made sure I didn't drink much more water after the first bathroom break. It was the worst bathroom spot we had encountered to date.

The nurse stationed at the clinic barely had any medicines, or anything of medical value, for that matter. It was ridiculous how the aid organization had left the building without even one hospital bed. Rest assured, the project managers had patted one another on the back after they had finished building the structure, however. They probably didn't think much about leaving the building with no furniture on their way back to Oz.

On the way back to Uepi from Cheara Clinic, we decided never to visit it again. Our time would be better spent visiting Chubikopi, Chea, or Patukae School. We wouldn't have to travel with our own furniture if we visited one of those places.

The group for this trip was great. There weren't any dramas, and everyone got along really well. On the last Saturday of the trip, we went on the all-day dive/snorkel excursion. Fortunately, we didn't have any boat accidents to attend to, so we were able to do all four dives. The P-38 Lightning was top-notch, as it had been in the past.

That night, after the dive excursion, Hal Gooch, one of our doctors, woke up at three a.m. with severe abdominal pain. He chose not to wake anyone and stayed still until morning. His roommate, Erik, had been to medical school but hadn't completed a residency program. Erik was working on a master's degree in public health and was doing some data collection on this trip. When Erik awoke, Hal shared the news of his acute belly pain with Erik. Erik started to poke on Hal a little until Hal said, "Stop touching me, and get Suzanne!"

Before breakfast, Erik came over and knocked on our door. He described the situation, and Suzanne grabbed her stethoscope to examine Hal. His belly was extremely tender on the lower right side. For a few minutes, Suzanne and Hal, both physicians, were likely thinking the same thing, but Hal let Suzanne continue without saying anything.

"Hal, I have to ask you a question. Do you still have your appendix?"

"I was afraid you were going to ask me that. ... Yes."

"Oh boy..." Suzanne replied calmly. There were no hysterics, but they both knew the depth of the situation. The good news was that Hal's vital signs were stable for the time being. The bad news was that Suzanne had no idea how long they would stay stable.

This was the last full day of the trip. The group was scheduled to get on the airplane the next day to fly back to the States. Suzanne called Kate for another opinion. Kate came to the same conclusion as Suzanne: Hal was suffering from acute appendicitis. This was really bad. Even worse was the fact that we were a long way away from an operating room in which we would feel comfortable allowing Hal to undergo surgery.

Suzanne and Kate called one of the nurses and asked her to start an IV on Hal. We were armed with several different IV antibiotics that we had for "oh shit" cases just like this.

After consulting with Jason, Jill, and Grant, Suzanne jumped on Uepi's satellite phone to call Hal's travel insurance company. Suzanne immediately began to explain the situation, and the person on the other line interrupted, asking, "Is the patient in imminent danger of dying?"

"No, he is stable right now," Suzanne responded with several caveats. She explained the situation and our location, and that we were scheduled to depart for Australia the next day. The person at the travel insurance company asked if he could call Suzanne back after they ran this through their medical officer. She pressed for action involving an emergency evacuation. The representative said he had to discuss the situation with the medical officer and they would call back.

Suzanne went back to Hal. She and Kate wanted to give him IV gentamicin. They discussed with Hal the possibility of hearing loss as a result of the medicine, but it was one of the stronger IV antibiotics they had. He was in agreement to use the drug.

The tension at breakfast was thicker than the Vegemite on the table. There was a lot of conversation going on about contingency plans. Plans for one final dive of course were on hold. The mood in the room was of uncertainty, and no one was happy with that feeling.

Shortly after breakfast, the quiet was broken by the ring of the satellite phone. Jason answered and gave the phone to Suzanne. She was not happy with the answers the representative gave her. The doctor for the insurance company did not agree with Suzanne and the other doctors' assessments that Hal needed to be evacuated. Suzanne continued to make her case, but the insurance company was not prepared to evacuate Hal at that time. They asked her to call back with an update of his condition later.

One thing was for sure: It was a good thing the insurance representative and medical officer were nowhere near my redheaded wife. They would have both needed IV antibiotics after she was done with them. Who were they to determine the severity of Hal's appendicitis? There were five other doctors on the trip who agreed with Suzanne's diagnosis and her assessment that this was a serious emergency requiring evacuation. Who were these people? Hal had paid a hefty one-time premium for travel insurance, which included emergency medical evacuation. The company was dodging its contractual responsibility—to save money, of course. This was borderline criminal, in my mind.

Suzanne didn't want Hal to be alarmed. She and Kate continued to monitor his status. He lay in bed for most of the morning and around lunchtime decided he would try to walk to the main house to sit out in the breeze and see the water. He walked slowly and methodically up the pathway, carrying his IV bag in one hand. He was in pain, but the acute stabbing had subsided for the time being. For the rest of the afternoon, he lay on the love seat at the end of the dining hall deck. His pain was coming and going. We had another twenty-four hours before our scheduled arrival in Brisbane.

Suzanne called the travel insurance company again to push for an evacuation. Of course there had been a shift change at the insurance company, so Suzanne had to tell the entire story over again. The conversation progressed a little to where the representative spoke about where a jet could land nearby and where the jet would originate. The representative kept talking about sending a jet from New Zealand. Suzanne tried to tell the person that there were several large cities in Australia that were much closer to the Solomon Islands than New Zealand was. Didn't these people have a globe or a map of the world on the wall? New Zealand? Yes, Americans in general are terrible at geography, but this was ridiculous and sad.

The insurance company had a hard time understanding that they would not be able to land a jet at the Seghe runway. Hello, the runway wasn't long enough for jet aircraft. An airplane or helicopter would have to be dispatched to Seghe to pick Hal up and take him to Honiara. Jets could land in Honiara and did land there regularly. The problem was that it was getting late in the afternoon. There were no runway lights at Seghe, and no helicopter would fly 110 miles to Uepi from Honiara at night; there was no coast guard in the Solomon Islands to rescue the pilot and Hal should the chopper go down in the water. Our window to get him out that day was closing quickly.

The eye doctor, Rachel, had brought her son, Richard, on the trip to assist her with the eye clinic. Richard was an attorney. That afternoon, Richard drew up a medical directive with Hal's guidance and blessing. Hal put me and Suzanne in charge of his medical decision making should he become incapacitated or not be able to make decisions on his own accord. I became nervous at this point. We were definitely preparing for a potential life-or-death situation. We had e-mailed Hal's two children, who were in Europe and the Middle East, to notify them of the situation. We had no idea if Hal was going to make it to an operating room in time. Had his appendix burst or leaked? We didn't have a definitive way of telling without advanced imaging. There wasn't even a CT scanner or MRI machine in the Solomon Islands. Hal needed to get to Australia, and fast.

The travel insurance geniuses continued to hem and haw without making a decision to evacuate Hal. Hal lay on the love seat all through dinner. Of course he was forbidden from eating anything so as to not further aggravate his appendix. He seemed to be in a strange limbo, teetering on the edge, but not writhing in pain, fortunately.

Darkness had fallen; no evacuation was going to happen. We gingerly escorted Hal back to his cabin to try to get some rest for the night. Suzanne and Kate checked on him regularly throughout the night.

During the night, Suzanne made a couple more phone calls to the insurance company, requesting an evacuation first thing the next morning. Those conversations ended without any decisions made in Hal's favor. It's not often I hear doctors talk about filing lawsuits, but the lack of action from the insurance company had a couple of folks in the group saying that a lawsuit would be appropriate in this case.

By the grace of God, Hal made it through the night. The next morning, we were at the point of needing to go to Seghe to make our regularly scheduled departure to Honiara and then on to Brisbane. Unbelievably, Hal was going to have to fly commercial. We notified the impotent insurance company that we were going to try to get him to Brisbane and that it was imperative that they have an ambulance waiting for him at the airport. That was the last contact we had with the insurance company prior to leaving Uepi.

Several people helped Hal get in the boat. The IV was still attached to his arm. There was talk back and forth about whether he should pull the IV before he got on the plane so the airlines didn't get suspicious. He said he wanted to pull the IV. The only problem was that should he begin to crash, the others wouldn't have quick access to his venous system.

After leaving Uepi, Grant sent a heads-up e-mail to one of the managers at Solomon Airlines. Grant notified the manager of Hal's condition and of the need to get him to Brisbane in an expedited fashion. Grant had a good working relationship with this guy, who worked in the Brisbane airport office of Solomon Airlines.

As we waited for the airplane at Seghe, we sat around and listened to Richard play his guitar. He sang some funny songs, and we collectively tried to keep the tension at bay. As the plane arrived, Hal decided to keep the IV in for the first flight but take it out once he arrived in Honiara. The nurses helped him hide the bag so it wasn't completely obvious.

When the Seghe flight landed in Honiara, Hal was still getting around under his own power. In the domestic terminal, prior to heading to the international terminal, the nurses pulled the IV. Hal remained strong as we took a cab to the international check-in.

As we all approached the check-in counter, Suzanne and Kate walked up with Hal's documents to check him onto the flight. I stood with them as the Solomon Airlines agent asked if we were the ones with the sick traveler. I explained that Grant Kelly had sent an e-mail through to describe the situation so Solomon Airlines would be aware and hopefully expedite the process of getting Hal on the plane to Brisbane.

"Yes, sir, I did see that e-mail, but that e-mail was sent to Brisbane. You are in Honiara, and we make the decisions on who can get on the plane or not," the gate agent responded in an obvious power play.

I couldn't believe what I had just heard. We had a man whose life was in danger, and this guy was going to start a pissing contest because the e-mail had not been addressed to him. This was unacceptable and rather scary, to say the least.

Suzanne spoke with the agent. "Is there a problem with Hal getting on the flight to Brisbane?"

"I'm sorry, miss, but since he is very sick, he cannot get on the airplane without a doctor clearing him to fly."

"Sir, I am a doctor, she is a doctor, and there are three other doctors over there. We all agree that he can get on the airplane to Brisbane," Suzanne said calmly but with plenty of sincerity flowing through her words.

"The Solomon Airlines doctor is the one who needs to examine him in order to get on the flight."

I couldn't keep my words in any longer! "We have been here for the past two weeks, taking care of Solomon Islanders in the Marovo Lagoon. We are a medical team, and this man, who is also a doctor, needs to get on that airplane today!"

Suzanne pushed me away from the counter because I was getting out of control. For one second, I saw myself being arrested at the Honiara airport for jumping over the check-in counter and choking the shit out of that little Solomon Airlines assistant manager. For one second, I looked at Hal and realized that I needed to keep my calm so as to not make him upset. He could obviously see that I was ready to go off.

I needed to regain control. I hastily looked around and saw an Australian Federal Police officer near the airport entrance. I walked up to him and pleaded my case. He understood our issue but said he was unable to pull any strings for us. Damn it!

"How do we get the Solomon Airlines doctor to assess Hal?" Suzanne asked the Solomon Airlines agent.

"I will call him now to see if he will come examine him," the man said as he dialed the phone. Suzanne's Pidgin had come a long way. As she listened, she could understand that the doctor was balking on leaving Honiara to come to the airport. The employee seemed unhappy with the doctor's answers. Suzanne asked to speak with the doctor on the phone, but the doctor declined. "He said he was in clinic and could not come down to the airport."

Are you kidding me? I was seriously going to hurt the man behind the counter and then track down the doctor and punch him in the appendix. This may have been the angriest I had ever been in my entire life. My body had more adrenaline running through it than ever before. What the hell good is it to have a doctor on call for the airline when the doctor won't leave the hospital to see one of the airline's patients? If this was Solomon time, I was going to devote the rest of my life to resetting their clock!

Suzanne kept her composure, but she was intent on conveying a few points. "Sir, do you understand that the National Referral Hospital does not currently have running water? I am not leaving this man here. Do you understand me? What do we have to do to get him on the airplane?" Suzanne knew the man had regulations he needed to follow. She also wasn't going to leave Hal in Honiara, and she made that clear.

The agent thought for a minute and then replied, "The only option he has is to take his case to the captain when the flight arrives from Brisbane. If the captain agrees that he can get on the plane, then we will need a written statement from you saying that he is well enough to fly to Brisbane. You will also have to accept all responsibility for his care."

"That's fine. I will be more than happy to speak with the captain. Please let me know when he is available," Suzanne told him.

Another half hour passed, and we heard the roaring jet engines from the Solomon Airlines flight that had just arrived from Brisbane. The situation was tense. I wasn't able to sit down. I paced back and forth behind Hal so he couldn't see my craziness.

After leaving the check-in area for about twenty minutes, the assistant manager returned and motioned for us to approach the counter. "I spoke with the captain, and as long as you sign the statement I mentioned, Hal can get on the plane."

Oh, the sweet, sweet, sweet feeling of victory at a time when we needed a win unlike any other! Thank you, Lord! Hal had to make it three more hours in the air to get to an ambulance that would take him to Royal Brisbane Hospital for surgery. The amount of stress I had caused myself had probably taken an entire year off my life. That was one of the few times in my life when I had felt like I was going to go berserk. I was thankful that I hadn't followed through on any of the crazy thoughts that had been flowing through my head.

The two pilots were older Australian gentlemen. Suzanne overheard them talking to one another as she boarded the plane. The one pilot said to the other, "Well, at least there are five doctors on the plane if he has a problem." That had been exactly our point! I'm glad these guys had some sense about them.

Finally en route to Brisbane, I looked back at Hal, who was several rows behind us. He was out cold, finally getting some much needed rest. Obviously, he was feeling just as much stress as we were, as he was the one with the appendicitis.

Prior to our arrival at Brisbane, Hal awoke and seemed to be doing quite well. As we taxied to the gate, I looked out the window for the ambulance. I didn't see any emergency vehicles or flashing lights outside the aircraft. What was going on? The travel insurance company had said they would have an ambulance waiting.

Before the pilots turned off the "fasten seat belt" sign, a small man entered the airplane and grabbed the microphone. He said that he was a quarantine officer and asked for Hal Gooch to come to the front of the airplane. Suzanne, Kate, and I got up and walked to the front with Hal.

There were no paramedics, not even an offer of a wheelchair on which Hal could ride. My blood started to boil again. The travel insurance company had not heard from me yet, but it was going to, without a doubt. As we walked a long way to immigration, the quarantine officer asked Hal some questions. He said an ambulance had been activated and should be waiting outside of baggage claim. Hal didn't receive any physical assistance and had to clear his luggage through customs just like everyone else.

We exited the airport. Kate had agreed to go to the hospital with Hal. I agreed to stay with Hal in Brisbane until he was well enough to travel home. The entire team stood on the curb outside of baggage claim, waiting for the ambulance. Twenty-five minutes passed without an ambulance showing. Hal started to complain that he was not feeling well. Unbelievable! Without an ambulance, we put Hal and Kate in a cab and sent them to Royal Brisbane Hospital.

Jo and Dave, our friends in Brisbane, had been alerted that I needed to stay with them for the next several days. They had no problem with Hal recovering at their house for as long as it took. The two of them were very good to us and never accepted anything in return.

Suzanne and I went out to dinner with Dave and Jo that evening. Kate sat in the ER with Hal. She reported to us that the ER doc had done everything that she had hoped she would. The doc had promptly loaded Hal into the CT scanner; the results had come back positive for rip-roaring appendicitis. The ER doc was concerned there may have been some leakage.

The next morning, Jo and I dropped Suzanne off at the airport to head home. Jo then dropped me off at Royal Brisbane to find Hal. There wasn't any room for him on any of the general wards, so he had been put in the neurosurgery recovery ward. He was happy to see me, even though he was still rather uncomfortable. It was surreal for me to sit there. Two patients across the room both had shaved heads and massive sutures across their scalps that resembled zippers. I didn't have to be told twice that we were in the neurosurgery recovery ward.

A case worker came in and took Hal's personal information and helped answer some questions for us. About an hour later, a nurse came to collect him and take him to surgery. I told him to hang in there and that I would see him in recovery.

Walking around Royal Brisbane was cool. There was a lot going on, and it seemed like a nice institution. It was a public hospital, which many Americans consider to be of the devil, but from what I had heard, Australia's dual public-private healthcare system seemed to have a lot going for it. As I had a bite to eat outside, I had a good time watching the young residents talking to one another in their snappy-looking clothes. They were all very hip, even though they were probably not making a lot of money as residents. It was a generational thing, I figured—it didn't matter if they didn't make any money; they just had to look good at all times.

After lunch, I made my way to the surgical recovery waiting room. I looked at magazines and watched Australian television for well over an hour, wondering what was happening with Hal. Not wanting to be a pest, I waited for quite a while between my first and second inquiries regarding Hal's progress. Finally, they let me go through to see him. He was still asleep when I got to him. I waited close to thirty minutes, but he never seemed to snap out of the anesthesia. I wrote a note and left it on the table next to his bed. I felt bad leaving, but it was five o'clock and I needed to get a cab to Jo's office so she could take me back to her place.

Riding on the other side of the road in Australia was a hoot. Not only was everything in the front of the car reversed, but the highways and intersections in Australia seemed alive. We drove under multiple structures possessing one type of automated toll device or another. The car beeped as we drove under the electronic toll booth perched twenty feet above our heads. Most intersections had cameras. There were red-light cameras and speed cameras everywhere. Why on Earth would anyone ever own a sports car in Australia? The police were filming their every move. The United States and Australia are similar in a lot of ways, but the differences in tolerance over public privacy issues were striking.

With Hal being in good hands at Royal Brisbane, Dave and I decided to settle another score. We walked to the shed, each grasping for a big win on the table tennis table. He had made quick work of me the past few times we had played, but my game had improved and I was going to give him my best. The hour of competition was fierce. Yelling could be heard outside the shed. I didn't want to get back on the plane a loser again.

Somehow, I finally beat Dave. I was glad he didn't pummel me afterward. Dave had been a boxer and had told me about many a barroom brawl that included his participation. He was a graceful loser, which was always the mark of a quality sportsman. We finished off the night with pizza and Crown Lagers. The beer was delicious. Dave knew I liked Crown Lager, and he had it for me every time Suzanne and I came through town: the mark of a true friend!

Jo was nice enough to drop me off at Royal Brisbane the next morning. There weren't any hurdles in my way to see Hal this time. He cracked a little smile as I walked into the room. His spirits were higher, although he did have some post-op pain. I asked him if the docs had shared much information about the surgery.

"Yeah, the appendix had leaked into my pelvis. Fortunately, they were able to do the procedure laparoscopically, but because of the leakage, it took ninety minutes to clean up all the pus." He took a breather for fifteen seconds and then continued, "It only took them fifteen minutes to do the guy's appendix next to me. Believe it or not, he's from Wyoming."

"That's crazy. What are the chances of a guy from Utah and a guy from Wyoming both having appendectomies on the same day at the same hospital in Brisbane, Australia? Wow. ... So have they given you any idea on when they think you can leave?"

"The surgeon said he was going to give me a letter certifying that I'm okay to fly."

"Good. The travel insurance company might want to see it."

The hospital discharged Hal later that afternoon. We took a cab to Dave and Jo's place. The speed bumps didn't sit well with Hal, but we had to get there. As always, Dave and Jo catered to our every need. Hal spent the next couple of days sitting in the recliner and slowly walking around from time to time. He ventured up to watch Dave and me have it out on the table. I knew he was getting better when he started to talk some smack about our game. He even threw it out there that we were lucky he was injured or else he would have beaten both of us. Strong words, Hal!

Three days after the procedure, Hal was feeling like he wanted to leave. He needed to get back to his practice in Salt Lake. The delay had definitely not been planned into his schedule. The time had come for me to get back on the phone with the travel insurance company. They started to use the same obstruction tactics they had used while we had been at Uepi. It was their opinion that Hal needed to wait a week before he flew home. What the...? Why? I faxed them the note from the surgeon who had performed the procedure; he had certified that Hal was okay to fly. Obviously, the crack medical team at the travel insurance company didn't trust the surgeon who had performed the surgery.

We needed to get home, and this crap wasn't going to fly! What was the company's problem? It was already facing the threat of a lawsuit because its people had chosen not to evacuate Hal during a life-threatening emergency. Now they weren't letting him get on the plane because there could be air in his gut that could expand and do bad things to him. Insurance exasperation had set in. Would this ever end?

Hal and I wanted another opinion. His medical background wasn't in surgery, and he didn't think flying would be an issue, but he wanted to double-check. Amazingly, within thirty minutes, we were able to get three surgical opinions from surgeons at St. Mark's Hospital in Salt Lake City. All three surgeons said there were no reasons why Hal couldn't get on the airplane immediately. All three of the independent opinions were contrary to the travel insurance company's policy. Hal wasn't sure what he would have done if one of the three opinions had not been in agreement. We told the travel insurance company to arrange the tickets because we were leaving the next day. I reminded them that they were facing a lawsuit because of the failed evacuation out of the Solomon Islands. Our insistence to leave and my threats forced their hand.

We showed up at the airport the next morning with Hal moving understandably slowly. He had requested an aisle seat. The woman responded that she was sorry but she had only a window seat. Without exploding on the ticket agent, we tried to remain happy as we explained the situation. The woman acted like we were blowing smoke for nothing. She then said, "You are in business class, sir."

"Oh, okay. That's fine then," we responded, both surprised and relieved. The insurance company had bought us business class seats because they were probably concerned about us suing their pants off. The entire case reeked of insurance company negligence and inaction.

Sitting in business class was good, but it didn't do anything to remove all the ill will I harbored against the insurance carrier. Needless to say, we would never be using that company again.

It was time to bring on the wine and mixed nuts! I needed to relax!

17

*T*hankfully, Hal and I made it home safe and sound. After the gray hair-producing ordeal, I came to the conclusion that I'd do it again for him. He was a quality guy and had provided excellent medical care to the people of the Marovo. If I had participants like Hal on every trip, my job would be a breeze.

I made contact with the representative of the US organization that had asked me to join them aboard the Bilikiki. The first thing my contact boastingly told me was that they had treated more than 5,000 people during the two-week tour. What? I wasn't sure what orifice that number was pulled from, but something smelled foul. How in the world could a team the same size as ours treat 5,000 people during the same number of clinic days? It was impossible! The only way I figured out that they could be coming up with such a large number was if they handed out free sunglasses to every person who came to the clinic. If they counted giving the free sunglasses as a patient encounter, maybe they could have reached 5,000 patients.

People like to hear big numbers thrown willy-nilly into the air after a medical or humanitarian team returns. Throwing numbers out wasn't important to me because the numbers by themselves didn't mean much. We had seen around 1,000 patients during most of our trips. The most important outcome I shared with people was that every person who had needed to be treated by a doctor had been. We didn't turn anyone away, which I thought was more important than making lavish claims about total numbers of patients seen. We did a lot more than just hand out sunglasses. Grow up!

The kicker to the conversation was when I tactfully brought up the issue about them leaving Seghe Hospital early. The big pot lay before me, and I was inserting a larger stirring stick! I explained that one of the village elders from the Marovo had expressed his anger to me regarding the team not sticking to its posted schedule. Silence. … "How dare him! He was lucky we came at all. He has no idea what it takes to put on a medical clinic like that … and for free! He should be ashamed of making a comment like that!" Wow, now I *knew* I was dealing with some arrogance. This woman was off her rocker. Her group had put out a schedule in an area where communication was extremely difficult. The locals were one hundred percent valid in their feelings of anger toward the group. Don't publish clinic times if you aren't going to stick to the schedule. It was a lesson learned for me as well.

Between the May and November trips in 2010, Suzanne and I decided to leave Salt Lake City. Suzanne's job was somewhat out of control. Her group of fellow gastroenterologists took way too much hospital call, and she didn't want to continue living her life that way. Doctors were normally required to take care of patients in the hospital for a certain amount of time every month, known as being on call. Her on-call time had become a monster that needed to be tamed. We had discovered a gem of a place. In 2003, I had found a B&B to visit in southeast Arizona, Casa de San Pedro. Birding was one of our favorite activities, and we had made several trips to Casa de San Pedro, along the banks of the San Pedro River. We had fantastic weekends there full of river walks and looking for rare hummingbirds in the Huachuca Mountains. Back and forth we went over a year or so about whether we could actually live in the area. I looked online and found that the hospital in Sierra Vista had been looking for a gastroenterologist.

The interview at the hospital went well, and Suzanne was excited about two aspects of the position. First, her call would be next to nothing compared to that in Salt Lake City. Second, she would be in practice by herself and wouldn't have to attend meeting after meeting about what the company logo should look like. The decisions could be made quickly, without forming committees or pulling teeth.

Since our first trip to the Solomon Islands, we'd had two fundraisers in Salt Lake City and a third one planned prior to our move in the fall of 2010. The first two fundraisers had been well attended. We were very grateful for the friends who had hosted the events. Donations helped us meet our programming needs. For the third fundraiser, we met with the owners of a swanky restaurant in town to see if we could hold an event there. The restaurant was known for holding large events, and Suzanne and I had been to a couple of events there that were nearly over the top. When we sat down with the owner, he thought of various ways to help us pull in more donations. We left there feeling like this would be a great next step.

Unfortunately, as time went on, we realized that there were a couple of things happening that were not in our favor. First, Salt Lake City was a tough town to get donations in. Mormons typically did not give to charities other than their church. The reason was that the church already required them to give ten percent of their income. That didn't leave them wanting to contribute to other charities. Second, we were small potatoes. Our operation was a mom-and-pop effort, and unless people knew one of us personally, they weren't likely to attend. The second thing working against us was that most Americans didn't have a clue where the Solomon Islands were located and thus didn't care.

In the spring of 2009, we had received some positive exposure from one of the television news stations in Salt Lake. A local network had done a three-minute piece about the solar panel story. It had captured firsthand experiences by interviewing people who had been on our trips. In addition, the network had interviewed children from the children's ministry at our church who had raised money to purchase four solar panels. I had been on cloud nine after the piece had aired. It wasn't until after I'd read the online piece that I had quickly returned to Earth. The negative comments posted at the end of the article were shocking. Some comments asked why we weren't providing care for Americans. It was hard to stomach at the time. We were treating human beings who were in desperate need of care. Even poor Americans could crawl into any emergency room in the country and receive basic medical care. That wasn't the case in the Marovo Lagoon. I wasn't happy with the comments suggesting that American lives were the only lives worth looking after. I've since learned not to look at comments posted by Internet trolls.

Working through our friends and colleagues to raise funds was not easy or appealing. I think development people have the gift of schmoozing and pulling money out of people's pockets—whether with a classy style or a sleezy slither. Suzanne and I were not trained in either of these techniques, and we relied upon the goodness of our friends to help us achieve our fundraising goals. Many people went out of their way to support our endeavors, and we were grateful to them. Then there were others who were really disappointing. I heard multiple times in church and other places that the wealthiest people tended to give the least. I agreed with those statements. I knew the human condition was a sad one. We are all fallen beings, and no one in the world is considered to be good, Biblically speaking. With that, I always hope for the best out of people. Sometimes my expectations are blown away, but often, they are let down. I can say the same about myself and my own conduct. Our last summer in Salt Lake constituted an overall donation letdown. We were unable to get enough people interested in a third fundraiser prior to our move. The event was cancelled. It was disappointing, to say the least.

Before we moved, we had a party at our house to say good-bye to our friends. We had been in Salt Lake for eight years. Leaving was bittersweet. Suzanne may have been the most sought-after gastroenterologist in town; it wasn't easy for her to leave all of the patients whom she had developed positive relationships with over the years. We had a lot of friends we didn't want to lose. The Wasatch Mountains were in our backyard, and the ease of recreation was hard to beat. Salt Lake's restaurants were fantastic and not dominated by cheap chains. It was a great city to live in, but it had serious growing pains of its own, and this was probably a good time for us to leave. With the city's serious air-quality issues, our lungs were about to thank us for the departure.

We also joked that Suzanne had had a big chunk of the congregation as patients at one point or another. We had developed several long-lasting friendships at our church. They were quality relationships, and we would miss those friends dearly. Sadly, the entire picture at church wasn't rosy. Again, I think we were leaving at a good time.

After our church had denied sponsoring us for the first group trip, I had failed to harbor a grudge. I needed to move on and take care of business in one way or another. It was very disappointing to look back on the time when Suzanne and I had struggled to get support to install the solar power system on the hospital without getting any support from the church leadership. No one had ever said, "This is a great grassroots effort from folks in our church, and we need to support this program." They had made donations to us, and we were very thankful for that and the other support we had received in Salt Lake, but I just didn't feel it was enough. Maybe everything happened the way it was meant to happen… puzzling.

Upon moving to Arizona in August of 2010, we started attending Faith Presbyterian Church, a great church in Sierra Vista. The congregation embraced us immediately. They were thrilled to have a new gastroenterologist in town, and they instantly took an interest in our work in the

Solomon Islands. The pastor, Virginia Studer, picked up on our mission immediately. Most Christian churches around the world celebrate communion together on one day of the year, called World Communion Sunday, in a celebration of unity. Within the first six months of our attending Faith, the session made a decision to support us by donating the entire World Communion Sunday offering—the individual offerings given by members of the congregation of our church for that day—to the newly established Marovo Medical Foundation. We were flabbergasted. It was the most incredible gift, both monetarily and in congregational support, that we had experienced. The economies of scale between the large church in Salt Lake versus this small church in Sierra Vista simply didn't add up, but maybe this was an additional reason we were meant to move to Sierra Vista. The session wasn't concerned about how far away the Solomon Islands were or how expensive it was to get there. There was no mention of having to get the church youth to the Solomon Islands, either. The congregation joined our mission full steam and pledged to lend whatever support they could. My energy level was renewed with the new congregation. It renewed in me a feeling that there were people who cared about truly providing beneficial improvements and services in the developing world.

Before our November 2010 trip, a friend of Suzanne's put us in contact with a gentleman who made documentaries, Doug Jardine. I spoke with him at length about the trip, and he said he wanted to come. His offer was great for us. In exchange for us paying his airfare, he would provide us with a high-quality video documentary. The program would be long enough to fit an hour television spot, and he would even make an abbreviated version for a thirty-minute spot. This was exciting! We didn't know how this would go or whether Doug would be intrusive in his filming practices, but we were excited about getting additional exposure.

We had a midsize project planned for this trip. The plan was to install screens on all the windows and marine-grade stainless steel ceiling fans throughout the hospital. The screens would slightly reduce airflow, so the fans would alleviate any stale air. Jason purchased all the fans and screens in Australia, and they were waiting to go for us when we arrived.

On our first full day in the Marovo Lagoon, we were speeding toward Seghe for the welcome ceremony. Doug had his big camera out and was filming from the get-go. I told the bishop not to worry if Doug put the camera in his face because he might soon be a television star in the United States. We had a good laugh, and the festivities commenced.

155

Doug wouldn't be able to film everything at the hospital during the welcome ceremony, we learned. After the customary speeches, Brenda, who had replaced Francis as the head nurse notified us that we would not be able to tour the main ward because a family was grieving the loss of a loved one. After a pause, she continued with information that the man had been attacked by a crocodile the day before while spear fishing at Viru Harbor, located forty-five minutes by boat from Seghe. Spear fishing was a way of life in the Solomon Islands. On our daily commutes through the lagoon, it was common to see unmanned dugouts floating over a patch of coral reef. Sometimes a head would pop up as we passed, and sometimes the free diver remained submerged. The crocodile victim hadn't been too far from shore when he'd been attacked by what we were told was a large crocodile. The man's son and friend had jumped in and aggressively beat on the crocodile to get him to release the man. They had been successful, but the damage had been done. The man had been brought to the outpatient clinic at Seghe but was dead on arrival.

As we walked around the hospital, I caught a glimpse of the dead spear fisherman in the bed. He was wrapped from head to toe in what looked like white gauze, but I wasn't sure what the covering was. The family stood around him, singing Christian hymns as they wept. It gave me chills. The waters in the Solomons were alive with beauty and, from time to time, danger. I prayed silently for God to comfort the family after they had lost their loved one in this sudden and horrific fashion.

The man's original home was not Viru Harbor but was on the island of Malaita. Solomon Islands custom was for the people of Viru Harbor to pay the man's family in Malaita because he had died while under their care, basically. There was talk of one of our doctors being needed to sign the death certificate, but that ended up not being needed.

Despite its somber start, the majority of this trip went smoothly. The last clinic day arrived quickly. During the previous two trips, we had tried to visit the remote village of Zaira, on Vangunu Island, without success. There were two main villages located on the weather coast of Vangunu. These villages were outside the protected waters of the lagoon. Jason said a straight line could be drawn on the map, without hitting land, from the village of Zaira all the way to Antarctica. This was the reason why the seas were always too rough to get a boat onto the shore at Zaira. Neighboring Tinge was a village that we had been to on previous trips. Villagers from Zaira had previously walked the six-mile trek to Tinge to see our doctors.

Jason told us that no medical team had ever visited Zaira, to his knowledge. That made the adventure even more exciting. To be part of the first medical team to ever visit a village constituted serious exploration and discovery, in my mind.

Our plan was to divide the team in two. We had enough doctors to pull it off. Half would go to Tinge, and the other half would continue to see if the water was calm enough to land at Zaira. Dividing the medicines was a chore, but we did the best we could. If the weather cooperated, we could even run medicines from one village to the other at the end of the day if necessary.

The morning breezes were calm. Weather conditions at Uepi were great, but if there had been swells originating far away in the Southern Ocean, we wouldn't know it until we got to Zaira. I knew there was potential for excitement when Grant made everyone going to Zaira get fitted with special life jackets. Going to this place could prove hazardous. The plan was to take two boats and proceed together to the first village, Tinge. From there, the other boat would continue a few more miles to Zaira. If the weather was too rough to land at Zaira, that boat would return to Tinge so the people on it could join the rest of the team.

Zipping past Seghe was magic. On our left was Vangunu, with the crest of its extinct volcanic crater jutting skyward. Forests on this side of Vangunu had yet to see a chainsaw. They were some of the most pristine intact forests in the country, and certain people were hard at work trying to keep it that way. The boats fast approached the transition zone between the calm waters of the lagoon and the rolling swells of the Pacific Ocean. On our right side, in the distance, was Tetepare Island. I wanted to visit Tetepare sometime to see the leatherback turtles and dugongs. It was supposedly a wild, untouched island.

As we cruised between islands, the bright aqua colors of the near-shore water brought a smile to my face. Folks on the boats would point at the beautiful water. Some were taking pictures of the splendor that was unrivaled anywhere, in my opinion. The commute was hard to beat. The only red lights were the occasional cardinal lorikeets flying through the trees.

Approaching Tinge, the first boat peeled off and worked its way to shore. I was shocked at how calm the sea was. I hadn't seen it this calm before. Conditions were favorable to potentially land at Zaira. We continued around a point of land where small waves broke along an untouched beach. Ten more minutes, and we were looking at the outside of the base of the volcanic crater. The view was mindboggling. The forests were painted the most inviting green my eyes had ever seen. The beaches were covered in dark sand. Palm trees lined the beaches as if a tourism catalog creator had placed them there by hand. It was the most beautiful forest-beach interface I had ever looked upon. Wow, this was Zaira!

I thanked God for calm seas. The water was like a bathtub with just a slight hint of swell coming through. Jason commented that he had never witnessed it as calm before. I knew there was divine intervention going on here. We were meant to visit this village on this day, and God had enabled it to happen. It was our third attempt to visit Zaira, and the third time was definitely the charm.

The water was too shallow for our boat to make it to shore, so we waited, sitting a couple hundred yards offshore for a while before we saw any movement on land. After they spotted us, villagers congregated along the shore. Before they could come get us, they had to put their boat in the water. It was a red and blue boat, made out of thick plastic, probably eighteen feet long. People onshore grabbed old brown palm fronds and lay them between the boat and shoreline for a makeshift boat ramp. Voices increased in number and volume as several men grabbed the boat and started to push it toward the water. The boat slid fairly easily on the rudimentary ramp. They continually cycled fronds from the back to the front so the boat continued to slide until it was in deep enough water to float. It was the most inexpensive boat ramp I had ever seen.

Two men jumped onboard the boat with paddles, one in the bow and the other in the stern. The waves were gentle, and thus there wasn't much haste in their strokes. The two strapping guys were happy to see our team. They asked for half of the group, carrying nothing but personal bags, to climb into their boat.

Before long, half the team was onshore without any excitement. I felt like I was sitting in a boat on a pond. I couldn't comprehend the calmness of the water. Since Doug was filming the event, I had hoped for a more exciting landing, as we were the first medical team to ever visit this village. As the Zaira boat landed onshore, it almost seemed anticlimactic, almost too easy. Then again, had the water been rough, the visit to Zaira wouldn't have even happened.

Of the villages we visited, some were clean and tidy while others needed plenty of attention. Zaira was beautiful. The village seemed spotless. Once we were all onshore, the school principal shared a brief welcome speech on behalf of the village. Our arrival was serious news for the inhabitants of Zaira. Not many foreigners had ever landed there, and as I've mentioned, we were the first group of medical folks to ever set foot on their soil.

An interesting point about Zaira is its proximity to the tectonic boundary between the Pacific and Australian plates, just twenty-eight miles away. The region is very seismically active and just two years earlier had witnessed an 8.2-magnitude earthquake within fifty miles. The villagers were well conditioned to run for the hills during a seismic event. If a tsunami were generated, the villagers would have less than a few minutes to get to higher ground before the wave energy descended upon them. We notified our team that in the unlikely event the ground started to shake, they were to drop everything and run with the locals to higher ground. That was a horror I hoped never to experience.

Throughout the day, the team commented on the fact that there weren't a lot of patients. Diabetes and hypertension patients were largely absent in this village. Maybe because they were so isolated, they continued to engage in more traditional types of food production and gathering, activities that would keep them fit. I didn't know if they weren't eating as much white rice as people in other villages, but whatever it was, they needed to keep doing it, because they were healthy.

Kate had only one or two dental patients. The first patient had one tooth left in his mouth. He was an older gentleman who looked like he may have been around during WWII. He joked on camera with Doug that he wanted his only tooth removed. Doug assured him that Kate could do the job. Kate was standing out on the beach overlooking the small bay in front of the village. Her two patients sat in a plastic lawn chair to allow her to do the extractions. At that time, there wasn't a better dentist's office in the entire world.

I think Doug was thoroughly enjoying himself. His filming techniques were professional and respectful of the locals, to say the least. I was ecstatic that he had chosen to come with us on the tour. Everyone from past trips had taken photos and video, but none of it had ever been put together in a professional documentary. Now I had a caring, professional filmmaker on the trip, and I couldn't wait to see what he was about to create. We had done a lot of work, and I looked forward to having a lasting memory of some of our work and encounters in the Marovo Lagoon.

Visiting Zaira was the best way to end the trip. After transferring back to the Uepi boat, we waved good-bye to villagers on shore. Cameras clicked like crazy, trying to capture the beauty of this isolated paradise one last time. A while later, we met up with the folks from Tinge and pulled the boats together offshore. It was time to celebrate the end of another successful medical tour. Jason opened the cooler, or esky, as they say in Australia, and pulled out beautiful green bottles containing Sol Brew. The beer was brewed in Honiara and was delicious, especially as we relished the fact that we had blazed new trails and encountered a previously unreached community.

Early in 2011 I would receive word from Doug that the documentary, *The Story of Marovo Medical: Yes We Make Island Calls* had been nominated for an Emmy Award. Holy cow! I couldn't believe it! How many people could say they were a part of a documentary that was nominated for an Emmy? I didn't know, and I didn't care. He said we were up against stiff competition. I didn't care if we won or not. For the rest of my life, I could say we had been nominated, win or lose. I had seen the documentary a couple of times, and I still had a hard time keeping my emotions in check. Boiled down, it was a love story, with the focus of our collective love being the community of the Marovo Lagoon. Doug did a great job telling the story. He was a true gentleman, and I would have him back to the Marovo any time. His plane ticket was worth every penny.

CHAPTER

18

*T*wo choices lay before us for the next capital building project at the hospital. Not only did the residents of the lagoon not have a doctor to see regularly, but they also didn't have any options for local surgical care. For the most part, only three hospitals were used regularly for surgeries in the Solomon Islands. The closest facility was Helena Goldie Hospital in Munda. Also part of the Western Province Health Service, Helena Goldie Hospital was nearly three hours by boat from Seghe. There was an OB/GYN who performed emergency appendectomies and other non-OB/GYN emergency surgeries. Most people in the lagoon went to Honiara for their surgical care, but some surgeries could also be done at the hospital in Gizo. From Seghe, getting to Honiara or Gizo required either a minimum of thirty minutes in an airplane or several hours on a ferry.

Having to travel to one of these hospitals created quite the financial hardship on the patient and his or her family. Not only did patients have to pay all the expenses of traveling and being away from their gardens, but they had to take a family member with them. None of the hospitals in the Solomon Islands had food service for the patients, so if patients didn't have family members looking after them, they wouldn't receive any food. This compounded the overall cost of a trip to a hospital for surgery. With boat fares, food, and lodging, a surgical trip to Honiara, for example, could cost someone traveling from the Marovo Lagoon several thousand Solomon dollars. That was often more than an entire year's worth of income.

Faced with the choice of building a new doctor's house or an operating room, Suzanne made a strong case for the operating room, and thus, we proceeded down that path. Prior to us leaving Salt Lake City, St. Mark's Hospital in Salt Lake had donated several surgical items to get the ball rolling. Neither Jason, Suzanne, nor I had ever built an operating room.

We were clueless about how to proceed and what to expect. We asked questions of surgeons, techs, and other surgical personnel. Gordon was a fantastic resource because of all the years he had spent working in the medical field.

After researching the dimensions and physical needs of an operating room, Jason got to work designing the building. We decided we would locate the OR in an open area between the maternity ward and the part of the hospital that contained the medical offices. It was a flat space with just the right amount of area for the structure. Jason sent designs back and forth, asking for our input. In February 2011, at the end of a whirlwind Central and North American holiday, Jason, with Josh, Uepi's assistant manager, visited us in the States. We were able to figure out other equipment specifications and needs for the OR such as oxygen, suction, cooling, and air movement.

After scouring the Internet and speaking with folks at medical supply warehouses, I figured out what type of wall mounts we needed for the oxygen, suction, and medical air. For the most part, we needed to use the same style of wall mounts for everything and then make sure that all the couplers for all the gadgets matched the style of wall mount. I was quickly becoming a well-rounded medical consultant, from procuring medicines to ordering the correct surgical supplies for an operating room.

Materials in the Marovo were in short supply. We specially ordered most things out of Australia. The general building supplies were sourced in Honiara, but things like the tubing had to come from Australia. If we weren't careful with our cuts and planning, we were screwed.

The solar power system had enough power to run most things during surgery, but we figured we needed a new generator to serve as the primary power source during procedures, as the original generator at the hospital had crapped out. The motor was in good shape, but the alternator had seen better days. We talked about getting it rebuilt, but the easiest thing was to start from scratch with a new unit. We were heading into uncharted territory with this building project. Installing a solar power system had been one thing, but building a functional operating room where people's lives would be in the balance added serious weight on our shoulders.

Had we raised enough money to build the OR in the previous year? Not even close. Were we going to proceed regardless? Absolutely! Suzanne and I knew from the get-go that the responsibilities for the improvements at

Seghe were our baby. We were invested with our hearts, souls, and bank accounts. Until this point, if there had been a budget shortfall, we had filled it. We had done it without thinking twice. Our complete devotion to nothing but progress and success extended to the OR.

*   *   *

During Jason and Josh's 2011 visit, Suzanne and I pulled out all the stops for them so they would have a great time and experience some great food and fun. One day, I decided to take them to Tucson. I told them to keep their passports in their pockets because, in effect, we lived in a police state. It wasn't all of the state of Arizona, but our house was south of the local Border Patrol checkpoint. For us to go to Tucson or anywhere else in a northerly direction, we were forced to stop at a federal checkpoint and to be checked out by Border Patrol agents.

For the most part, I didn't have a problem with the situation. It did, however, rub me wrong when they would sometimes ask, "Where are you headed today, sir?" *What?!* Yank me out of the car. Strip-search me, although be gentle with the cavity search. Let the drug dog take a dump on my back seat, but whatever you do, don't ask me where I'm going. I always wanted to say, "None of your damn business! I'm an American, and I don't have to tell anyone where I'm going!" I understood their strategy of having choke points on roads that were heading north from the border, but if we were really concerned about illegal border crossings, it seemed like those guys should be down on the actual border and not letting the people and drugs come through. But that's not the way they do it.

As the three of us approached the Border Patrol checkpoint, I confirmed with them that they had their passports in hand. I didn't plan to draw any attention to them, but I never knew what question I was going to be asked. The patrol agents often asked if I was a US citizen. I told Jason and Josh that we weren't going to lie if asked.

Approaching the checkpoint, I could sense there was a little excitement in the car. It wasn't a big deal, but there were road signs notifying us that we had to stop and federal officers would be present. I slowly proceeded over the three small speed bumps and came to a stop next to one of the agents. It never failed that as I was talking to the agent on the driver's side, another agent was peering in my other windows without me noticing.

I rolled down my window, and the agent looked in at us and said, "What's happening today, guys?"

Suzanne was totally correct; I always offered too much information to people in government uniforms. I'm not sure why, but I did. "I have a couple of friends in from Australia, and I'm taking them up to see some things in Tucson."

The mood changed on a dime. "You have Australians in the car? Sir, please pull over."

Jason erupted in laughter like I had never heard. I pulled over in front of the mobile office unit. Jason and Josh were still cracking up as the agent approached but were ready with their passports. The agent looked at both passports and confirmed that my friends had in fact officially cleared customs at LAX. After the agent let us go, Jason started laughing again. "Allan … ask him if he'll come back and do it again. I want to get it on camera. That was hilarious!" He mimicked the agent as he laughed. "You have Australians in the car? Sir, please pull over." We had a ball with that incident for the rest of their stay.

CHAPTER

19

Three months after Jason and Josh's visit, we embarked on our sixth group medical tour. During the May 2011 trip, we continued tweaking the site plan of the OR. Jason's plan was to start construction after the medical tour ended. We tentatively planned to do the first surgeries on the May 2012 trip. There was a lot of work to do to meet that goal, but we were fully committed to getting the facility up and running.

It was a thrill and delight to have Hal Gooch return with us on the May 2011 trip. He was back in the saddle one year after nearly succumbing to appendicitis. The travel insurance company's incompetence had seemed to indicate they were fine with him keeling over, but fortunately, it hadn't been his time. He was excited to be back and even brought his daughter, Cara, with him to help with the clinics.

For the first time, we had two Australian doctors on the trip, Chris Hannon and Dora Lee. They were fantastic docs, and the international team worked together flawlessly. I wanted more Australian doctors to join us. It was my goal to incorporate more Australian medical and helper personnel on future trips. It was so much closer, easier, and cheaper for them to get to the Solomons than for US docs; the entire trans-Pacific flight could be eliminated for them.

This trip also included another first-timer. Chloe McKenna was not only Australian but also the first nutritionist to join our ranks. She proved to be a valuable asset. I had heard a statistic that in the States, only about six percent of doctors received nutritional training in medical school. I think this probably happened over the years as drug companies grew and exerted more and more influence on medical schools. That may be one of the reasons why western medicine was so focused on treating symptoms instead of first addressing nutritional inputs into the body. It's okay, though, because then the drug companies save the day with a little pill to cure every ill. (Please help us!)

Chloe arrived in Honiara a few days before the team. She spent her time there meeting with the head of the Nutrition Department for the Ministry of Health. This individual provided Chloe with a fantastic and comprehensive set of resources to use during the tour. At the village clinics, we had all patients with diabetes and/or hypertension visit with Chloe after meeting with the doctor. Chloe figured out what they were eating and tried to steer them toward making food choices that would ease their diabetes or hypertension symptoms. In addition to addressing those chronic diseases, Chloe helped several mothers address malnutrition issues with their children. Thankfully, there wasn't a lot of malnutrition in the Marovo, but Chloe provided great treatment plans for the few cases she saw.

On one of the weekend days, I went on a morning dive at Elbow Point. Elbow was known for hammerhead sharks. Suzanne enjoyed scouring the vertical submarine wall for small colorful creatures, but I found my thrills fifty yards off the wall, hovering in 800 feet of water, waiting for big sharks and pelagic fish to swim past. Being out in the deep blue was challenging if you couldn't see land, but fortunately, an 800-foot-high wall loomed directly in front of me for reference. I had yet to see a hammerhead on all my dives at Uepi.

Suzanne passed on this morning dive. Lamai was our dive master, and he and I got along really well. I asked him to bring the shark caller, consisting of a ribbed plastic water bottle and metal rod. Underwater, Lamai would rub the metal rod along the ribs of the bottle, producing a strange sawing noise. Evidently, it had been used many times before to entice the hammerheads and other large fish to come closer.

We descended to a hundred feet, give or take, and made our way to the point. Lamai pulled out the bottle and started to make noise. I hovered around with him for quite a while. Our dive computers allowed us to explore at that depth for around twelve minutes. Following the computers' recommendations, we slowly ascended up the wall. After fifteen minutes, Lamai gave up and put the shark-calling instruments in his pocket. We continued ascending the wall, swimming back and forth around the point.

At about sixty feet, I looked below me and was shocked to see the unmistakable outline of a large hammerhead shark. It was cruising well below me along the wall. I looked around and didn't see anyone to point the shark out to, so I yelled in my regulator as loud as I could, "Whewwww hoooooo!!!!" In an instant, I realized that may have been a serious mistake. Lamai had heard me, but he wasn't the only one. The hammerhead turned on its tail and headed straight up the wall in my direction. *Oh shit*, I thought. *What have I done?* The shark looked cool from a distance, but now it was obviously swimming quickly upward to see what creature had made the strange noise. Obviously, the shark thought my underwater exclamation was a creature in distress, and it clearly wanted a piece of the action. On its initial path, the shark had likely been fifty to sixty feet below me. Upon hearing me and turning dead vertical, it had come closer and closer. I backed up against the wall as it continued its rapid ascent. It closed half the distance between us in a few seconds. As I considered my options, the shark abruptly leveled out and turned to continue on its original course. No way! That was intense!

Back on the dive boat, Lamai and I had a good time laughing about the experience. I said, "You don't need to use the bottle anymore. There's a new shark call … whewwww hoooooo!!!!" I exclaimed. He laughed and made the same noise a few times. It was nice to share an experience like that with one of the dive masters. They likely saw a lot of the same things day in and day out. Having something different thrown into the mix proved to be a good time. Personally, I was glad the shark turned away; after all, it was a lot bigger than me.

Even with the close call with the hammerhead, the trip was largely devoid of any major calamities, which was probably a relief to Hal. He thoroughly enjoyed his second trip. He, too, was falling in love with the Marovo Lagoon community. At least this time, one thing he didn't have to worry about was his appendix going bad on him.

* * *

Time flew by after we returned from the May 2011 trip. At the end of September, I had a lot going on, as usual. My father had been very helpful along the way with the OR project. He had spread the word about our Solomon Islands work to many people. When I mentioned we needed to find some big items for the OR, he turned me onto an online auction website. He mentioned that he had seen several unused anesthesia machines up for auction. The site handled the entire US military surplus contract. When the military didn't need things anymore, it was the responsibility of this company to auction the items to the highest bidder. Fortunately for us, there were a lot of surgical items available.

A couple weeks prior to the online auction, I realized I was scheduled to be on a flight at the time the auction was to close. That wasn't good. I had a lot riding on getting one of these machines for a good price. After all, they were military field units that came in bomber shipping cases. Plus, from what I could ascertain, they had never been used. I hoped they would go for cheap. My father was willing to handle the auction for me. I told him I wanted two units so we had one for spare parts. I told him I didn't want to pay more than $3,500 per unit.

The auction site had another item that we desperately needed—an operating room table that had supposedly never been taken out of the box. There was a lot that could be said for the government purchasing an operating room table and never taking it out of the box. All government cracks aside, if I could get my hands on it, the table was going to go to a good cause and would get a lot of use.

In addition to the OR table, there was a brand-new field surgical scrub sink available. We needed a scrub sink as well, so my radar was locked on both items. Fortunately, I would be back home for these auctions and wouldn't have to bother my father to do my dirty work.

After my flight landed, I called my father. "Hey, Dad, what happened with the auction?"

I could sense something was amiss as he hesitated to respond. "Well, I've got good news and bad news."

Shoot, my initial thought was that he had gotten only one machine. I really needed two because we were operating in the middle of nowhere and a backup machine would be indispensible.

"What happened?"

"Well, there were actually twenty-four anesthesia machines up for auction today, and the bidding got a little crazy. I was bidding on more than one machine, and it was hard to keep track of which lots I had."

"And…"

"I ended up buying three of them."

Silence was all that came out of my mouth. I didn't have money for three anesthesia machines. "Okay, how much did they cost?" I asked after a pause.

"I think I got each one for around $3,200 or so. With the auction charge, I think it will end up being just over $10,000."

Gulp. Oh man. At some point, Suzanne and I needed to start thinking about saving for retirement. This wasn't going to help. The units were located in Norfolk, Virginia, and I had to get them to Los Angeles to get on a ship. In the meantime, I had to find someone who would store them for me until I was ready to ship all the equipment together.

I shared those concerns with my father, and he mentioned that he had a friend who owned a trucking business in Richmond, Virginia. "I'll call my buddy for you and see if he can help you with the shipping. I'll let you know what he says." I hoped his contact would come through, because we didn't need to hemorrhage any more money with the OR equipment. I hoped the OR wasn't going to destroy us financially. At least with the solar power system, I had known what all my costs were up front. Building the OR was different. Finding operating room equipment could prove to be a slippery slope financially. There was a lot of surplus equipment available, and I wanted to outfit the place with everything available, but my desires weren't realistic. We needed to focus on securing basic equipment because it was going to take years before we would be able to do more than general surgeries.

Three months went by as I worked on various aspects of acquiring items for the OR. In the meantime, I heard great news from my father. His buddy who owned the trucking company had agreed to pick up all the equipment in Norfolk and hold it at his warehouse in Richmond until I was ready to ship to the Solomon Islands. He donated the freight charges and delivered the items to Los Angeles, which included the anesthesia machines, operating room table, field surgical sink, and a few other pallets of supplies and equipment. Prior to our departure in November, all three anesthesia machines had been transported to Los Angeles with the other items.

Since I was unable to get rid of the third anesthesia machine, our new plan was to keep two of the machines at Seghe and donate the third to the Ministry of Health. They were in need of working anesthesia machines, and I was happy to be in a position to donate the machine. As with other things, we just had to eat the $3,500 and move on.

We were back in the Marovo Lagoon for our seventh group trip in November 2011. Jason and some local guys had been hard at work since we had left in May. The sights at Seghe blew my mind. Fantastic progress had been made with the OR. The entire concrete slab had been poured, and all the walls were framed. A lot of work needed to be accomplished to get a roof overhead, but Jason was confident the guys would be able to nail down some roofing material before the end of the trip.

We had another great group of folks with us. Doctors Grace Lin and Ian Harris from San Francisco were with us for their second trip. A paramedic firefighter from Arizona, Marianne Reiber, decided to join us. She was a Kiwi who had lived in Sierra Vista for the past fifteen years. It was always fun for me to see Kiwis and Aussies interact. They loved to take the piss out of one another, to use one of their expressions. One of Suzanne's previous partners from Salt Lake City, Dr. Wes Keller, and his wife, Jean, also joined us on the tour. Jean was a nurse practitioner, and she and Wes had both just retired. We had spent many good times with them and were thrilled that they had decided to join us.

Bishop Kurepitu was happy to see us yet again. The friendship we had created ran deep. He told me that he still possessed the original handwritten solar power proposal that I had hastily drafted and given to him four years earlier. Wow, that meant a lot to me! He couldn't hide his excitement with the OR. He had witnessed the solar power installation and how it had changed the facility and community for the better. Now he was about to witness another major event with the first OR under construction at Seghe. He continued to assist and provide his support whenever he had the opportunity to do so.

Sadly, this would be our last medical tour with Bishop Kurepitu. He was moving up in the world. It was great for him and hopefully not bad for us. He had been chosen by the United Church of the Solomon Islands to serve as the moderator. This meant that he and his wife had to move to Munda, the headquarters of the United Church. He would be, in effect, the CEO of the United Church. He would be the big boss.

Bishop Kurepitu had served the faithful of the Solomon Islands with fervor and conviction. He was a young man in his late forties, maybe the youngest to ever be appointed to the position of moderator. He had served in a few different posts prior to landing at Seghe. Possibly his most influential posting had been in Honiara during the civil war, or "tension." He had shared stories with me of leaving his family in the morning during the tension and not knowing if he would be killed during his daily travels and meetings. He and many others had worked tirelessly to broker peace between the two sides. He served the Lord and his fellow Solomon Islanders in a humble and dignified manner. I felt honored to be considered one of Wilfred Kurepitu's close friends. I wasn't about to let the friendship slip away.

It wouldn't be the same without him in Seghe. Fortunately, our working relationship would continue, thanks to the ties that existed between our group and the church. I was happy for him, but I was definitely going to miss our interactions at Seghe. Visiting him in Munda was a must. Finding the time to make a detour to Munda would be the tough part.

When we got to Seghe on this trip, the hospital looked great! Two full-time cleaning people had been doing a great job in maintaining the facility. Fortunately, the nurses no longer had to spend any of their time cleaning and were able to focus on their nursing duties. In December 2010, Anthony Jonah had been hired as the full-time hospital administrator, replacing Jason as the interim administrator. Anthony was a great guy and genuinely cared for the facility. Jason was thrilled with his level of personal integrity. Anthony had grown up just around the bend from Seghe. He hailed from Bareho village and knew the area and local people very well. This was my first time meeting Anthony, and I gave him a multi-tool as a welcome and thank-you for all his hard work thus far. He was thrilled to have the gift, and I knew it would get a lot of use around the hospital.

During the first week of the trip, the former superintendent minister of the United Church passed away. He served below the bishop in order of local church hierarchy. Word made its way to Uepi that the bishop and the superintendent minister's family had requested that Suzanne and I attend the funeral. Jill explained that they must have felt strongly for Suzanne and me to be invited to the funeral, which would be on the first Saturday of the trip.

No one likes to go to funerals. That is reality for sure. A big part of me didn't want to go to this funeral, either. Suzanne and I tossed the idea back and forth. Jason and Jill encouraged us to attend. We didn't know what to expect, but we decided to do the right thing and accept the invitation.

The minister and his family lived in Patutiva village, which was located directly across the channel from Seghe. A boat driver took us from Uepi to Patutiva on the day of the funeral. We tied the boat to the run-down wharf, and a gentleman standing nearby led us up a long hill. The sun was beating down as if we were standing a couple of inches from a heat lamp. We continued past a couple of school buildings and then down the backside of the hill. We entered another residential area and could see a place where people were gathered. The new superintendent minister greeted us and thanked us for coming. He told us we had to wait for the group that was currently in the house to leave and then it would be our turn. I didn't know what was going to happen when it was our turn, but Suzanne and I were there to show our support, regardless.

Twenty-five minutes later, around a dozen people emerged from the house. They were all very sullen and obviously distraught. In the group waiting to go in were several women who were wearing some sort of United Church women's uniforms. My efforts to try to see what was written on their uniforms were in vain. As we were led into the house, the scene changed in an instant. The women led the way and stepped up on the deck. At once, they all began to wail at the top of their lungs. The hair went up on the back of my neck. Wow! They were extremely loud and theatrical, to say the least. I'm not inferring that the scene was without sincerity, but it definitely made me do a double-take.

Entering the house, surrounded by eerie wailing, we sat down around the casket. I had never seen anything like it. The minister's body was in an open casket in the middle of the room, covered in a green cloth or screen of some sort. Surrounding the casket were orchids and flowers three feet deep. I didn't know if the flowers had a dual purpose or not. Flowers were present at all funerals that I had been to. The climate was harsh on everything here, and the Islanders had no way to preserve the body. It is Solomon Islands custom not to bury a body until all family members have arrived to mourn. Obviously, people knew they needed to get there as quickly as possible because time was of the essence. I wondered if maybe the flowers were therefore also present to mask any potential smells from the body.

The wailing continued nonstop for nearly twenty minutes. Suzanne and I sat cross-legged on the floor, looking at the flowers and the floor, more or less. Then, as if a switch had been flipped, the wailing came to an end. There were a few random outbursts, but for the most part it ceased. Another minister was in the room and began speaking. He was speaking in Pidgin, and thus, I couldn't understand everything he said. A couple of prayers were recited, and then the minister's widow began to speak. She seemed to be addressing Suzanne and me. Her words recalled her husband's last few days from a medical perspective. She explained what had happened to him before he died. From the sound of it, he had likely died from a heart attack. The widow thanked us for being there and then surprised us both when she asked us to say something. *What?!*

Suzanne had learned Pidgin much better than I had, so I sat there quietly and let her take the lead. She expressed how we had enjoyed the meetings we'd had with the superintendent minister and how we were very sad that he had passed. She did a very nice job and spoke excellent Pidgin. The people in attendance would have understood traditional English, but it was more meaningful that she had spoken in their common language.

After reflecting on the minister's life and passing, our group was escorted back outside. It was at this point that all the conjecture surrounding Solomon Islanders' rice consumption was verified. A couple of people were standing behind a table set up in the brush. They dished out massive plates of white rice. The amount of rice doled out per plate had to have been the equivalent of nearly two cups of uncooked rice—four to six servings! The plates were full from side to side and mounded at least four inches tall in the center.

I couldn't believe what I was seeing. It was diabetes on a plate. It was hemorrhoids on a plate. These two ailments had likely not been very prevalent in the Solomon Islands prior to the importation of white rice from Southeast Asia. It was ridiculous. They put a little canned beef on top of the mountain of rice. The poor dietary shift had reached epidemic proportions, and the people of the Solomon Islands needed to get a grip on this, or else they were all going to die a slow and miserable death from diabetes. The reliance on rice as a major food source in the Solomon Islands was troubling to me. It was amazing how one food could do so much damage to the health of an entire nation.

As they served our plates of rice, we told the server we didn't need a whole plate full. An entire plate of overcooked white rice was nothing more than bulky sugar with little to no fiber. This wasn't a healthy meal to eat once, twice, or maybe even three times a day. No wonder people were blowing up like balloons and having to have feet and legs amputated. The importance of nutrition education had just moved up a few notches on the list. This experience validated for us the need to have a nutritionist or someone trained to do a nutritionist's job on every trip we made to the lagoon. If we could change what the islanders put in their mouths—and that's a big *if*— we could really reduce the need for diabetes medicines. It was so simple in my mind, but I wasn't in the islanders' shoes.

As hard as it was, and funerals were never easy, Suzanne and I were glad we had gone. We had become somewhat of a fixture in the lagoon, and it was very nice that we had been included. I would have preferred it had been a wedding, but who knew, we might get our chance for that someday.

During this trip, Gordon was able to knock out the majority of the wiring for the OR. I planned to stay longer than the rest of the group yet again to help with additional items. We had specially ordered copper tubing for oxygen, suction, and medical air lines. Setting up the oxygen lines and interconnections was going to be tricky. Jason and Gordon knew a lot more than me about plumbing and the properties of the gases. I wasn't thrilled to hear about the volatility of medical-grade oxygen. Evidently, oxygen can combust in the presence of grease while under pressure. That meant that all of our tubing and fittings had to be ultra-clean to prevent a big boom when we pressurized the oxygen system. Yes, it was the first operating room any of us had ever built, and when variables including explosions were thrown into the mix, it got real.

Figuring out how to design and manage the three systems had taken some serious research ahead of time. Many steps needed to happen before we were ready to test the systems. We had made an oxygen manifold that could hold three G cylinders of oxygen. After consulting with a few anesthesiologists to determine normal oxygen flow rates and typical oxygen usage during surgeries, we figured that three tanks would be a good fit for the facility. Getting the oxygen cylinders there was going to be a challenge, as the Ministry of Health seemed to circulate cylinders around and didn't have any spare tanks at the time. We had time to get the tanks, but we couldn't wait too long. Our gung-ho timeline included doing the first surgeries six months later, during the May 2012 trip. There was a tremendous amount of ground to cover to meet the timeline, and Jason and I needed to stay on top of the folks at the Ministry of Health to make sure we were going to actually receive the oxygen cylinders prior to that trip.

We purposefully planned to wire the OR with 110V and 240V power so we could run equipment from either Australia or the United States. The Solomon Islands follow the Australian power standard, 240V 50 Hz. The solar power system had been purchased from the United States, but we'd had it configured to produce 240V 50 Hz electricity. Most of the American appliances that had been donated ran on 110V 60 Hz. The plan was to install a 4KW voltage transformer in the ceiling to knock down the voltage from 240 to 110. That was easy. The 110 coming out of the transformer went to all the American wall outlets in the OR. Next to the American wall outlets were Australian 240 outlets. The only issue was the frequency. Voltage was easy to transform, but frequency wasn't easy to change. It took us a while to figure this out, but we had to have equipment that would run on either 50 or 60 Hz. Motors that were designed for one speed of hertz didn't run well on the other frequency. They wouldn't last nearly as long and wouldn't run at optimal speeds. This one parameter would shape our equipment purchasing and acceptance or rejection of donations from then on.

A festive mood hung in the air on the last Saturday of the group trip. Jason and his parents were throwing a farewell celebration for Bishop Kurepitu and his wife, who would be moving to Munda. When the morning of the festivities arrived, the resort was out of fish. Jill and Grant dispatched a couple of boats out to the FADs to bring back some fish. The FADs, or fish-attracting devices, were located about twelve miles out in the Slot. The FADS had been installed by governmental and nongovernmental organizations to aid the commercial tuna fishery. They were anchored a few thousand feet down, and each had a buoy on the surface. Below the buoy was some sort of metal framework with nets that hung off the line to serve as structure in the water. The structure attracted fish—often big fish. Jason spoke of huge tuna being caught out there. Wherever big tuna hang out, there will often be big sharks. He said the sharks out there included silky sharks, oceanic whitetips and some big bronze whalers. It was a different scene than the near-shore waters of Uepi. You didn't want to unintentionally end up in the water if there happened to be fish struggling on a hook below. Landing a fish out here before the sharks attacked them sometimes proved challenging.

The lines holding the FADs had enough slack in them to allow the buoys to swing in a circle up to a kilometer or more in diameter. The local guys used the islands as reference points for navigation. They didn't rely on GPS. They could judge distance and direction by triangulation. They continually looked behind them at the islands of New Georgia and Vangunu to make sure they didn't venture off course.

Sixty to eighty people were expected for the festivities, so the pressure was on the fishermen to produce. Solomon Islanders didn't seem to get too uptight about an impending deadline for an event or festival. Things seemed to be taken care of magically right before the start time. It was uncanny, but I had seen it happen more than once. This day was no different. Not long before the bishop and others from Seghe arrived, the guys pulled up with their catch. They had done well. There must have been between twenty to thirty fish in the bottom of the boat. Several species were present. It was an impressive catch. Yellowfin tuna, rainbow runner, dolphin fish, and Spanish mackerel combined for a hundred pounds or more of delicious bounty from the sea. The main course had arrived at the eleventh hour … of course.

Suzanne and I cleaned up and then sauntered down the sandy path to the main house. We could see smoke through the layers of green foliage in front of the kitchen. Not only had the guys caught the fish, but they had cleaned them and cut them into steaks. Iron grates full of fish fillets sat a foot above a large hot wood fire. The sizzling tuna and mackerel looked incredible. I almost couldn't contain my excitement for the upcoming meal. I was a barbecue nut. The traditional Solomon Islands barbecue before me was a sight to behold. There were no frills, just wood, iron, and fish. Nothing else was needed. Fire and fish … an excellent combination.

The festivities kicked off with some traditional Solomon Islands dancing. I knew a few of the dancers. They were clothed only in loincloths. Their dark bodies were covered in white paint. The contrasting white paint was stunning. I didn't know what the paint designs signified, but they looked pretty cool. They danced a couple of numbers, and everyone clapped and cheered in appreciation. The third number the dancers did was different. In the middle of the dance, they called people out of the audience to dance. The first to be called was Brenda, the head nurse. She jumped right up and danced with full animation. She looked at the lead dancer as if jokingly mocking him. It was obvious he was trying to control his laughter. He danced away from her to keep his composure. The entire crowd was beside themselves with laughter.

After an incredible buffet of barbecued fish, crayfish, sweet potatoes, beans, and dessert, the program continued. Of course there were speeches. We had a surprise for the bishop. Josh's mother, Jenny, had been visiting for a few weeks. She was a fantastic artist. She and John Baticolo, a nurse from Seghe, had painted a couple of murals on the walls in the pediatric ward of the hospital. The playful scenes with dolphins and smiling children really helped to brighten up the space. Jason had asked Jenny to paint a picture of the new operating room as it would look when finished. He had described the building to her, and she had gone to town. Not only did she paint a beautiful rendition of the OR, but she put Suzanne in the picture leaning over, holding the hand of small Solomon Islands child. It was hard to hold back my tears when I saw the beautiful piece of art.

The piece was not for Suzanne and me but for Bishop Kurepitu. We, along with the Kellys and the staff at Seghe Hospital, agreed that the new operating room should be named after Bishop Kurepitu. The painting from Jenny was a gift from all of us. It served as a kind and uplifting reminder of the incredible dedication that he had shown in helping make Seghe Hospital a hospital that people would want to visit. A lot of the projects that we had been able to complete at the hospital had happened because of the bishop's support, guidance, and facilitation. No one else deserved to have his name on the building more than the bishop.

Upon being presented with the painting, the bishop was obviously touched by the gesture. He couldn't believe the facility was going to be named after him. He knew it was going to be the best operating room in the country, and he had to feel good that it would bear his name. There were many wet eyes in the room when the painting was unveiled, a moment I won't soon forget. It was a fantastic way to wrap up the seventh group trip.

CHAPTER

20

A couple of months after the November 2011 trip, we determined that we wouldn't be ready for surgeries in May 2012. Our goal had been overly ambitious. The next logical plan was to bump it back to November 2012. Suzanne and Jason were more optimistic than me regarding the new timeline. That wasn't surprising, since Suzanne considered me to be more pessimistic. I considered myself to be more of a realist, but I knew I could be Chief Poopy Pants more often than I should. Jason, Suzanne, and I joked about who was the CLO, or chief logistics officer. Suzanne somewhat jokingly would put the title on her shoulders, and Jason and I would immediately laugh and tell her that there was no way she was the CLO. Overall, CLO responsibilities fell on my shoulders, but in the Solomons, Jason was definitely the boss. Without him and his parents, our efforts would largely be in vain. Of course, Jason had a lot of other things on his plate, like running a sustainable timber business. He was giving his all for Seghe Hospital, but realistically, the chances of meeting the next planned opening date for the OR were fluid.

There were things that we didn't have in place, such as the OR light, the new generator, and air conditioning, to name just a few. Getting these things took time and a lot of coordination. Most importantly, it took money to make it all happen. We'd been having fundraisers that had helped a great deal, but we continued to make up the difference. I hoped a benefactor would fall out of the sky. … I really did.

I had a solo trip planned to the Solomons coming up in April 2012. I was going by myself because I had a plane voucher on Air Pacific that needed to be used. The timing of my trip coincided with the arrival of our latest shipment of supplies. Let me backtrack just a bit here.

I had sent a shipment of equipment the year before, which had been the first shipment after the solar panel shipping saga. I had avoided using Redtail Shipping again. They were a major player in the international freight forwarding business, but I figured there were others. Searching the Internet, I had found a company out of Seattle that would pick the goods up at our house and ship them all the way to Honiara. I wouldn't need to burn any brain cells worrying about it. After the goods were on the ship, I had received the bill and the final paperwork for the shipment. To my surprise and horror, the company had simply charged me $2,000 more than Redtail would have ... just to place the items in the hands of Redtail Shipping. What?! This had to be some sadistic joke. I was so done with the Seattle company. Thankfully, the goods had arrived at Uepi without incident. I had been taken by the middle man on that one. Note to self ...

Fast-forward to 2012 and the most recent shipment of large OR items. This shipment contained the OR table, three anesthesia machines, and the surgical sink. At the time of shipping in January 2012, Redtail Shipping actually gave me the cheapest bid for the shipment. I decided to take my chances and ship with them again. Maybe I wasn't thinking straight?
Prior to arriving at Uepi in April 2012, I received mixed messages about how many pallets were in the shipment. I had personally packed three pallets from our house in Arizona. I had visited a medical warehouse in Ogden, Utah, and gathered two more pallets of supplies there in January 2012, and the military surplus items from Richmond were supposedly four pallets, but I didn't have total confirmation of that number.

The shipping story gets more interesting. ... I had contracted a large freight company, which I'll refer to as Off-Guard Freight, to pick up the two pallets in Ogden. I coordinated this shipment with the three pallets from our house, through the company's Tucson office. Sandi, the agent in Tucson, was helpful. She looked at our foundation's website, created a couple of years earlier, and did all she could to ensure we would get the best rates. I paid the Tucson office for the pickup from my house in Arizona and the pickup in Ogden. These five pallets were to meet at the freight forwarder in Los Angeles. In LA, they would, hopefully, be integrated into the same container with the goods coming from Richmond. My goal was to put multiple pallets from three different parts of the country into one container in LA.

I wasn't sure what the pallets from Richmond looked like, so I asked the agent in LA to send me pictures of my goods. In the batch of photos he sent, there were two pallets stacked with strange-looking boxes that looked out of place. Everything else was there, but these two pallets looked like they were stacked with boxes of wine. I immediately replied to the agent that those two pallets weren't mine. He responded by saying he had sent those pictures by mistake. Okay, problem solved, other than the final bill of lading suggesting that I had eleven pallets when I could account for only nine pallets. Regardless of the total number of pallets, our stuff was supposedly sailing toward the Solomon Islands. The international shipping crapshoot had begun again. How many pallets would show up at Uepi? The bookies in Vegas wouldn't have touched those odds.

A couple weeks prior to my departure, I received a phone call from the Salt Lake City office of Off-Guard Freight. The agent described the need for me to pay an amount that was due. The amount was nearly the same as what I had already paid Sandi in the Tucson office. I hastily explained that it had been paid through the Tucson office and they would likely be receiving their payment soon. I figured this would be a quick conversation and I would be on my way.

"Mr. Daly, we received the funds from the Tucson office," the agent told me. "These charges are additional freight charges."

"Additional freight charges ... for what?"

"We inspected your cargo and found items that we didn't consider to be donated medical supplies."

"I'm sorry ... like what?" My defenses quickly turned to offense as I prepared to explode through the phone into this woman's tympanic membrane.

"Sir, we found items such as pillows and scrub sponges that we did not feel constituted donated medical equipment, and thus we need to charge you an additional rate."

I looked around our foyer in utter disbelief and scorching anger. My pacing accelerated. I had picked up these items from the Swanson Family Foundation medical supply warehouse. Everything in that shipment was destined to be used at Seghe Hospital. It was so on the up and up that it was absurdly squeaky clean.

I held back from blasting the agent off the other end of the phone. "This is completely unacceptable," I said. "Those items are destined for a rural hospital in the Solomon Islands. They were donated from a medical-relief warehouse and thus are donated medical goods."

"I'm sorry, sir, but the $735 charge needs to be paid."

"This is bullshit, and you know it," I exclaimed, and then hung up the phone.

What hospital in the United States doesn't have pillows for its patients? Show me one hospital in the United States that does not use cleaning sponges to keep the hospital clean. No, the items were not needles or stethoscopes, or bandages that obviously screamed "medical supplies," but they had been donated from a medical-supply warehouse and were going to be used by the patients and cleaning staff at Seghe Hospital. This charge was absurd! It was rampant abuse of big-business power over the little guy, and I wasn't going to stand for it. Without hesitation, I e-mailed Sandi in the Tucson office, explaining my total outrage over the additional charge. I notified her that we had received positive press coverage when we had lived in Salt Lake City and I was going to call all the media outlets to cover this story. Off-Guard Freight was trying to make me bend over and take it when I had done nothing improper in the first place. What recourse was there in the shipping business if things didn't go right? For a little guy in the shipping world, I felt like I was peeing into the wind.

Sandi and her office manager fought a long fight for us. They had many conversations with the office manager in the Salt Lake City branch, and somehow, the charges were dropped. It's hard to believe they had to fight within their own company to get a resolution. The case was so simple and obvious. The manager in Salt Lake either wasn't the brightest bulb in the bunch or was hell-bent on making his monthly bonus by screwing a small charity. Thank you, Sandi!

*　　*　　*

In March 2012, we received great news from the IRS. It had taken nearly eight months for our application for nonprofit status to be approved, but Marovo Medical Foundation had been officially launched and we were a legitimate 501(c)(3) entity. Having our own nonprofit was going to streamline fundraising along with making the purchasing of equipment and supplies more efficient. This was a big step in the life of our project. We were thrilled to promote Marovo Medical Foundation and its mission of expanding the health care options available to the people of the Marovo Lagoon.

A month later, in April 2012, I had the joy of navigating another customs clearance in Honiara. Slipping through the customs gauntlet, I rounded the corner to see a familiar face. Jason was there to meet me for a couple of days of meetings with the Ministry of Health. Standing next to him was Anthony, the Seghe Hospital administrator. I think Anthony was happy to have his feet on terra firma, as he had flown for the first time earlier that morning. I asked him how it had gone, and he rolled his eyes and laughed a little. Also there was Atkin, the Kelly family's personal driver. Atkin stood out from most Melanesians, as he was tall and thin with lighter skin and a more angular face. I had met Atkin several times by this point, and he greeted me with a smile and handshake.

Until this point, my experience in Honiara was minimal. Several participants from past trips had had either scheduled or unscheduled overnight layovers in Honiara. I had lucked out thus far and hadn't spent the night there. Henderson Field was several miles outside of town. The roads into town were interesting, to say the least. Roadwork was being done at a feverish pace because Honiara was about to host two big events. The Pacific Arts Festival was ready to descend upon the city in a mere three months' time. An entire village area was being constructed to house representatives from every Pacific island nation. Each country would have an opportunity to highlight its cultural diversity through dance, sport, and other means. From my vantage point, they had a serious amount of work to finish prior to the event.

Driving into Honiara troubled me on many levels. First, trash was ubiquitous. Crossing a couple of the bridges yielded views of terribly trash-laden rivers extending to the Pacific. It was disgusting, to say the least. The buildings were as grungy as one could imagine. Their exterior walls were often covered in dirt or green algae/moss. A lot of structures resembled a corrugated iron shanty town, like pictures I'd seen of Rio. The outsides looked horrible. I couldn't imagine what the insides harbored. Finally, the dogs … oh, the dogs. The dogs wandering the roads were heartbreaking to me. I think the dogs were more numerous in Guatemala, but these dogs didn't look good at all. The city needed a vast spay-and-neuter campaign, but the chances of that happening were slim. I pondered if it would be more humane to take the approach of Belize. There, the government notified people to bring their pets inside on a given night. After most had gone to bed, officials distributed large amounts of poisoned food around the streets. I'm not sure what chemical they used, but I was told the animals succumbed quickly. Before morning dawned, a crew went around and picked up the carcasses of the dead animals. That was probably why the stray-dog situation in Belize was much better than that just across the border in Guatemala.

Downtown Honiara was a cluster of cars and people going every which way. Shop after shop lined the streets. They were almost all owned by Chinese businessmen. I thought it was both strange and also a shame that more Solomon Islanders weren't able to run and/or interested in running businesses. I'm not sure if it had to do with financial constraints or cultural issues.

We were staying at the Kitano Mendana Hotel, supposedly one of the nicer establishments in town. The lobby impressed me. It was open-air, with beautiful hardwood desks and tropical décor. We ate dinner that night in the hotel. There wasn't much to do after dinner, so we had a couple of beers and called it a night.

Jason and Anthony were in Honiara to finalize some aspects of a grant that Jason had received from the EU. Along with coordinating all the work surrounding the OR construction, Jason was also coordinating the construction of several new staff houses at the hospital with the money he had received from the EU. He had applied for the grant and assumed the leadership responsibilities himself and secured a healthy amount of funding to see the project through. The process had been deathly slow and rife with bureaucratic red tape and incompetence. The initial grant had provided enough money to construct five staff houses, but the EU office in Honiara had dragged its feet so long that by the time it had come around to issue the check, prices had gone up so much that Jason could afford to construct only four houses. What a crying shame! Surprise, surprise … more sad news regarding international aid projects. Jason was obviously mad about it, but after living in the Solomons for a large chunk of his life, he was used to the nonsense.

Anthony was in town to receive final training on how to administer the grant funds for building the staff houses along with tracking and reporting the costs associated with purchasing equipment and paying wages. After we had dropped Anthony at the EU office in the morning, Atkin took Jason and me to the offices of the Ministry of Health. Jason had secured a meeting with Permanent Secretary of the Ministry of Health, Dr. Lester Ross. The MOH office complex was a somewhat secure compound. A guard had to open a gate for us to proceed into the lot. Communication with Lester had been a little sketchy. The meeting had been arranged by the head anesthesiologist of the MOH, Dr. Kaeni Agiomea. It wasn't a good sign that Lester's secretary didn't have any record of the event when we got there. After walking down to his office, she came back to inquire about the nature of our meeting. When Jason mentioned that Kaeni had set up the meeting, Dr. Ross's secretary raised her eyebrows and briefly closed her eyes in acknowledgment that Kaeni had bypassed her and called Lester personally. After another trip down to Lester's office, she waved us through.

Lester was a jovial short and stocky man. He hailed from the Marovo Lagoon, seemingly a good thing for us. We explained that we were there to introduce ourselves and to give him some background on our involvement at Seghe along with our plans to finish the OR and eventually hire our own doctor for the hospital. His reception was positive, and fortunately, he didn't have any problems with our nonprofit and the Kelly family's nonprofit teaming up to hire a doctor for the facility. That was a relief! Truly, we hadn't known how much power the MOH wanted to wield over the hospital and future personnel decisions. The doctors at the Helena Goldie Hospital in Munda were employed by both the United Church of the Solomon Islands and the Council for World Mission from England. The precedent had been set, and I was glad we weren't treading on unchartered waters.

The meeting ended with Jason asking Lester for a name at the National Referral Hospital in Honiara to provide us with a tour of the facility. Lester Ross had been a delight to meet with and was appreciative of all our work for the people of the Marovo. He asked that we keep in touch so he could stay apprised of the progress on the OR and other projects. I walked out of his office on a high note—much higher than I had anticipated.

At the NRH, we found the nurse who would be showing us the facility. I had heard stories of the hospital's extensive tuberculosis ward and knew that was one part of the facility I would not be entering. On first inspection, I saw that the facility was a sprawling campus of one-story buildings that went on and on. One of the first things I noticed at the NRH was the amount of equipment and beds clogging the various wards. The representative of the medical team from the United States who had asked me to join her group and then proceeded to leave Seghe without following the schedule had bragged to me about the million dollars' worth of equipment they had donated to the NRH. Obviously, the hospital was not suffering from a major lack of equipment. Of course, there were high-tech items they could use, but without trained personnel to use such equipment, those items would just clog the halls like all the beds and tables that we dodged on our tour.

In each ward, we asked questions of our nurse tour guide and gleaned information that didn't paint the facility in a positive light. The place was a mess, to say the least. From my vantage point, the entire complex needed a thorough washing from the most powerful pressure washer on Earth. One of the wards we visited was the ENT, or otolaryngology, clinic. The clinic was staffed by two ENT-trained nurses. There was no ENT physician in the country. The clinic wasn't able to do much for patients other than perform ear exams and the removal of foreign bodies. If there was something out of the ordinary or in need of serious ENT work, the patient would be put on a list and possibly receive a trip to Brisbane to have the condition dealt with by a fully trained ENT doc. The chances of them receiving care in Brisbane were as good as winning the lottery. There weren't many slots available for care in Brisbane for people from the Solomon Islands, and thus, most folks went without resolution of the problem unless it was as simple as removing a stick or berry from their ear. I found it rather disturbing that there was no ENT doc in a country of more than 600,000 people.

As the tour went on, the list of medical subspecialists not available grew and grew. At the time of the tour, the list of medical subspecialties for which the Solomon Islands had no specialists or practicing physicians was extensive:

Otolaryngology
Gastroenterology
Cardiology
Neurology
Pulmonology
Hematology
Oncology
Nephrology
Rheumatology
Optometry
Podiatry

More or less, if it was an "ology" of some sort, the specialty wasn't available in the Solomon Islands. At the time of our tour, there were roughly fifty-six doctors in the country, and the vast majority of them were general practitioners. The other doctors fell into the following categories:

1 ophthalmologist
3 general surgeons
1 orthopedic surgeon
3 anesthesiologists
2 pediatricians
3 OB/GYNs
1 radiologist
1 pathologist, who dealt only with gross anatomical specimens from surgeries
1 psychiatrist
2 speech therapists

The medical scene was bleak. One of the main reasons for the terrible picture was that the Solomon Islands government paid their physicians lower wages than any other country on Earth. They paid a lot of money to send people for medical training in Papua New Guinea and Fiji, but when those people returned, they didn't stay long. It didn't take much thought for them to realize they could earn a higher wage in another Pacific nation. This fundamental shortfall in the system had to be changed before the issues with access to quality and adequate health care could seriously be addressed.

As we continued on the tour, the nurse pointed out the TB ward on our right. I didn't venture near it, knowing the scene inside was likely not pretty. Tuberculosis was a serious issue in the Solomon Islands and was getting worse. The government required patients who were positively diagnosed with TB to receive one month's worth of drugs under a supervised treatment program. After the first month, the patients were allowed to return to their villages and then continue on the medicines, unobserved, for the next two months of the three-month treatment regime. I had my doubts about how well the treatment plans were being followed once the patients left the hospital.

We made our way to the prosthetics lab. The room was full of woodworking equipment. Slabs and planks of wood were strewn about. Not only did the lab construct prosthetics, but it made a lot of crutches as well. There was a pile of long almost 1" x 1" pieces that the lab workers cut and bent into crutches. A side room in the lab contained several wooden and plastic leg molds. The lab had the ability to make a custom wooden leg for a patient. I didn't know if the legs they made had the ability to bend at the knee, but it was obvious the lab workers were doing the best they could with the resources they had.

We made our way out to the hospital waste collection and disposal area. After the scene Suzanne and I had encountered at Seghe a few years before, my interest in the system at the NRH was piqued. Several large trashcans of different colors were lined up inside the fenced waste-collection area. A building with a tin roof sat adjacent to the cans. Behind the fence was a rusted-out medical-waste incinerator. The nurse explained that it had come from the UK and worked for nearly six months before it had broken.

"If it's broken, where are they incinerating the hospital waste?" Jason asked.

"There's an open pit up on the hill where they burn the medical waste."

I looked at the nurse incredulously. "An open pit? What about the sharps?"

"They are burning them in a concrete pit," she responded.

The needle skipped across the record. This was bad … really bad. The main hospital for the entire country did not have proper waste-disposal capabilities. Talk about a serious issue. Suzanne and I had seen the hospital waste-disposal issue on a very small scale at Seghe, where probably a couple thousand patients a year were treated. The NRH treated tens of thousands of patients a year.

The old incinerator building was situated along the shoreline of Guadalcanal. The water was lapping against the shore nearly twenty feet from where we were standing. The shoreline was full of trash and debris. I looked toward the ocean to see a massive yacht parked well offshore. The ship was huge. The hull was a deep blue color, and the superstructure above was white. The color contrast was striking and not very common in the world of luxury yachts. While standing at the scene of a nonfunctional medical-waste incinerator and hearing the story of how the main Solomon Islands hospital was inadequately disposing of its medical waste, I was struck by the dichotomy between the mega-rich person who owned the ship and an entire nation's medical system that was literally in shambles. It made me sick to look at the yacht. How could one person use so many resources while so many people standing around me in Honiara and the entire Solomon Islands were often not able to get the medical care they needed to sustain life? Jason told me the yacht belonged to one of the founders of a massive computer company. They had inquired with Uepi to dock the ship outside the resort, and Uepi had declined. The yearly operating budget of the vessel was likely several times the operating budget of the Ministry of Health of the Solomon Islands. Sickening!

After the eye-opening tour of the hospital, I was eager to get to Uepi. Our time in Honiara had been well spent, but we needed to get back to the Marovo to continue working on the operating room.

*   *   *

A few days after we had left Honiara, shade slowly enveloped the wharf at Uepi as the April sun slipped below the rainforest canopy. The *Western Star,* a barge, slowly steadied itself against the crosscurrent of Charapoana Passage, the body of water adjacent to the main buildings at Uepi. The passage on the Uepi Island side was considered to be one of the best snorkeling reefs in the world. The barge was about to hover over incredible biodiversity and pristine marine conditions. *Western Star* was larger than the usual supply ship, the *Santo Star.* The captain precisely used the bow thrusters to maintain position as he simultaneously lowered the front landing deck. Uepi staff gradually materialized at the end of the wharf. I filmed the barge as the deck came down and helped bring the boat to a screeching halt … literally. The deckhands passed a couple of large ropes down for the Uepi employees to secure to the wharf.

Jason stood on the loading deck and yelled back to me, "How many pallets?"

"I'm not sure. … Either nine or eleven!"

The diesel engines hummed as they continued to keep the ship in place. One of the deckhands jumped in the cab of the fire truck to move it aside. A small twenty-foot container sat behind the fire truck at the base of the bridge. I was thrilled that all our things had been placed in the container. Glenn, the new manager of Silentworld, was taking good care of our items. Glenn knew they were medical supplies destined for Seghe Hospital and that they needed special attention.

A forklift on the barge roared to attention with the turn of a key. Jason and several of the Uepi workers met the forklift as it deposited some of the lighter pallets on the wharf. They surrounded the pallets and picked them up one by one, depositing each at the other side of the wharf to make room for the next one. Each anesthesia machine was in two large military cases. One pallet contained all three machines in six stout dark-green cases. I cringed as the forklift operator swung the machines over the side of the starboard side of the boat. These expensive medical devices had made it all the way from Norfolk, Virginia, and I didn't want to see them take a dip while being unloaded. The machines dangled over the water for a few seconds before the driver backed up and straightened out to come down the ramp. The driver dangled a couple of other pallets over the side to maneuver the forklift around the boat. He was skilled behind the wheel and didn't let anything get damaged, except my nerves.

We were almost finished. The driver brought down two final pallets that were tightly wrapped in black plastic. I counted everything on the pallets and realized that I had everything with nine pallets, not eleven. As the driver dropped the first big pallet of black plastic-wrapped mystery off, I said to Jason, "Hey, this isn't our stuff."

"Don't worry about it. Let them get it off. They won't take it back right now, anyway. Let's figure out what it is, and then we can deal with it later," he replied.

The deckhands positioned the final two pallets at the end of the wharf. I signed for everything, and then the *Western Star* shoved off and headed to Gizo. The next part was the hard part. All the items needed to be transferred to Seghe. We didn't have enough secure storage space at Seghe to store all the goods, which was why we'd had it all dropped at Uepi. Some of the goods would be stored at Jason's warehouse, located at the other end of Uepi Island, until they were needed.

There were still two unknown eight-hundred-pound elephants sitting on the end of the wharf. I walked over to one of the pallets and ripped a hole in the top. I could see a blue box with gold lettering and markings. *Oh no*, I thought. *I've seen this box before. These are the boxes the shipping agent in LA sent me pictures of.* I had explicitly told him that they were not my goods. I reached inside one of the boxes and pulled out a strange-looking plastic water bottle. It was shaped like a Phoenician amphora. It was clear plastic except for a tan plastic top that resembled a cork.

"What is this?" I said as I held it up. Jill and Jason were standing next to me. I reached back into the large box and pulled out a smaller box that contained the water bottle.

Jill read the box out loud. "Jar Zam Zam water. … What is Jar Zam Zam water?"

I went to the other pallet and opened the top. Sure enough, we had two full pallets of Jar Zam Zam water. What in the world was this stuff, and why was it in with my medical supplies?

Jill headed straight to the office with one of the bottles of Jar Zam Zam water. Before long, she returned with her computer research findings. "Well, the Internet says that Jar Zam Zam water is bottled at a holy spring in Mecca, Saudi Arabia. It is Muslim holy water."

"Jason and I looked at one another, and I said, "Why couldn't it have been French wine?"

I told everyone that we probably didn't want to plaster this all over social media in case some extremists got a wild hair and wanted to come looking for the water. We didn't need an international incident in the Marovo Lagoon over a bunch of holy water that I wanted nothing to do with. One thing was for sure: This was going to provide a lot of comedy for the next trip and beyond.

There were a few problems with receiving the Jar Zam Zam water. First, I figured I had paid around $900 to ship the water from LA to Uepi. Yes, I had been charged for these two pallets even after I had told the freight agent that the items weren't mine. Second, Uepi didn't have a lot of storage space where the water could be kept until we could figure out if anyone was going to come and pick it up. Finally, if no one was going to come get it, how was Uepi to dispose of two full pallets of plastic water bottles? We were in a very ecologically sensitive part of the world. Uepi wasn't going to throw the bottles in the ocean, and there wasn't any plastics recycling in the Solomon Islands.

After having flashbacks about the horror of dealing with Redtail over the lost solar panels, I had to e-mail them to let them know that I had received two pallets of Muslim holy water that did not belong to me. They responded promptly and as they had in the past with their trademark response: "We're looking into it and we'll get back with you." Here we go again, except the situation was a little different this time. I had received all of my goods in fine condition but had overpaid $900 to ship a bunch of water halfway around the world, and it didn't even belong to me. I had to start the process to get a refund. In addition, I told them they needed to do something about getting the two pallets of bottled water out of the pristine Marovo Lagoon.

Some of the items in the shipment were so heavy that we needed to have a full team in place to move them. The largest item was the OR table. The pallet containing the table weighed one thousand pounds. It was too heavy to pick up as it was. We had to dismantle half of the box so we could lift the table and put it into Jason's barge. I couldn't believe it. … When we pulled the box apart, we found all the cushions inside in mint condition; they had never been removed from their original packaging. The table was truly brand-new and unused. We had scored big with this find! It had been sold to the US government for around $22,000, and I had been able to get it for $5,000. The table was manual, not electric. That was perfect, because I didn't want additional bells and whistles that could break.

During this trip, Jason, some local guys, and I did a lot of work on the OR. We finished hanging and painting all of the fibro sheeting that was used for the walls. It was white ant-resistant and a quality building material. When we were finished, there was still a lot of work to be done in the operating room before the OR table and anesthesia machines could be moved in. I had sent several boxes of epoxy concrete sealer with the shipment, as we planned to seal the concrete floor with the epoxy. It was a durable finish and would allow us to use a steam cleaner or chemicals to clean up between surgeries. But that would have to wait for the next group trip.

My solo trip had been successful, although we still needed to get some serious business done. The list of items that we needed to collect continued to grow. The biggest big-ticket item I had yet to purchase was the new generator. It would take some research and bargain hunting to get a quality unit within our budget. While I was at Uepi, we scoured some global marketplace websites for new generators. It didn't make any sense to purchase the generator in the United States, since the alternator needed to produce Australian 240V 50 Hz power. I knew I could get it cheaper from overseas as well. I expressed my interest on one of the websites for either a genuine Cummins or Perkins diesel generator from 25 to 35 KW. The next day, I was inundated by manufacturers in China touting genuine Cummins and

Perkins generators. What a bunch of crap! Genuine Cummins and Perkins generators have certain color schemes that have been used by the manufacturers for years. The pictures that these manufacturers sent of the various "genuine" generators looked nothing like the real thing. The prices were great, but what was I buying? What recourse would I have if something went wrong with it? The level of risk with buying such a big-ticket item out of China was a little higher than I wanted. I needed to do more research before I could feel comfortable about making such a big purchase.

Research about the generator would have to wait a while longer, as my time at Uepi had come to an end. Unbelievably, it would be only another month before I would be returning with the May 2012 medical tour. I couldn't get enough of the Marovo Lagoon, and I felt blessed to have visited more than ten times already.

The way the flights worked out, I had one night in Honiara on my way home. I was excited to go to dinner with the Solomon Islands eye doctor, Mundi Qalo. He and his team planned to join us on the tour the next month to do cataract surgeries at Seghe Hospital. I invited him to meet me at the Japanese restaurant in the Kitano Mendana Hotel. I thought he seemed very young, although I still had a hard time judging age with Solomon Islanders.

During dinner, we talked about a lot of things, including physician pay in the Solomon Islands, medical students training in Cuba, and the excitement associated with him joining us on the next tour. He was obviously distressed at how low the wages were for physicians in the Solomon Islands. He explained that physicians were considered civil servants and were paid on a civil servant pay scale. He looked me in the eye and said, "Do you know how much they pay me?"

"No, I don't have any idea."

"They pay me 400 US dollars every two weeks."

After a quick calculation, I figured he made just under $10,000 a year. That was unfathomable! It was no wonder the Solomon Islands government couldn't keep any doctors around. The only docs in the country were ones who were truly convicted to stay and help their people regardless of the nonlivable wage they received. Mundi continued telling me that he took locum jobs around the South Pacific from time to time to supplement his income. This was atrocious. Solomon Islands doctors were the lowest-paid doctors on the face of the earth—dead last.

It didn't make any sense. Jason had told me that the Solomon Islands were the most heavily leveraged international aid country in the world. Where was all the money going? With a struggling national health care system and poor infrastructure, it was plain to see that a lot of those dollars were likely being siphoned off somewhere higher up on the government food chain.

Another interesting discussion point was that several Solomon Island medical students were being trained in Cuba. Mundi didn't know the specifics of how the program had come about, but evidently, Cuba has had a very good medical system for quite some time. There must have been some arrangement made between the two governments for this to take place. From our conversation, I could tell Mundi was skeptical about whether those medical students would stay in the Solomon Islands upon their return. He didn't think there was any money to pay them. The government was paying to have medical students trained not just in Cuba but in Fiji and Papua New Guinea as well. Many of the newly trained doctors would return to Honiara or Gizo for a little while and then leave because they weren't making a livable wage. In effect, the Solomon Islands government was paying for these doctors to be trained and then was losing them to other countries for nothing in return. It was a double waste of money ... ridiculous.

From having dinner with Mundi, I had learned a lot of information about the current system. I had also learned that one of our initial goals of hiring our own doctor for Seghe Hospital could actually become a reality. Of course we would offer more than the Solomon Islands did, but even at $10,000 to $15,000 a year, we could afford to pay a doctor to be at Seghe. If we provided the doctor a nice house with amenities, the package might look really appealing. In addition, we were building what we hoped would be the nicest operating room in the country at Seghe. The new OR would also likely help in attracting a new doctor. I left the dinner with sadness for the medical situation in the country but with excitement because I knew the dream of having a doctor at Seghe could definitely happen!

CHAPTER

21

Prior to our departure for Marovo in May 2012, I still hadn't received any word from Redtail Shipping regarding a refund for the Jar Zam Zam water. I felt bad that the stuff had been at Uepi for nearly a month. It consumed valuable space at Uepi. Redtail Shipping didn't care about it being there and clearly didn't really care about trying to get it to its rightful owner. The shipping shell game didn't surprise me anymore. After the solar panel saga and Off-Guard Freight trying to bend me over, I knew not to expect Redtail Shipping to care about the situation. After all, the situation wasn't costing them any money. Marovo Medical Foundation's money was on the line, and we were small potatoes.

I decided the battle would have to wait until after the May trip, though. I had some plans up my sleeve if Redtail didn't respond to my e-mails, but I needed to give my brain a rest and put my anxiety in check for a few more weeks. I hoped I would get the $900 back, but I knew there weren't any guarantees.

As planned, I arrived at Uepi several days before the medical team. There were a lot of things to get ready prior to the medical team's arrival. All the medicines had to be taken out of locked storage at Uepi and arranged in alphabetical order in our cabin. After the first group trip in 2008, we had learned that the Solomon Islands Ministry of Health would provide medicines for our tours. Since then, we had been ordering through the MOH for each trip. Normally, a week or two before the team arrived, the medicine shipment from Honiara was delivered to Seghe Hospital with Suzanne's name on it. Whatever medicines they were not able to provide, we had to purchase in the States at the last minute and bring with us. Before every trip, we have to inventory the medicines from Honiara to make sure we received what had been ordered. We weren't sure we would ever completely figure out the medicine ordering system. Quantities of items could sometimes be hard to figure out. One time we ordered silver nitrate sticks and thought we were ordering one package of them. Digging through the order, we had found one stick in a paper bag. Obviously, there were glitches in the system, but the MOH had made great strides with their pharmacy supply chain since we had been involved with them.

The bags of nursing supplies and reading glasses, which we'd been bringing since the second group trip, had to be put in the cabins of their respective keepers. We had several tackle boxes that were used as doctor kits. Each doc would get a tackle box that contained items that they might need during clinics, such as a flashlight, an otoscope/ophthalmoscope, Lidocaine, needles, a scalpel, and ear loops. Batteries needed to be charged, and bulbs needed to be checked. All the dental supplies had to be taken to the dentist's cabin. Dental tools needed to be resterilized prior to the first day's clinic.

Three days before the team was scheduled to arrive, Jason's workers loaded the bottom of one of the dive boats with timber to be used to cover the walkway between the OR and the main ward. Once the boat was full of timber, Jason and I took it over to his warehouse to load the boat to the max with additional medical supplies. While we were loading the items, the weather changed rapidly. The sky grew dark, and the clouds became more dense and ominous. We secured a couple of tarps over the boxes of supplies. We didn't have a choice. The items had to be at the hospital, and more work had to get finished.

We didn't get a mile away from Uepi before the intense wind and rain hit us like we were attention-seeking weather reporters standing out in a hurricane. The tarps violently flew toward the stern. Jason stopped the boat, and we hastily refastened the tarps to prevent the supplies from getting soaked. That worked until we started moving again. We made it another few hundred yards, and then the tarps loosened. It was a crazy scene. Jason and I were yelling to try to be heard above the wind and rain.

The middle of the lagoon is a lonely place in the middle of a squall. There were several miles to go before we hit Seghe. The tarps would not stay down. We tried to secure them under the heavy timbers lining the floor of the boat, but the wind was too strong. I was in my bright orange raincoat and decided to lie on top of the tarp at the bow. We had to get going, and there wasn't any other way to keep the tarps down. I was spread eagle with my face being pummeled by the driving rain. At this point, I knew I never wanted to be a hood ornament again. Jason continued to manage the rear tarp while my torso and four limbs did a good job of securing the front tarp. As we approached Seghe, the storm passed. All in all, it was actually a cool experience. Had it been freezing cold, I wouldn't have been nearly as happy, however.

Prior to the arrival of the team, we secured support beams above the walkway between the OR and main ward. Nailing through the tropical hardwoods was a challenge. It wasn't pine. Construction workers doing framing in the States have it pretty easy with their air hammers and soft wood. Many a thick nail was bent and thrown out while we tried to connect two thick timbers together. The wood was so dense, it was unbelievable. I was way out of practice with the hammer. Jason had a few good laughs while I crunched my thumb multiple times.

Jill and Josh came over that day after we'd put the support beams up and helped put the finishing coats on the concrete floor. The team would not be able to walk on it, but they would get a good view. All the lights worked, and the OR really popped with the shiny tan floor when Jill and Josh were done.

The tour consisted mostly of newcomers this time. Kate Wilson was thrilled to have two friends from medical school on the tour with us: Doctors Keith and Elizabeth Toms, plus their two children and Elizabeth's mother to watch the children during the days. Dr. Jack Iliff and his wife, Sally, joined us from Maryland. Jack was a recently retired ophthalmologist who was eager to help. He had been in touch with Mundi and was eager to see the small-incision cataract procedure done. Eye docs in the United States typically employed a different approach to cataract surgery. Two friends of Jack and Sally, Dr. Chris Murphy and his wife, Laura Norton, decided to jump on board with them. Chris was a dentist and Laura was going to be our runner to coordinate patient flow in the villages. Chris had never done bush dentistry, so he had communicated with Kate ahead of time to get an idea of what he could expect. His upper body would definitely be stronger at the end of the tour from all the teeth he was about to pull.

A friend of ours from Arizona, Dr. John Chiakmakis, took a big leap and signed up. John had never been out of the United States, other than the Caribbean, so this was a huge step for him. He had recently retired as a podiatrist, and we were thrilled to have him and all of his surgical expertise. I looked forward to spending time with him. John was a great storyteller, and I was always looking for a good laugh.

We had only one RN for this tour; Ed Wicker from Salt Lake had come through for me in a pinch. He and his wife, Nicole, had been with us on a previous trip, but only Ed came as a last-minute addition. I knew I could rely on Ed to keep the triage portion of the clinic running. He was completely dedicated to his profession and his patients.

For this trip, we did a brief welcome ceremony at the hospital after the group arrived. Walking from the airstrip to the hospital was a lot of fun. Kids jumped out of the bushes dressed in leaves and warrior outfits. Some of the ladies from Seghe made sun visors out of grass and local materials. Each person in the group was given a visor. It was a delightful gesture.

After the brief welcome, we walked everyone around the hospital. Jason and I were excited to show off the OR. Suzanne's eyes opened wide at the sight, and her smile was vibrant and full of joy. She cried a little bit at the beauty of the facility. It had really been her decision that we build the OR. She was blown away to see how good it looked, even though it had a ways to go before it would be finished.

The first day's clinic was, as always, at Seghe Hospital. There were patients waiting for us upon our arrival that morning. Dr. Mundi Qalo and his team had already been busy doing cataract surgeries when we arrived. The cataract patients were lined up outside the main ward, sitting in chairs. They were all senior citizens. When we walked by and looked into their eyes, it was obvious they were there for cataract surgery. Their eyes were milky gray. A few of them had cataracts so bad that they could barely see anything. Mundi invited Jason into the dental office, which was an office that had a dental chair but had never permanently housed a dentist. The patient was already lying in the chair when Jason came in. Mundi allowed Jason front-row access to the procedure. Jason captured incredible video footage of the process. The procedure was truly amazing, and Mundi was highly skilled.

Unfortunately, we wouldn't be there for the removal of the patient's bandages, but Mundi explained that it was always a watershed moment for everyone involved. Talk about a procedure that had a nearly instant life-changing effect. These people who, for the most part, had had their vision significantly impaired, suddenly could see as clear as when they were five years old. I hoped to witness the event someday, but the timing wasn't right on this trip.

After seeing several hundred patients, we finished the first week. For most of the group, the weekend was the time to relax and explore the island and surrounding water. On Saturday, some of us went to Jason's warehouse and loaded Uepi's large boat, *Triton*, with medical supplies. These were the supplies that had arrived the previous month. Earlier the same morning, the guys from Uepi, along with some of Jason's employees, had broken their backs to get the OR table onto Jason's timber barge. The barge had long since left. It was slow, and thus it took more than an hour to get to Seghe.

By now, the epoxy floor coating had dried enough to accommodate the several-hundred-pound OR table. While the barge slowly chugged along to Seghe, those of us in *Triton* made several trips back and forth from the boat to the OR with supplies. It almost seemed a shame to clutter the pristine-looking facility, but it wouldn't be a true OR without all the accoutrements needed to successfully cut someone open and sew them back together.

When the barge finally arrived at Seghe, the task was to figure out how to get the massive and heavy OR table to the hospital. The manual said it had wheels but the wheels had only a quarter inch of clearance. Jason had hoped the table could be taken apart, but unfortunately, it didn't come apart easily. We would have to carry the table one hundred yards to the hospital. Once on the concrete floor outside the outpatient clinic, we could remove the table from the crate and wheel it to the OR.

Jason assembled a crew of guys, including Ed Wicker, to get the table out of the barge and up the hill. Large timbers were put down from the side of the barge to the rough coral jetty. Fortunately for me, my back wasn't in the best of shape, so I relegated myself to filming the episode. After some serious yelling and energy expenditure, the massive box was up on the timbers. Jason wet both of the boards with seawater to act as a lubricant. The half-ton box slid easily down the timbers to the coral below.

Four large timbers were placed under the pallet in a cross pattern. Jason commandeered more local men to help. In all, it took fourteen men to pick up and carry the OR table up the hill. They were obviously struggling and had to stop once on the way. They dropped the table at the top of a series of steps. The hospital sat close to five feet lower than the pathway outside.

Someone found two long metal poles about four inches in diameter. They placed the poles at the top of the hill. Incredibly, the poles were just long enough to make it to the foot of the concrete pad at the front door of the hospital. The box slid down the poles perfectly. Once the table was on the concrete pad, folks cheered the successful move. That was a serious team effort!

As far as drama went, we had one blip on the radar screen during the trip. We were greeted at Telina village by another great show. The villagers didn't need to do anything for us, but inevitably, they put on an elaborate welcome ceremony. It was always a highlight for our group.

Halfway through the clinic day at Telina, Suzanne couldn't find her cell phone. We figured she had put it down somewhere or that one of the other docs had grabbed it to look up medical information. As the day went on, however, it became more apparent that no one on our team had picked up the phone. No, this couldn't have been theft. The people at Telina were always good to us, and we good to them. There had to be another explanation. No one wanted to believe that the phone had been stolen; these people were so appreciative of our care. Still, when the day came to an end, Suzanne's phone was still gone.

We brought the situation to the attention of a couple of the village elders. They were beside themselves with sadness. They cancelled their ceremonial war canoe presentation. They made a speech expressing their sincerest regrets for what had happened. Finally, they said they would do everything they could to try to find the phone.

There were a few problems associated with the missing phone. One thing I couldn't fathom was the fact that the majority of Solomon Islanders didn't have a toilet to sit on to go to the bathroom, but they didn't seem to care about that issue. As a whole, they were voluntarily choosing to skip toilets and to jump straight to cell phones. They seemed to be unaware of the potential consequences of a growing population without adequate sanitation. We saw it time and again, children out swimming and playing in the water only a hundred yards down from the community toilet—an area along the shoreline where people congregate to urinate and defecate. Swimming and playing in water where people also go to the bathroom would eventually prove problematic. Unfortunately, the population seemed more concerned with getting status symbols like cell phones than with toilets. If only toilets were considered status symbols, the locals might be able to prevent an impending health disaster. Cell phones weren't going to help prevent sanitation-related illnesses. Solving this problem was definitely in our purview but had to wait until we finished upgrading Seghe Hospital to an acceptable and sustainable level. First things first.

The other problem with the missing phone was that it was probably the only iPhone in the entire lagoon at the time. Anyone who saw this phone would realize that it was different from all others. The thief also probably didn't realize that he or she had taken the phone of the leader of the group. The sheer fact that someone had taken Suzanne's phone was a blow that she had a hard time managing.

A few days after Suzanne's phone disappeared, the carvers descended upon Uepi. Suzanne had been upset about the cell phone, and for good reason. She had no desire to buy carvings on this day, as many of the carvers were from Telina. We knew the village as a whole was full of people who were genuinely thankful that we visited on each trip, but still, the theft was hard to stomach.

Jason came to us and told us that we had been summoned to the dining hall. It was a strange exchange, and we weren't sure what to expect. As we arrived, we saw four elders from Telina village sitting in the lounge area. Jason, Jill, Suzanne, and I sat down in front of them. They went through a few customary speeches, each expressing sincere regret that the phone had been stolen. Suzanne had properly diagnosed an ectopic pregnancy on one gentleman's wife the year before. His wife had made it to Honiara but had not been given proper care and had, unfortunately, died. He knew how important it was for us to visit their village twice a year. He and the other elders were horrified that the phone of Suzanne, the chief medical officer, had been stolen.

After we had been sitting there for nearly fifteen minutes, wondering where this was going, Kerry, one of the elders, started to speak. In slow, dramatic fashion, he pulled a white cloth from his bag. Our eyes were fixed on the cloth. He slowly opened it and revealed Suzanne's phone. Her eyes opened wide in amazement. Jill was dumfounded and completely blown away that the phone had reappeared. She had thought for sure we would never see the phone again.

The elders explained that the boy who had taken the phone would be dealt with and punished appropriately. We hoped that it wouldn't involve physical violence, but we couldn't be sure. The elders knew the ramifications of the incident, and Suzanne made it clear to them that we would continue to visit their village. They collectively sighed in relief when she told them we would return to Telina on the next trip. Prior to the meeting, we had decided that we would return to Telina, regardless of whether the phone reappeared. We weren't going to let one bad apple spoil the scene for the nearly 200 people we treated there each trip.

On the lighter side, a funny story came from one of the clinics. Elizabeth mentioned to Suzanne and me that a patient she had seen had an interesting primary complaint. She said the patient had explained, "I have a tumor in my asshole." The patient hadn't beat around the bush and obviously had jumped to conclusions with her immediate tumor self-diagnosis. Fortunately for the patient, it was just a hemorrhoid, potentially the result of too much white rice in her diet.

The story was funny, but it really spoke to the lack of general knowledge that the people had regarding their bodies. Now, I'm sure many people in the developed world have thought the same thing about feeling an external hemorrhoid, but this type of reaction from the villagers mimicked other age-related ailments. We had people who only needed reading glasses but thought they were going blind. Many people still considered accidents, such as crocodile attacks, to be the result of improper living. Even though Christianity had been firmly in place for one hundred years, there were still a lot of beliefs that drew upon pre-Christian traditions and practices.

We knew we needed to create a general health information booklet for the people of the lagoon. Our plan was to have the booklet written in their native language, Marovan. Pidgin and Marovan seemed to be spoken interchangeably in the lagoon. Solomon Islanders from outside the lagoon spoke a different native language and thus would communicate with people of the Marovo in Pidgin. I heard only English being spoken when locals were speaking to non-Solomon Islanders.

A health booklet would go a long way to educate the population regarding basic fundamentals of health and the human body. It would also address dietary issues and the causes of Type II diabetes and other lifestyle-related diseases. Having the booklet published in Marovan would be key to the successful dissemination of the material in the villages. We had started to put key elements of the book together, but there was still a long way to go on that project. Because Marovan was a language with around 15,000 speakers, the United Nations considered it a language with the potential of being lost, so we hoped the United Nations would be interested in funding such a publishing project, but we had to finish the book first.

The medical tour, meaningful and successful, came to an end. Everyone in the group left, except for John Chiakmakis and me. We planned to do some more work at the hospital over the next few days. It was always strange staying on later after the team left. The entire resort had been ours for the two weeks. Now, suddenly, our folks were gone and a new set of people, many of who didn't care about our medical work, showed up to dive. John and I started a conversation with a couple from Brisbane, Peter and Margaret Fletcher, who were there to dive. They had visited Uepi many times. It turned out Peter was a general practitioner and Margaret a recently retired PhD in education. The meeting was serendipitous. Peter expressed his desire to participate in a medical mission very similar to ours but said he had yet to find one that suited him. The advertising for Marovo Medical never stopped. Only a couple of days after our group had left, John and I were busy trying to recruit Peter and Margaret to join the next trip in November. Turns out, I was successful. Prior to John and I leaving, Peter and Margaret let us know they were almost a lock for the upcoming tour. Yes! I always needed new doctors, and Australian doctors were in high demand. It made so much sense to have increased Australian participation because the Solomon Islands were much closer to Australia than the States in so many ways. I would bet nine out of ten Australian children could easily identify the Solomon Islands on a map. On the converse, most likely, nine out of ten American children, or even adults, would be unable to easily identify the Solomon Islands on a map.

During my additional days at Uepi, I took some time to think about something the documentary filmmaker, Doug, had mentioned to me. I had briefly mentioned to him something about a reality television show centered around our work in the Marovo Lagoon. I remembered his response being unequivocal and immediate. "You want a reality show? All I have to do is make one call to my friend at one of the cable networks and you'll have a contract an inch thick in front of you before you know what hit you." He obviously knew the local sights, experiences, people, and intrigue would come together to make an incredible and real reality show. The thought wasn't continually in the forefront of my mind, but since he had made the comment, I hadn't forgotten his words.

Wow, what could a reality television show mean for us? Maybe it would help to fund the foundation and create a truly sustainable health care program in the Marovo Lagoon. The show would have actual meaning. It wouldn't be about country hillbillies making moonshine, animal calls, or even spoiled housewives. It could educate the American masses about how life is outside of the United States. Americans needed to travel to the developing world. They needed to see that big-box America existed because less fortunate people around the world lost their resources for pennies so our products could be inexpensive. The idealist side of me wanted to showcase the suffering that happened when people didn't have access to doctors or dentists. Illustrating the ravages of cheap big-box furniture on third-world communities would really make my day. I saw so much potential for educating the simple, misinformed, and uninformed masses in America. What could go wrong?

The more I thought about it, though, the more I realized maybe it wasn't such a good idea. Where to start? I wasn't a fan of drama, and we had previously hosted some drama queens on the trips. The only thing that made people want to watch reality television was drama. They wanted to see someone causing trouble and the resulting confrontation. Our trips ran the best with little to no drama from our participants. There was always some sort of medical drama, but I didn't need additional contrived drama that would inevitably happen when cameras started rolling. One didn't have to watch too many reality shows to realize that people make serious asses out of themselves when a camera is in their faces. Any shred of integrity that people may have prior to the television show, in many cases, quickly evaporates. They seek attention, and the more ridiculous their behavior becomes, sadly, the more attention they receive.

For some trips, it had been really difficult to secure enough doctors, nurses, and support personnel to make the tours operate smoothly. A reality show would open up the floodgates to a lot of people who genuinely wanted to help, but probably to a lot more people who just wanted to get their fifteen seconds of fame. Backstabbing would start on camera. Most reality shows love to interview the cast in private and ask provocative questions about other cast members to try to get them to say nasty things or make improper judgments about one another. That type of third-grade behavior has no place on our trips.

Finally, and most importantly, I wouldn't want the show to change the local culture. I often walked around the clinics, filming the locals. Others took pictures here and there. That was no big deal. If we brought a film crew with six or eight cameras into a village and every time a doctor spoke with a patient, they had a camera in their face, it might start to cause friction. The cameramen and producers might even egg the children on to get them to do things that would otherwise be considered rude or unacceptable in normal village life. Bottom line: the cons definitely outweighed the benefits of doing such a show, in my mind.

*   *   *

Back at home, the task of putting together the November 2012 trip was before me. As hard as it was, we had decided to delay opening the operating room yet again. A few of the large vital components had yet to be purchased, including the generator and main surgical light. Making the decision to delay opening a little easier was the fact that we didn't have a surgeon lined up to go with us on the November 2012 trip.

Of course I still didn't have a refund from Redtail Shipping in LA. My repeated attempts to get answers were continually met with their standard response: "Sir, we are looking into this." I figured they were a large multinational corporation that had the ability to figure out shipping errors in less than four months' time. It was time to employ my next strategy. Yes, I've said drama was never high on my list, but now I needed some drama on my side to force the hand of Redtail Shipping to return our $900. I drafted press releases right and left. I didn't hesitate to make the headlines as crazy and dramatic as possible: "Muslim Holy Water Dumped in the Solomon Islands and Arizona Charity Stuck with the Bill!" or "Shipping Company Charges Mom & Pop Charity for Shipping Muslim Holy Water to the Solomon Islands." Of course I was trying to create some excitement surrounding the holy water. I needed the company to be held accountable and to resolve the situation. Not only were we out $900, but Uepi Island Resort had to dispose of two full pallets of plastic bottles that Redtail Shipping didn't want to share any responsibility for dumping on their doorstep.

I sent the press releases everywhere I could, including media outlets in Tucson, Phoenix, and Los Angeles. I knew it wouldn't be long before my phone was ringing off the hook and sweet justice would ensue.

Unfortunately, no one wanted to touch the story. Living in southern Arizona, I had learned that the Tucson media outlets had little to no interest in covering stories that weren't local. The folks in LA were probably too busy covering the latest reality-star scandal or high-speed chase to care. I had two final options in front of me. First, I decided to file a Better Business Bureau complaint against the company. Second, I sent one last press release to a newspaper in Sierra Vista, Arizona.

Incredibly, the next day, I received an e-mail from a vice president for Redtail Shipping, which read

Dear Alan,

I was made aware of a BBB complaint referencing the above booking. I researched and found your claim to be valid and have asked _____ to get in touch with you to see if you can prepare some sort of bill we can reimburse the $900 dollars to you against.

This really looks like a very silly error from what I've found. Without having all the facts, the important ones are these pallets were delivered to us extra, by your trucker, in error. With the pictures you got, it was identified this was not your cargo and it should have been stopped and we should have reached out to your trucker informing them we had 2 pallets that don't belong to you.

What happened was when you wrote that they were not yours, customer service assumed the pictures you sent were not of the cargo going to you, but of something else, so basically ignored it. It was something that frankly is a bit amazing and I've never seen something like that before.

With the details I got it was very easy for me to make this decision to reimburse the $900 to you. I wish my staff had elevated this to me earlier so we could have settled this for you earlier.

Please add my name to your contact list and let me know if you have any other issues requiring senior management intervention in the future.

I apologize for this error and the frustration you experienced in getting resolution.

Best regards,

_____ ____

Unbelievably, as I was halfway through reading the e-mail, my phone rang. It was the editor from the newspaper in Sierra Vista. He said he would like to do a story regarding the press release I had sent him. I told him his timing was uncanny, as I was reading an e-mail from the company explaining that they were going to resolve the issue and reimburse us for the $900. That was wild timing right there. Now I knew how to get results with any shipping company in the future. File a BBB complaint and they would respond lickety-split! Another shipping company battle had come to an end. Now I could get back to focusing on planning the next trip and securing the last big-ticket items for the OR.

CHAPTER

22

Our church in Sierra Vista, Faith Presbyterian, had donated the entire World Communion Sunday offering to Marovo Medical Foundation for the second year in a row. It was a tremendous gift, and enough money to purchase a new generator for the hospital. The new generator was key to the hospital being able to do surgeries. Gordon had designed and wired the system to seamlessly switch back and forth between the solar power system and the generator. On a daily basis, the solar power system met all the electrical needs of the hospital. During surgeries, however, the solar power system would serve as a backup, and the generator would serve as the primary power source for the entire hospital, including the OR. It would easily be able to accommodate the additional loads created by the air conditioners and air compressor.

The hospital electrical system was designed to operate on 240 Volts and 50 Hz. This was the type of power used in Australia. As I've already mentioned, most generators sold in the States are based on 110 Volts and 60 Hz. The voltage isn't as big a deal as the hertz. Motors are normally designed to run on one or the other. Running a motor on the wrong hertz would slowly deteriorate the motor, so purchasing a generator out of the States was basically out of the question because almost none of them were made to operate at 50 Hz. I didn't have any faith buying anything from China, and I wasn't about to stick my neck out and use our precious donation money to purchase something for which I had no way to verify authenticity.

Grant at Uepi gave me a couple of names of companies in Australia. I contacted the first company on the list. They were a genuine Perkins dealer, and my references said I could trust them. Initially, their quotes were a little high. I had only around $10,000 to purchase a 30KW generator. The first two quotes the gentleman at this company gave me were around $13,000 and didn't include shipping. The Chinese models were much more affordable, but I just couldn't go there in good conscience. I needed a reliable unit, and Chinese manufacturers, of myriad products, often produced inferior goods. I didn't need to hear another news story about dogs dying in the United States from tainted Chinese-made dog food to cement my negativity toward Chinese goods.

I told the salesman I couldn't spend $13,000 on a generator. A few days after our initial e-mail exchange, he sent me another message. He had been able to find a clearance unit at one of their other stores. It was a genuine Perkins unit rated to produce just the right amount of power that we needed. I almost fell over when I read the price: $8000. Yes, yes, yes, I'll take it! He confirmed the unit was in fact brand-new but they were no longer carrying the specific model. Score! This was a serious victory for us. Thank you, Faith Presbyterian! The power plant for the operating room was on its way.

Prior to leaving for Brisbane, I had another win regarding OR equipment. We had designed the suction system to run using a Venturi machine with a medium-sized air compressor. Jason identified the compressor model, and I called the company in Brisbane, Boss Compressors. They didn't have a website purchase option, so I called them from the States to order the unit. I explained to the lady what I needed and that it was going to be used at a rural hospital in the Solomon Islands. I provided all my contact information with the credit card number. She was a delight to speak with and reassured me that the unit would be delivered to the freight forwarder straight away.

The next day, I received a confirmation e-mail from the woman at Boss Compressors, a family-run business. She had looked at our website and shared it with other members of the family. I was shocked when I read her e-mail.

Hi Allan,

This morning I looked up your website and was very impressed and touched by the help you bring to others. We would like to donate this air compressor as we gather every little bit helps. (no funds have been drawn on your credit card)

I will include a set of air filter elements and spare set of cylinder gaskets(just in case a repair is ever needed) Also a free Boss Kit as advertised.

I can supply a bottle of oil for service—but I'm not sure if this is a problem for shipping, it would be inside a box and won't leak. Let me know if you don't want this included.

I have attached a Tax Invoice and will make sure this gets to your shipping company.

All the best for the future.

Boss's gesture blew me away! These people didn't know me, Suzanne, or Jason at all, yet they had seen the story and decided to act. Donations were extremely important to our operations, although the time needed to sort them out was often in short supply. A donation that was given to us without us having to ask was the best kind. I planned to stop in to the store on my way through Brisbane to personally thank them for their gift.

I left several days ahead of the group prior to the November 2012 trip to make sure all the medicines and supplies were set up and ready to go upon the team's arrival. After working for a few days to prepare for the team's arrival, I was finally ready for one of my personal highlights of each trip to occur. The plane was due to land at Seghe with the participants ready to embark on the ninth medical tour of the Marovo Lagoon. I stood back, filming as the plane arrived. Off came an incredibly hot redhead with beaming confidence and a smile that got my motor running. Suzanne was my earthly rock on these trips. She had the medical know-how and confidence to put my mind at ease in any medical situation. Jason and I busted our asses to make sure all the logistics were covered, but the medical side of things was her baby, and I knew she had it covered. Her presence in the Marovo was indicative of the fact that it was time to get down to business and start treating the sick. Let's go!

Peter and Margaret Fletcher climbed off the plane behind Suzanne. Our relationship was a new one but seemed to hold a lot of promise for future collaboration with Marovo Medical. Behind the Fletchers were Ian Harris and Grace Lin returning for their third trip. Every time Ian was in the country, he was the only cardiologist for 600,000 plus people. The people of the Marovo had no idea of the caliber of doctors that we had for them.

In the end, though, that didn't matter. The important thing was that these medical professionals all came to freely give of their time and talents to diagnose, treat, heal, and cure ailments and give hope. At least that's what I thought about everyone at the beginning of the trip. ...

The trip started smoothly. It didn't take long for me to realize that some members of the group had their own agendas, however. For only the second time in nine trips did I have folks who weren't team players. Unfortunately for us, more than one person was causing trouble this time. One of the nurses on the trip, Shelly, and two of the medical practitioners seemed to be there for reasons that I was unable to figure out. I didn't want anything to do with petty crap. Adults need to be able to put their mental crap in the backseat for two weeks to be able function as a cohesive medical team. Oh, the perfect world I try to live in.

The first Thursday of the trip took us back to Batuna Clinic. We always visited Batuna on Thursdays because the Batuna market occurred that day and there were loads of people in attendance. The area also had a trade and business school on the hill, where Suzanne and I were paying for little Allan Daly's mom to go to business school. I hoped little Allan would show up with his mom so I could see how big he was getting.

Working in the pharmacy, I could often discern when something wasn't going quite right inside the clinic. When a serious medical case presented itself to one of our clinics, people moved more quickly and docs could be seen talking together with very serious expressions on their faces. I liked to keep the atmosphere light as much as possible, but sometimes we were faced with situations that could not be taken lightly. I knew, even without knowing the full details, that this was one of those situations.

Peter Fletcher came out to ask about some medicines. I could tell by his demeanor that they had a serious situation inside. "Peter, what's going on?" I asked.

"We've got an eight-month-old baby in there with a serious heart defect. I don't think she'll make it another twenty-four hours unless we get her to Brisbane for surgery."

"What's next?"

"Jason has been on the phone working on our options," he replied with a look of despair on his face.

I wasn't thrilled that cell phones had made inroads in the Marovo Lagoon, but in this case, they seemed to be a good thing. Jason spoke with Brenda, the head nurse at Seghe, to get phone numbers of the Provincial Health Service in Gizo. He then connected with a pediatrician in Gizo. He briefly explained the situation to the pediatrician, and then Suzanne and Ian both spoke with her to provide additional medical information about the diagnosis and the child's condition.

To further coordinate the logistics, Jason got back on the phone and tried to navigate getting the baby into the referral system. The pediatrician didn't think that step was necessary because she knew there was nothing that could be done for the child anywhere in the Solomon Islands. The pediatrician even questioned whether there was any point in moving the child because there was a serious possibility that the child wasn't going to make it much longer.

Several minutes after the conversation with the pediatrician ended, the phone rang again. It was the pediatrician from Gizo again. She had given Jason's number to the National Referral Hospital and RAMSI. Thankfully, she had requested that a helicopter be dispatched to pick up the child. It was amazing that we had navigated the nonexistent emergency medical system in the Solomon Islands to the point that Jason had ended up on the phone, speaking to a helicopter pilot from RAMSI.

The clinics weren't ever easy. Some days had fewer patients than others, but inevitably, one or more patients had serious ailments that needed immediate attention. Incredibly, on this trip, we happened to have Dr. Ian Harris, a congenital heart defect cardiologist, with us for the third time. Unbeknownst to the mom or the little girl, the child was being cradled in the best hands possible. Along with Ian, Peter was a top-notch, highly skilled general practitioner from Brisbane with decades of pediatric experience. The two of them were collectively going to give this little girl the best chance she had at getting to a pediatric cardiac surgical center in Brisbane. Our loaned portable ultrasound unit had a cardiac probe with it, so Ian did a heart echo on the child. The results of the echo showed that she likely had two heart defects. Ian told me that these things would normally be fixed at birth or shortly thereafter in the developed world. Sadly, Solomon Islanders—the majority of the world's population, for that matter—didn't have that luxury.

Ian commented that the pediatrician on the phone had seemed like a deer in the headlights at hearing his diagnosis. After the pediatrician had heard that Ian was a cardiologist and that he was in the country, she had asked him to come by and read some cardiac studies for them. Sadly, we knew that wasn't going to happen.

Before the helicopter crew lifted off from Honiara to come our way, the pilot called Jason. They had been informed they were going to uplift one person out of the Marovo and wanted to know where the most suitable landing site was. Jason notified them that the child and mother would be at the Seghe Airport and that would be the best site for medical evacuation.

A few minutes later, Jason spoke to the pilot a second time and notified him that there was a possibility of landing at Batuna. The pilot declined to land there, as it was an unconfirmed landing zone and it would be close to dark at the time of pickup. The ETA for the pickup at Seghe was scheduled around 6:00 p.m.

Jason rang Brenda to let her know the baby was coming. Ian, Peter, Mom, baby, and the boat driver sped off to Seghe. The baby actually rallied during the boat ride and was feeding on her mom's milk. They started furosemide on the baby at Batuna to remove unwanted fluids. The team didn't have oxygen with them, although they knew the chopper would have it.

Upon landing at Seghe, the medical crew approached and assessed the patient. The anesthetist commented on how bad the baby looked. Ian replied, "She actually looks much better than she did an hour ago." The anesthetist was taken aback. The chopper team knew they had a serious case on their hands. I'm sure they've been called in before and found that the patient's status has been exaggerated. In this case, sadly, there were no exaggerations.

The next day's clinic went by without much fanfare. It was obvious that the fate of the baby was prying on the minds of everyone in the group. Information, and correct information at that, could be very hard to come by in the Solomon Islands. Fact verification wasn't always held to as high a standard as it should have been.

Saturday finally arrived. It was time to relax and enjoy a two-day break from the clinics. Everyone needed a respite, both physically and mentally, from the work in the villages. Unless participants had been with us on previous trips, they were unaware that a special party was going to happen Saturday evening. As a celebration of all the hard work the team does, the Kelly family throws a barge party for us the first Saturday night of the trip. Uepi staff spend all afternoon outfitting Jason's barge with palm fronds, flowers, furniture, and even carpet.

The party was always a blast and people inevitably had a good time. That was … up until this trip. At breakfast, we notified people to show up at the boat jetty at five p.m. for the barge party. Later in the afternoon, I heard some chatter that a couple of participants seemed to have a problem with the barge party. Evidently, they weren't happy that I hadn't notified them ahead of time that there would be a fun evening cruise on a party barge. *What?!* Who gets bent out of shape about not being told about an incredible evening party celebration on a barge in the Marovo Lagoon? Are fun happy surprises that bad? Who doesn't like drinks and appetizers under the stars in bathtub-calm water in one of the most beautiful places on Earth? Who gets upset at not being told days ahead that out of the dark was going to appear a boatload of Uepi staff members playing traditional bamboo-band music? Who would get upset about the boat, the music, the magic, all appearing out of nowhere, seemingly the perfect capstone experience to the first draining week of work? Who, who, who? A few people in our group, that's who.

Even though all those things were an affront to a few people, the barge party started off with fantastic news. Two regular Uepi guests, Darcy and Neil, had joined us at Batuna Clinic to help in various ways. Taking time away from their vacation to help out in our clinic put them at the top of my list. It really showed that they were genuine, caring people. Darcy and Neil had flown back to Australia the day before the barge party. As the barge shoved off on its usual terrible voyage, Jason stood up to share some good news. "I received an e-mail today from Darcy and Neil. On their flight to Brisbane, they happened to sit next to the helicopter pilot who flew the baby to Honiara. He told them that a med-evac jet was waiting at the airport and the baby was transferred to Brisbane." Cheers, applause, and many tears flowed with that incredible piece of information. Wow, at least she was going to get the best chance possible at fixing the defects and living a normal life. What a way to start the barge party!

Sunday was spent relaxing and sleeping off any alcoholic and barge party-induced hangovers. Spending the day snorkeling or diving was a great way to unwind. The second week of clinics was less than twenty-four hours away, and I cherished the relaxation. Snorkeling during the hot afternoon was a great way to cool off. The plethora of fish swimming around in their normal routines was soothing, to say the least. I had enjoyed having fish tanks as a kid, although after I had snorkeled and dived in an incredibly diverse ocean, the allure of keeping fish in a tank had faded into oblivion.

Monday was our usually scheduled day at Telina Village. We heard that there wouldn't be any war canoe welcome or warrior dancing ceremony upon our arrival, because a beloved member of their village had passed away the day before. The facts regarding his passing were murky. A somber tone hung over the clinic, which seemingly added more humidity to the already oppressive weather conditions. The day wasn't anything special—actually somewhat boring, in my opinion.

Boring was about to get a very sad makeover, however. That evening at Uepi, news that could only be described as crippling and tragic began to spread around the dinner table. It seemed that the helicopter pilot had unknowingly given Neil and Darcy erroneous information regarding the baby from Batuna. The true story was that there had been a med-evac jet sitting on the tarmac in Honiara. Unfortunately, the flight had not been for the baby. Someone else had gotten on that airplane to Brisbane. The baby had been taken to the National Referral Hospital in Honiara. Sadly, the baby had died the next morning. The emotional roller coaster left us at the bottom of the track. How could this be? Collectively, we had thought we'd won a big one. Evidently, by the time we learned the news, the mother had already returned to the Marovo and buried the baby. Our hearts went out to the mother and the rest of the family. I wish we could have seen the baby earlier, because she may have had a real chance.

We had to keep going despite the sad news. There were three more days of village clinics before we were finished. The villages were planning on us coming, so no matter how bad the news had been the day before, we were off to Viru Harbor. Viru, Tinge, and Zaira were the only three villages we ever visited that were not inside the Marovo Lagoon. We drove past Seghe early in the morning and wove through the mangrove-lined channels of the Bapata canoe passage. The entire ride to Viru was amazing. The open ocean between Bapata and Viru teemed with hundreds of spinner dolphins. The town was aptly named; the towering cliffs on either side of a well-protected anchorage shouted "harbor" to anyone passing by. The cliffs on the left side of the harbor still housed Japanese artillery from WWII. One cannon sat in its original position. The other lay at the bottom of a massive bomb crater with just the tip of the barrel sticking out of the pit. Evidently, an aircraft from Seghe had come in very low on a raid. Allegedly, it had been flying lower than the big guns could shoot. The pilot had climbed the wall in a steep maneuver while dropping his bomb on one gun. The massive bomb crater proves just how good of a shot the pilot was.

Viru Harbor was the birthplace of the Seventh-day Adventist Church in the Solomon Islands. The village housed the largest building in the country that I had ever seen. It wasn't a church but served as a meeting and event hall. It seemed almost as big as a big-box store in the States, although it was an open-air pole barn-type structure. The village hung sheets in areas to create privacy for the doctors and patients. The lab and pharmacy seemed to be a football field away from the doctors, dentist, and triage. Our folks were going to get some good exercise at this clinic.

Halfway through the day, I noticed a few of the docs in somewhat of a huddle regarding a patient. I knew from Batuna that this wasn't a good sign. We had several point-of-care diagnostic testing tools with us, but they were still fairly rudimentary and limited in scope. The patient was a young girl, probably younger than ten. She had thinning hair, and her overall malaise was more pronounced because of her gaunt appearance. After a few physician huddles, the team determined that the girl likely had lupus. With our limited blood-testing capabilities, they couldn't be one hundred percent certain, but they were in agreement that it was likely lupus. Autoimmune-type diseases were not conditions that we were able to effectively treat. We had prednisone, but we didn't have any of the latest infusion therapies that might be more effective with this type of disease. The parents were out of sorts regarding the girl's condition. They wanted answers, and they obviously had their hands full providing full-time care for the young girl. They were even concerned about whether they had caused the problem from disciplining or smacking her as a child. The doctors reassured them that it wasn't the result of anything like that. Another reason to finish the health-education book. There wasn't a lot we could do, and the girl's future seemed dim. We dispensed her medicine and hoped for the best. Her condition and the obvious stress that her parents were under unfortunately wouldn't leave my brain.

Sadly, out of nine trips, I placed this one tied at the bottom of the enjoyable scale. It was tied with the trip when I'd had so many issues with Char. For me, the quality of the experience I had was often indicated by the amount of video I shot during the clinics and our time off. It hadn't taken long on the ninth trip before I'd put the camera away for good.

To add insult to injury, Shelly chose not to assist with inventorying our medical supplies at the end of the trip. It was vital to us that we know what we had and what we would need for the next tour. On the last evening, Suzanne; Lynnette Griffith, the lab technician; and Kate were forced to count all the nursing supplies. There was one bag left to count. After she, Lynnette, and Kate had counted the majority of the supplies, Suzanne asked Shelly, the one nurse on this trip, to count it and give her the tally the next morning. At breakfast, I watched in horror as Shelly told Suzanne that she hadn't counted the items but knew what was in the bag. I thought Suzanne's red hair was going to turn into a flamethrower and vaporize Shelly while others calmly ate their breakfast. It wasn't like it was the end of Shelly's trip and she needed to spend as much time as possible pursuing leisure activities before going home. Almost everyone else was going back to the United States or Australia to go back to work. Not Shelly. She was going to be touring around the South Pacific for another two weeks. Her unwillingness to help was totally unacceptable. *Go, go, go, I thought, and don't ever come back!*

I left the Marovo trying to forget many things about this trip. To have people spend all that money to volunteer their time and then act like "little shits" rubbed me wrong. Thankfully, we were able to take good care of people during the trip, but the personnel dramas took their toll on Suzanne and me. I knew I couldn't handle many more trips like that. These folks had even been recommended to us. I couldn't and didn't want to imagine what kind of personalities would volunteer and come out of the woodwork if we had a reality television show. It was time to forget about it and close my eyes on the flight back to America.

CHAPTER

23

In February of 2013, I made another solo trip to the Marovo to help Jason prepare the operating room for the grand opening. There wasn't much time left, as the opening ceremony and first surgeries were scheduled in ten short weeks. For the record, my physical labor contribution to the OR was about .01 percent. Jason and the local guys built the facility, and they did an incredible job. It was likely the best-built structure in the entire country.

Several hours after eating my normal Brisbane Airport breakfast of potato wedges and orange juice, I touched down at Seghe. Jason and Anthony, the hospital administrator, were standing outside as the plane came to a stop. I climbed down the stairs and greeted them. We pulled my two suitcases off the airplane and handed them to the Uepi boat driver, and then the three of us jumped on the Solomon Airlines Dash 8 and headed another ten minutes to Munda. Since Bishop Wilfred had become Moderator Wilfred, he had moved to the headquarters of the United Church in Munda. Munda was not only the headquarters of the United Church of the Solomon Islands but also the site where Christian missionaries from Tasmania had first landed around 1900.

At the Munda airport, we were met by a church staff member who was driving a white Toyota truck. The white Landcruiser bounced us up and down as the driver did his best with the pothole-filled road. We came to a T intersection, where the driver parked the truck to wait for the Moderator. To pass the time, we walked the few streets of Munda and found a little takeout café. There were places for about eight people to sit. The business was owned by a young couple—she a Solomon Islander and he originally from Australia. Their café was called the Leaf House. The owners exuded a lot of energy toward their fledgling business. The sandwich I had blew my mind. It was simple, but one of the best I had ever put in my mouth: fresh avocado in a grilled cheese with thick, homemade bread. Wow, hello Munda! I knew we had to eat there again.

After the delicious sandwich, we headed back to the truck to meet the moderator. He emerged from his meeting and, as always, greeted us joyously. We jumped in the truck and headed down the road to his office alongside the Helena Goldie Hospital. After showing us his office, he took us out to the water to point out the small island where the first missionaries had landed. The coastline was beautiful, and the stories he shared were intriguing.

The moderator arranged a tour of Helena Goldie Hospital for us. He let us go so he could take care of more work. The hospital had been built around 1970 and didn't hide its age well. At the hospital, we met the secretary of health for the United Church and a couple of administrative assistants. An old acquaintance, Soso, a dental assistant, was there with his tall, thin frame and snow-white smile. Soso had joined us on a couple of previous trips to the Marovo, assisting our dentists.

A few minutes after we met the secretary of health, Dr. Jenny Longbottom entered and introduced herself. Her husband, Dr. Graham, wasn't far behind. They were Methodist missionaries from the UK. We had a lovely discussion about the hospital and all the difficulties the Longbottoms experienced in providing care. A lot of the stories were all too familiar. Munda was the closest hospital to Seghe that had a doctor. At this time, Helena Goldie had two doctors and two surgeons.

Graham led us on a tour of the facility. It didn't take me long to realize that the facility needed more than paint and a serious cleaning. It really needed a bulldozer makeover. Jason had told me that Seghe Hospital was awesome compared to Helena Goldie, but until I had seen it for myself, I'd had to take his word for it. The wards were dingy and dark. The overall feeling I got was of filth. The facility actually had an operational film-based x-ray machine. It was very old, and the kicker was that the rotting walls surrounding the x-ray machine were not lined with lead. The outpatient clinic waiting area was outside the x-ray room. If any of those people came within six feet of the outside of the wall, they could very well be receiving radiation without knowing it. In most places, that wouldn't be considered acceptable. Dr. Graham explained that the government had turned them down for a grant that would have paid to have the room lined with lead walls. I would have considered that a priority over other projects.

As we walked through the wards, I couldn't help but recognize a face. It wasn't that the face had been haunting me, but there was no way I would forget her. The little girl from Viru Harbor with lupus was lying in a hospital bed. Her family was there. The looks of despair on all their faces hit me hard. Why? Why was there nothing that could be done for this little girl? She wasn't even ten years old. Her young life held so much promise, yet this disease that we had no way to effectively combat was robbing her of the dreams she may have had. We spoke with the family briefly, and Dr. Graham agreed that he also felt she had lupus and there wasn't much they could do. She should have been out jumping rope or splashing in the water with her friends. It wasn't fair, but unfortunately for her, she would likely languish in a hospital bed until she died. Sometimes I was able to walk away and not think about sad things that I had seen in the Solomon Islands, but this little girl's hopeless look wasn't going to leave my brain anytime soon. It's those memories that make me want to continue the good fight to help this fledgling health care system grow and improve.

A brand-new hospital had recently opened in Gizo. The hospital had been built by the Japanese and was rife with problems from the get-go. Millions had been spent on the project. It was supposedly a nice facility, but as usual, a foreign aid organization had come into the Solomons with its own ideas of what was best. The hospital had some serious power-supply and cooling issues associated with the design. The arrangement had been for the aid organization, the Japanese government, to build the facility and the Solomon Islands Ministry of Health to outfit the inside with equipment and supplies. Evidently, the MOH had simply moved all the old medical equipment from the old hospital into the new facility, so it had ended up being a new building with old equipment. It was a shame that part of those millions spent to build the hospital couldn't have gone to Munda to build a new hospital there. Helena Goldie Hospital seemed to be begging for a bulldozer to put it out of its misery. With the desperate need for new health care infrastructure and the funds to adequately pay health care staff, I couldn't help but think back to the mega-yacht parked off of Honiara. Hundreds of thousands of people in the Solomon Islands could not get access to adequate health care, yet one man could spend hundreds of millions of dollars on a huge boat. Oh, how I would love to stick that punk's nose in one of those old mattresses at Seghe Hospital.

Later that afternoon, the driver picked up me, Jason, and Anthony to visit the moderator at his home. We had been invited for a meeting and dinner. The drive took us from our lodge, down past the hospital and church head-quarters, and around the far end of the runway. The bumpy dirt road took us out of the open and under the forest canopy for a short while. The driver slowed the vehicle and made a sharp left turn. The engine groaned a little as the driver navigated a steep, rock-strewn hill. Near the top, we emerged into an opening in the forest to see the moderator's house and an adjacent meetinghouse. Prior to the house along the road was the garden, with beans and pumpkins growing along the hillside. The view was impressive. The house sat overlooking the middle of the runway and the entire Rendova Lagoon. It was, without a doubt, a view to cherish.

Out came the moderator and his wife, Roselyn. His beaming, infectious smile left us with no option but to be happy and smile in return. We exchanged pleasantries yet again and proceeded into his house to start the meeting. Jason and I had brought Anthony with us because he was the hospital administrator and we were concerned that the church was not formally recognizing his authority. All the staff at Seghe were government employees except for Anthony and the cleaning staff. The church, in effect, was in charge of the facility. Certain people on the hospital staff didn't want to recognize Anthony's authority because he was not a government employee. We needed the church to side with us and put their full faith and backing behind Anthony so the government employees would recognize and respect his authority. The moderator understood and generally agreed with our position.

When the moderator had been the bishop at Seghe, Jason and I had had many conversations with him regarding the importance of finalizing the relationships between the nonprofits and the church through a Memorandum of Understanding. Up until this point, we had not had the time to put the document together. More or less, we wanted formal support on an informal basis until we could get the MOU together and signed. At the end of the meeting, we invited the moderator to participate in the opening of the new operating room the next month. We were confident he would attend, as the facility had been named in his honor.

Regardless of the business that needed to be done, I always enjoyed spending time with Wilfred. The bond between fellow believers can be great, and I feel as though Wilfred and I had great mutual respect and appreciation for each other in our business and spiritual relationship.

The meeting was followed by a fresh dinner prepared by Roselyn. The table was covered in fruits, vegetables, rice (of course), fish, and some sweets. I found it interesting that Roselyn didn't join us for dinner. I had heard that married couples in Melanesia often didn't eat dinner together. She sat in the other room, watching us eat. She smiled and waved when I thanked her for the wonderful meal.

*   *   *

Back at Uepi, we had a couple of days before the head anesthesiologist for the Solomon Islands, Dr. Kaeni Agiomea, was scheduled to arrive. He was a kind, very helpful man, originally from Malaita. He had served the people of the Solomon Islands for years. His dedication to providing good care to his fellow man was evident through our e-mail correspondence and the stories he had shared. I had asked him to fly out to help set up one of our anesthesia machines. Folks at Suzanne's hospital told me that it was best to have an anesthesiologist set up the machine and test it prior to doing surgeries. Jason and I didn't have any experience with anesthesia machines, so I was thrilled when Dr. Kaeni agreed to fly out for one evening to set up the machine. I told him that we had ended up with three anesthesia machines, and he was thrilled when I told him we were donating one of the machines to the Ministry of Health. I could see the excitement in his eyes as we unpacked the machine. His willingness to join the team in May to assist with the first surgeries was very comforting.

Jason and I spent several days organizing all the medical supplies in the OR. We had an Uepi guest, Katrina, who gave up a day of her vacation to help us sort and count items in the OR. She was an enthusiastic helper and vowed to assist in participant recruitment from Sydney. She also had her sights set on joining us on a future medical tour. I loved that type of spirit! Through all the organizing and thinking about where things should go, Jason and I jokingly agreed the surgical team had better not make too many changes. Deep down, we knew changes would be made because neither of us had ever built or outfitted an OR. For that matter, neither of us had ever even spent much time in an OR other than as patients.

I left the OR on that trip feeling really good about being where we needed to be to finish prior to the grand opening. The generator and compressor were on their way from Brisbane with a scheduled arrival well before I was supposed to return at the beginning of May. The generator needed to be installed and tested. The compressor needed to be installed and the suction system tested. The medical air and oxygen systems also needed to be finished and tested.

At the end of the trip, Jason flew back to Honiara with me to take care of some business at the National Referral Hospital. Suzanne had been given a load of orthopedic tools and supplies from the Wilcox Hospital in southern Arizona when it had decommissioned its operating room. Needless to say, the instruments were worth tens of thousands of dollars.

Jason and I had met the only fully trained orthopedist serving in the Solomon Islands a year before. It was a pretty funny encounter. The nurse taking us around the hospital had taken us into the fracture clinic, where the orthopedist had been seeing a patient. I had looked at him, and the image of the stereotypical jock orthopedist had popped into my head. He was standing, talking to the patient behind a partially closed curtain. In both his ears were white earbuds attached to a phone or something in his pocket. He was talking to the patient while wearing the earbuds in his ears. I cracked up laughing, but not out loud. I had never seen such a thing, but the fact that he was an orthopedist had taken it to another level of comedy in my mind.

We had waited a few minutes, and the nurse had asked the orthopedist if he had a minute to speak with us. She introduced us, and the look on the orthopedist's face was classic. It was obvious that international-aid types had been in there before to waste his time. He looked at us like he didn't care one bit about what we had to say. That was until two words came out of my mouth. I told him I had a couple of fragment sets in my basement. The fragment sets contained special plates and screws to join broken bones back together. His head turned back to me, his eyes opened wide, and a smile showed bright white teeth. He had put his hand back out and reintroduced himself and asked Jason and me our names again. I couldn't blame him for his initial response. He had probably thought we were from another international-aid group that was going to deposit a bunch of rusty beds or outdated equipment in his lap. I had learned too much about the mistakes that other aid organizations had made in sending their garbage to the third world to know better than to do that. The orthopedist had been excited to hear about the fragment sets from Arizona and had shared his e-mail address so we could keep in touch.

Back to the present, when Jason and I arrived with a seventy-pound box full of premium orthopedic equipment… The four orthopedic residents looked at the box, full of anticipation. Unfortunately, the doctor we had met before was not in the hospital that day. There were a bunch of leg splints and soft items in the top of the box, so it took a few minutes to get down to the meat of it. As the fragment set came into view, a couple of the residents leaned over to see what I was about to pull out. As my hands emerged with an aluminum case, smiles and excitement flowed between the residents.

When Jason and I opened the case, the docs were thrilled, to say the least. The chief resident pulled out the screwdriver and said, "Now, this is the only one of these in the country. We were using a drill before. That was not the proper tool for the job. We have needed one of these for a long time."

Wow, that was a meaningful donation. We had just changed the way these guys would be able to put broken bones back together. The smiles didn't lie. They were truly grateful for the donation. It was a targeted donation that was very important and useful. Aid isn't about people giving what they think someone needs. It's about asking the folks on the ground what they need and then finding a way to deliver the goods. Just because I have something that I think is useful doesn't mean it will be useful in a developing country. This is where we needed to remove our egos and *listen* to the locals and let them tell us what they really needed. It's not about us; it's about them!

I said good-bye to Jason and flew back to Brisbane on a Thursday afternoon. Peter and Margaret Fletcher had jumped onboard Marovo Medical Foundation with reckless abandon, and I couldn't have been happier. After going on one trip with us, they had decided to hold a fundraiser at their home. The plan was to hold the event in their beautiful front yard. All their children came together and assisted with providing the food. Margaret's brother, Scott McDougal, a well-known artist in Australia, brought over twenty original paintings to sell. He was so kind as to donate a big percentage of all sales to the cause. Peter and Margaret's sons sold raffle tickets throughout the evening. They worked the crowd really well to maximize the raffle ticket sales.

At the end of the night, a $15,000 painting had sold and the donations totaled about $20,000. It blew me away. We had never raised that much money through any of our fundraisers in the States. With their first event, the Fletchers had knocked it out of the park. On top of all that, the residents at a nursing home where Peter worked had decided to donate a brand new $5,000 EKG machine. Was there no end to what the Fletchers were capable of producing? My heart went out to them for putting on such a high-class and successful event for a cause that was so new to their hearts.

Because of the success of Peter and Margaret's fundraiser, the thirteen-hour flight to Los Angeles didn't bother me one bit. I was returning home on a high note. I needed that high note to last as long as possible because things were about to get hectic and stressful.

*   *   *

We were only three weeks away from leaving on the tenth medical tour. Not only was it the tenth tour, but it was the grand opening of the operating room at Seghe and the first surgical tour. Gordon and I were going to go two weeks in advance to help Jason finish last-minute essentials. Many items needed to be crossed off the list before we could operate on someone. The generator had arrived but needed Gordon's electrical prowess to make sure it was hooked up properly. The compressor and Venturi systems needed to be completed and tested. The true test would be whether we could suck a cup of water dry with the suction unit. Friends of the Kellys, Jack and Bar Graham, planned to join us a week in advance of the tour and to stay to help throughout the tour. Jason told me that Jack was a guy who could engineer anything and maintain it in top-notch working order. I liked the sound of that. Jack and Bar had been to Uepi many times. Their children had grown up with Jason and his brother, Wes. Along with several other families, their ties were so close that they were called "the tribe." I'd heard a lot about the tribe but had never met any of the non-Kelly members until now. Jason was thrilled that Jack and Bar were participating in the trip. He gave Jack the specs on what we needed for the medical air system, and Jack took care of designing and compiling the vital components.

Multiple systems needed to work flawlessly for the surgical team to perform successful surgeries. Gordon planned to leave a day or two before the team arrived, so I was counting on Jack to be there should any of the systems go down. The ins and outs of surgery were not my forte. I wasn't sure what systems were vital and what systems could be done without in a pinch. I just wanted everything to work because there was a lot riding on this. Jason had spent more than a year building the facility. He, Gordon, and I had figured out how to engineer the oxygen, suction, and compressed-air delivery systems, and Jason told Jack ahead of time what he wanted in the form of a medical air system.

A few days prior to my departure for Uepi, I received an e-mail from Dr. Kaeni Agiomea, the head Solomon Islands anesthesiologist. The e-mail made me nervous because it stated that he had to pull out of the upcoming tour at the last minute. He explained that the Solomon Islands had an agreement with several other small South Pacific nations to provide anesthesia coverage should one of them be without an anesthesiologist. The country of Nauru, to the northeast of the Solomon Islands, was without an anesthesiologist, so Dr. Agiomea had to meet the obligation and leave for Nauru. I wasn't about to argue with that. Dr. Kaeni was a great guy, and I was thrilled that he had plugged his number two into his spot to join us. We had two anesthesiologists coming with us, but we really wanted involvement and collaboration from the doctors from the Solomon Islands. It was their country, and their participation was paramount to the local people trusting the new operating room.

Not long after I received Dr Kaeni's first e-mail, I received a second message from him saying that the Solomon Islands' surgeon was switching places with another surgeon. They were keeping me on my toes. I couldn't complain about any of our work in the Marovo being stagnant or boring, that's for sure. I didn't know what was coming next.

We had a lot of new personnel to find room for at Uepi. An operating room tech, David Brownstein, was joining us from Suzanne's hospital. He had never been on this type of trip and was excited, to say the least. Several months prior to the trip, David and a colleague, Sarah Lion, had visited our home a few times to identify and group the various surgical instruments that the Wilcox Hospital had donated. Suzanne had known what a lot of them were but, not being a surgeon, had needed David and Sarah to set us straight on what we needed and how to group the instruments for various procedures. David was looking forward to seeing the instruments again at Seghe.

The new surgeon's name was Dr. Douglas Pikacha. The last-minute musical chairs seemed to be standard for the Solomon Islands. When I e-mailed Jason to let him know the name of the new surgeon, his response was noteworthy. He said Dr. Pikacha was the most senior surgeon in the country and was from Telina village in the Marovo Lagoon. Awesome! Having a truly local surgeon for our first surgical tour couldn't have been better scripted. Surgeries were uncharted territory for the group. Bad things could happen during operations, and it was good to have the local hero from the Marovo Lagoon there in the event of a bad outcome.

The usual pre-trip frenzy was in full swing. During the month prior to our departure, Suzanne painstakingly sorted through the medicine lists. We always had to wait until the last minute to hear from the National Medical Stores in Honiara about what medicines they had in stock. Whatever medicines they were lacking, we had to purchase locally and take with us. Because I was leaving two weeks early, I needed to know the medicine answers immediately. Showing restraint in e-mails was not my forte, and I had sent some forceful e-mails to the folks in Honiara to get the lead out and give me the answers I needed! The remaining medicines and supplies that we needed to take had to be distributed to all the participants. Physicians only ever carried medicines, and nonmedical folks normally packed supplies for us. Suzanne didn't have time to ship the items, so I burned the midnight oil to take care of business. She had enough on her plate with trying to take care of patients at her practice in Arizona, let alone all of her patients in the Marovo Lagoon. Her stress was evident, and adding the surgical component ratcheted the pressure to near-explosive levels.

Gordon and I met at LAX. I don't think we had flown to the Solomon Islands together since the first group trip. I was tense, as usual. Gordon told me many times that I needed to lighten up. For some reason, I always seemed to get mentally mired down when it came to dealing with heavy responsibility. I was at a crossroads in my life. Things between Suzanne and me were at the lowest they'd been in the ten years of our marriage. We knew we needed help, and we were going to get it. I may have let the seriousness of the Solomon Islands medical project take me down further. I took the project seriously, to say the least. Since having left a university faculty position to become a domestic stallion, this project had become my calling in life, and I gave it everything I had. Unfortunately, I had other things that needed to be sorted out so my marriage and the Solomon Islands project could thrive. Suzanne and I commented that we had found our hearts in the Solomon Islands but may have lost our relationship there. I hoped that wasn't the case.

As had come to be the pattern on my several recent trips through Australia, Peter and Margaret took excellent care of Gordon and me. Margaret had a knack for putting together the most simple yet delicious meals ever. The crab in fresh avocado blew my mind. The lamb she threw in the oven induced taste-bud euphoria. I was blessed to have such good care taken of me while stopping in Brisbane. Their hospitality toward our transient team members and their intent desire to help us improve the health care scene in the Marovo made their true caring nature as evident as the bright sunshine. I looked forward to more fun and meaningful interactions with the Fletchers.

At Seghe, there was no option but to hit the ground running. The generator had arrived and needed to be installed. The old generator sat in a small shack of a building outside the main ward. The walls were covered in corrugated iron, and the concrete pad was fully saturated in diesel and oil. Spider webs and dirt were ubiquitous throughout the 5' x 8' shack. Over the years, I had seen many different things in the tall grass around that building, some disgusting and some interesting. This morning, I saw a small python slowly stalking through the blades. I made sure the snake was far away without telling Brenda, the head nurse. It was her day off, and she had come up to help, wielding a machete. Solomon Islanders do not like snakes, but I knew how beneficial pythons are for eating rodents and other critters, so I didn't want to alert the bush knife-wielding matron to the location of the serpent. Brenda ripped the machete back and forth to cut down the grass around the door of the shack. She made quick work of a couple of saplings that were impeding our access. Unbelievably, she cut through some thick boards that we needed to move the generator. Not only was she an incredible nurse, but I would have picked her over anyone in a knife fight.

Jason grabbed several of the workers who were building EU-funded staff houses. As they arrived at the shack, Gordon and I finished removing the nuts that held the generator to the concrete pad. The control panel and gas tank were then removed. The only thing left was to pull out the heavy diesel motor. We set up two boards to slide the motor down to the ground. The floor of the shack sat close to twelve inches above the ground, so sliding the compact, yet densely heavy, motor was a much better idea than trying to carry it. As the workers slid the motor down the boards, it quickly became evident why they didn't want anyone on the downhill side of the unwieldy block of steel. When the motor was halfway down the hastily assembled ramp, the ramp began to buckle. Fortunately, the motor wasn't needed, because at that instant, the board on the left snapped and the motor tumbled to the ground. That was one way to make room for the new generator.

With the old one out, it was time to bring the new generator into the shack. I stood back and filmed while the same group of guys, with Jason in the lead, pulled a 2000-pound generator across a grassy field. They had attached a large tow strap to the steel skids on which the unit was mounted.

A few pipes and boards had been gathered on which they rolled the unit along. It was as if I were watching the pyramids being built. They slowly and methodically pulled the generator over the pipes, and then the person in the back pulled the other pipes forward. The unit slid nicely, with the only serious consideration being that it be kept upright without tipping over. As they approached the narrow, elevated doorway, more and more jostling and repositioning took place. Each movement seemed to require more energy. Half the guys jumped into the shack with the tow strap. In a well-choreographed effort, they lifted one end of the one-ton generator onto the edge of the doorway. The testosterone-filled chorus erupted in shouts and grunts as they heaved the rest of the machine through the narrow doorway. In true Solomon Islands fashion, the guys started laughing after expending all that energy. They worked hard and enjoyed themselves in the process. Happiness during manual labor could be hard to find in a lot of places in the world, but it was almost always a given in the Marovo.

With the generator in place, Gordon needed to make all the electrical connections. When he had designed the solar power system, he had mentioned that the wiring needed to be done correctly so the inverters would instantly recognize the electrical input of the generator and then allow the generator to serve as the primary power source for the hospital. The generator was, of course, going to provide the primary power during surgeries, but it would also quickly top off the batteries if they happened to be low. We turned the generator on first to make sure it would run. It was a beautiful sound.

Jason and I couldn't stay because we had to continue sorting items in the OR. An hour or so later, Gordon came in to the OR and said with a smile, "It's hooked up and running. I was a little nervous turning the breaker over on the inverter to accept the AC input from the generator, but it took it without a problem."

What a relief! We told Gordon we hadn't seen the lights flicker or anything click on and off. It had been a seamless transition from the solar power system to the generator. We had removed the main albatross from around our necks. The other systems had to wait until Jack arrived in a couple days time.

Fortunately, customs didn't cause too many problems for Jack as he carried a large haul of shiny stainless steel parts into the country. After I met

Jack and Bar at Uepi, Jack opened the suitcase containing nothing but OR bling. The shiny metal was attractive, to say the least. It didn't take me long to realize that Jack was the man! He had hit a home run for us, and I hadn't even worked with him yet. I looked forward to getting to know him and Bar over the next few weeks.

Jason's brother, Wes, had also arrived early. He was supposed to have been at Seghe a couple of days before, but because of an incident on his flight, he had been delayed. His flight from Brisbane to Honiara had been only thirty minutes from landing when the windshield in the cockpit shattered. There were multiple layers of glass, and fortunately, only one had broken, but the bad news was that they had to turn around and fly three hours all the way back to Brisbane. There were no maintenance facilities available in Honiara to fix that type of a problem. It had taken Solomon Airlines several days to replace the glass because the replacement glass had to come from another country. They had to lease a plane from another airline in order to meet their flight obligations. I'm sure Wes was happy to finally be in the Marovo.

The slogging at the OR continued, literally. We had some serious rainfall as we worked on finishing the final critical systems. The rain was coming down so hard that the water coming off the roof alongside the OR was getting close to running over the foundation. Some of the guys quickly dug out a deeper and more effective drain that ran along the entire front of the building and around the back to the drainage ditch. The water started to move and recede, which was a relief. We'd done too much to have water infiltrate the building a few days prior to the grand opening.

The concrete walkway was as muddy as muddy could be. Our last project prior to the group arriving would be to coat the entire concrete walkway with epoxy concrete sealer the same product we had used on the concrete floor in the OR. It was marketed in the States for garage floors and worked really well for these applications too.

Jack and Jason installed a big stainless steel plate that held the master air pressure and suction gauges. The plate was on the wall near the OR table so the anesthesiologist had quick access to the air and suction main switches. The gauges were a couple of millimeters too small in diameter to completely cover the holes in the plate, so we had quite a difficult time getting them lined up and fastened tight. We moved the air compressor into the small room adjoining the back of the OR. We named the building adjoining the OR Tank Command, as it held the three G cylinders of oxygen, the scuba tanks for the medical air system, and the Boss air compressor. The collective tank pressure in the room was a little scary. We definitely needed to put some "no smoking" signs around there so an unintentional oxygen ignition wouldn't propel the entire building to the moon.

Jason and Gordon hooked the surgical scrub sink up to the water line and thoroughly tested it. The sink was another piece I had purchased from the government surplus auction website. I don't think the sink had ever been used before. The pump flushed a lot of rusty water, but it was working well and the rust would be eliminated. The sink had a pump, so we didn't need to provide the sink with pressurized water. That was a huge score. The sink also had a heating unit: a major bonus. Things were looking good.

The lack of guttering around the entire OR roof was causing a lot of mud, and there was a water tank in front of the OR that wasn't plumbed properly, which caused additional water to pool in front of the building. The outlet of the tank wasn't set up to properly take water out of the tank, so when it rained, the tank overflowed. Fortunately, there was a fair amount of downspout pipe lying around, so Jack launched into another project. His batteries didn't seem to need recharging. Jack and a few of Jason's helpers dug and slogged in the mud for several hours. I could hear the sweat squelching in Jack's boots as he walked by. We all laughed at how dirty he was. There weren't many square inches of his body that weren't covered in mud. Talk about taking one for the team. Jack was on my A list from there on out. It was a privilege to have someone so energetic and dedicated to a project that he had just become involved with. The world needs more Jack Grahams!

The final patch of concrete, for the walkway, that we poured on Saturday had cured by Monday morning. The entire walkway connecting the main ward to the OR was ready to be cleaned and painted with tan epoxy. The team was scheduled to arrive Monday afternoon, but they would be bypassing the hospital and heading straight to Uepi. We had only until three in the afternoon to finish everything. The opening ceremony was the next day.

We vacuumed the entire OR. All surfaces had been wiped down, and the place was spotless. It looked incredible! I didn't have a lot of time to stand back and ponder what Jason had built, but damn, that boy had skills! Impressed was a strong word, but not nearly strong enough to sum up my feelings regarding the capstone project in Jason's four years of volunteering at Seghe Hospital. His blood, sweat, and tears, along with a lot of his hard-earned money, had gone into Seghe Hospital. I think culturally it may have been hard for the locals to understand how much of his life Jason had put on hold for the hospital. I hope they knew that it was his devotion to improving the facilities at Seghe that had made that OR a diamond in the rough. Suzanne and I had coordinated the medical, international logistics, and fundraising from the beginning, but Jason had been the domestic coordinator, construction manager, cheerleader, referee, personal therapist, and chief negotiator. Suzanne and I were very proud of all he had done, and he was only twenty-six years old. I can't even remember if I cared about anyone but myself at twenty-six. Jason's elevated level of caring and commitment to the Marovo Lagoon community continued to chart new highs in my book of respect. He hadn't stopped working on the community's behalf, and I hoped he had a lot more energy in him.

Time flew by on that last workday. It went so fast that we were late greeting the Solomon Airlines flight from Honiara. On each trip, I liked to videotape the team emerging from the aircraft, but when I ran up to the terminal, they were all waiting, as the plane was about to depart. As I introduced myself to the folks I hadn't met before, it became apparent to me that nearly half of the group was missing. David Brownstein explained that their flight from Brisbane had been delayed and they hadn't made it to the domestic terminal in time for the flight to Seghe. Wow, that was exciting. There we were, supposedly ready for the opening ceremony for the OR the next morning, and half the group was stuck in Honiara for the night. One thing was for sure about air travel in the Solomon Islands: Nothing was for sure.

Jason spoke with the Solomon Airlines agent, who reassured us that the others would be arriving around 8:30 the next morning. I couldn't figure out why the Solomon Islands' surgeon, Dr. Pikacha, hadn't been on the first plane. Bata, the anesthesiologist, said he had been at the airport and then had gone home. Bata figured Dr. Pikacha would come out on the next flight with the rest of the group.

I wanted to see Suzanne, but she was stuck in Honiara with Hal Gooch and some others. I hadn't seen her in a couple of weeks, and I was looking forward to her smile and rock-like presence within the medical team.

Later that night, I found it hard to fall asleep. Knowing that Suzanne and the other part of the team hadn't made it as scheduled threw a variable in my brain that I didn't want to address. The grand opening of the operating room was scheduled in just a few hours, and one of the stars of the show was still a hundred miles away. I reminded myself that I had to have faith that they would make it on the next morning's flight.

CHAPTER

24

*B*efore breakfast the next morning, Jason and I busily collected supplies and equipment to take to the hospital. Not only were we going to celebrate the opening of the OR, but we would also have a half day of clinic at the hospital. All the equipment, including the portable EKG machine, blood analyzer, and portable ultrasound, were on the boat, ready to go. Several bags of nursing supplies and medicines were also packed and ready for the twenty-minute ride to Seghe.

The boat ride to Seghe had never been filled with so much anticipation and excitement for me before. The extreme clarity of the water paralleled the clarity in my head. Yes, yes, yes, everything was fitting into place. All the time and money put into this project had definitely been the right thing for the people of the Marovo. All of the hard work over the past eighteen months was about to be made public. The operating room at Seghe was to officially open in just over an hour. I could barely contain myself!

I hadn't heard anything about Suzanne and the rest of the group that morning, so I hoped Solomon Airlines would come through and deliver them to Seghe as planned. Between conversations with folks on the boat, I gazed at the passing water. The coral heads zipping by below held great intrigue in my mind. I knew there were so many discoveries to be made below the surface. I almost wished we could slow down to get a better look at what was scurrying below.

The water's surface was like glass. It was a calm morning in the Marovo, and the stage was set to knock some people's socks off after the ribbon cutting. I couldn't wait to see Suzanne's face. I had spent a lot of time away from her, helping to coordinate various aspects of the project. Hopefully, the splendor within those four walls would engender a certain sense of happiness toward all our efforts.

As we passed Patutiva village, I had no idea if the plane had arrived. Even if the plane had arrived, had our team members been on it? If not, the word buzzkill would have fallen short in capturing the true level of my disappointment. There would be no option but to delay the ceremony if the plane didn't arrive. The ceremony wouldn't be the same without Suzanne. She and I had gone down this road together. It had been her idea to build the operating room in the first place. Yes, Jason and I had playfully cursed her name many a time during the construction process, but her presence was nonnegotiable for the ceremony to be complete.

Thinking back about the conditions that Suzanne and I initially saw on that first trip to the hospital left me speechless. Comparing those images to the inside of what was surely the nicest operating room in the entire country created a dichotomy of epic proportions. Together, we needed to relish this moment like no other. The progress had been swift and effective. Jason's businesslike demeanor and surefire resolve to build nothing but the best was going to propel us into a celebration of grand proportions. I had made a special purchase at Duty Free in Brisbane and knew that the three of us needed to find the time at the end of the trip to reflect and celebrate.

As we got closer to the hospital, my focus shifted to filming our arrival at Seghe. I knew there would be some fireworks of some sort, so I had my lens at the ready. My eyeballs were focused on the hill leading to the hospital and thus didn't even see the boat zip in behind us. Before I could see it, I heard Suzanne's voice say, "Hello!"

I said quietly, "Thank you, Lord!" The ceremony could proceed.

Most of the folks on the two boats didn't know one another. The group size, including local nursing staff, was going to be near thirty on this trip. It was our largest group by at least eight people. I filmed as people exited the boats at Seghe. Handshakes and introductions occurred at a rapid clip. I gave Suzanne a brief hug and kiss. Public displays of affection were frowned upon in Solomon Islands customs.

As the team walked up the short hill to the hospital, out came the warriors. There were several of them, and they were wielding handmade hatchets and shields. Their clothes were minimal. Paint covered their bodies, and their voices echoed loudly with incoherent fighting words. Hatchets cocked and ready to strike, they approached members of the team with fervor … for a few short moments. Before long, they were laughing and running away. One of the warriors was John Baticolo, one of the nurses at the hospital. John's quiet, reserved demeanor was in stark contrast to his thespian take on vintage Marovo headhunters.

I was last to the hospital. My efforts to capture as much of the event as possible were paying off. Reverend Moderator Wilfred Kurepitu and Jason were standing by the entrance to the outpatient clinic as I approached. Wilfred had a big smile for me, as usual. Because I was filming them, he told a joke to Jason while pointing at me. He was a godly man, yet his feet were planted firmly on terra firma. He and I came from two different worlds, yet we had a common bond in faith. I knew that if I needed to bend his ear, he would provide not only that but also his heart. I valued his friendship immensely, and I was thrilled that he was present to cut the ribbon to his namesake operating room.

I was the last to walk up to the building and was also the last to have a lei put around my neck by one of the local girls. It was a string of tightly packed, intensely fragrant frangipani.

Out in front of the hospital was a bamboo band playing beautiful, crisp notes. The melodious tunes filled the tropical air with a sense of welcome like no other. The players used rubber shoe inserts to strike the ends of various lengths of bamboo to evoke a hollow tubular tune. A set of bamboo pipes consisted of anywhere from five to ten pipes of bamboo or even PVC of varying diameter and length.

Every person I looked at in our group wore a big smile. People were filming the band and enjoying all the fanfare. Inside the patient waiting area were a couple dozen plastic chairs fanned out. When the band stopped, Jimmy, the malaria technician, asked everyone to be seated. He served as the master of ceremonies for the event. As was customary, he introduced one of the local clergy, who started with the invocation. After the prayer, Jimmy asked us to proceed out to the front of the operating room. Holy cow! The entire walkway leading from the main ward to the operating room was covered. The roof was held up by a series of 6" x 6" posts. Every post was decorated in a beautiful assortment of hibiscus, orchids, greenery, and balloons. The scene was stunning. Jason told me the hospital staff had been up all night preparing the decorations. Emotions ran high. Smiles were ubiquitous. I had known the nurses were proud of the hospital, but this was a level of pride I'd had yet to see in the Marovo. A great deal of time and energy had been spent gathering all the flowers and vegetation to make the beautiful decorations. No one had paid the nurses to do this. These gestures of gratitude and celebration were from the heart and came with no strings attached. I personally knew all the nurses, and I would have been mistaken to think they didn't love their jobs and love working at the much improved Seghe Hospital.

Upon our arrival, Suzanne had been notified that she would need to make some remarks. Public speaking was not her bailiwick, but she had become very proficient at impromptu public addresses. In the Marovo, we never knew when we would be asked to say a few words. Most of the time, this fell either on Jason's shoulders or on mine because we were operating in a male-dominated society, but this time, someone had gotten it right. They knew who the real boss was, and I was glad they had asked her to address the gathering. She had probably treated more patients in the Marovo than any other doctor in history. The number of patients in the Marovo Lagoon who considered Suzanne to be their primary care doctor was large and growing. The continuity of care that she and the other docs with Marovo Medical provided was one of the driving forces behind our success. The people of the Marovo knew we weren't a one-and-done medical team but were the real deal and were here yet again to put a lasting mark on the community's medical facility. Suzanne was trusted by many in the lagoon, and her words were invaluable to everyone in attendance.

After speeches from several people, including Suzanne, Jason, the bishop of Seghe, and the moderator, the moment of truth was before us. The moderator and the bishop gathered in front of the red ribbon and bow that were stretched between two poles leading to the OR. Well over seventy-five people were in attendance, yet at this moment, silence dominated the scene. The moderator held the pair of scissors in his hand. The bishop laid his hand on top of the moderator's hand in unity. After a few more moments of silence, the moderator prayed, "In the name of the Father, Son, and Holy Spirit, I pronounce this operating theater open!" Cheers and applause followed the cutting of the ribbon. The moderator held the scissors and one side of the ribbon high for a couple of extra seconds. He was beaming from ear to ear. I was choking back tears, trying to keep it together and keep the camera steady. All the pain, mental anguish, and dedication I had felt over the course of this project flooded my brain and filled my heart. Man … we had done it!

Now all the team had to do was successfully knock someone out, cut them open, and sew them up and this would be a real operating room. Jason and Suzanne were dueling for who would make the first incision. We knew it wasn't going to be Jason because he didn't have a medical license, and Suzanne was needed in the villages, so neither of them would get the honor.

The next day yielded the first incision and thus the first in a series of surgical cases. With the oversight of Dr. Douglas Pikacha, Dr. Emily Huang, a third-year surgical resident at the University of California San Francisco, had the honors of doing the first surgery at the OR. I had met Emily while I was lecturing at the National Youth Science Camp (NYSC) in West Virginia the year before. I was thrilled she had the honor. I had quite a history with NYSC, and Emily was one of several past camp delegates and staff members who had joined us on one of the medical tours. I was scheduled to speak at NYSC a month after the surgical tour, and I couldn't wait to deliver the news that the first surgery had been performed by a former NYSC delegate. Emily was at the top of her field, and I was thrilled she could add this little interlude to her quiver of life experiences.

The first case wasn't a big one, just the removal of skin lesion slightly larger than an inch in diameter, but it was what we needed to get the ball rolling. The doors were open and we were in business, so to speak. Anthony was charged with making sure all the systems were running properly—most important was ensuring that the generator didn't run out of diesel. We had instructed the team on what to do in the event of a generator shutdown.

A major bonus was that we had four surgeons on the team. The plan was to take either Emily or Stephanie Lin, the vascular surgeon, with us to the villages each day. Douglas would stay at the OR to help with any local angst about having surgery at the new facility.

Having a surgeon in the villages with us really helped with efficiency. Up until this point, if a wound, large boil, or laceration trauma had walked in the door, one of the medicine docs had to stop seeing medical patients to attend to the surgical issue. There was no question they could address the problem, but it slowed down the efficiency of the clinic immensely. Having a dedicated surgeon in the villages was like traveling in style! The surgeon could also prescreen potential surgical cases to be sent to Seghe.

Stephanie and Kevin Fukuda, the anesthesiologist from San Francisco, had both done multiple international surgical trips. They were fantastic assets in helping us figure out items in the OR. They pointed out things that would work well, and a fair number of things that needed to change or were lacking. Jason and I had to take all their recommendations and concerns at face value. I had been primarily responsible for outfitting the operating room with the equipment, and Jason had been primarily responsible for designing and building the facility. It wasn't easy to hear that things needed to change, but throughout the entire creation process, we'd never had someone who had worked in an operating room visit the facility to give us guidance on, for example, where the autoclave should be located. We needed to hear all these things, but after eighteen months of hard work, we also wanted them to be excited for the place and flexible with how the facility was set up. I think they were genuinely impressed with what we had put together without any prior surgical knowledge or guidance. Their recommendations were invaluable, and we would make changes … after the trip. I couldn't have asked for a more experienced surgical team for the first trip.

Two days after the opening of the OR, two more members of the surgical team arrived. Grant Mills was our third anesthesiologist, or anesthetist, depending upon where you are from. Grant brought a colleague, Nigel Peck, a general surgeon who specialized in surgical and nonsurgical procedures focusing on the upper digestive tract. Nigel brought his portable ultrasound and nearly a dozen pieces of abdominal mesh for use in hernia repair. Mesh was expensive. I liked these guys already!

The first full clinic on Wednesday was at Chea village. Chea and Chubikopi were adjacent to one another on Marovo Island. Chea was Seventh-day Adventist, and Chibikopi was United Church. Our tours had switched back and forth between the villages from one trip to the next. The SDA villages were often better kept than the United Church villages for one reason or another. The SDA as a whole seemed to be much more controlling of its members' lives than the United Church was. For instance, word in the lagoon was that SDA members were not allowed to chew betel nut. I heard that many of them did chew betel nut but had learned to brush their teeth to eliminate the telltale red stains. By far, the SDA folks did have better-looking teeth than the United Church folks. I didn't know a lot about the origins of the SDA church, but it seemed almost too squeaky clean for me. Maybe that was just my eighteen years of living in Salt Lake City speaking for me, though.

At Chea, we set up shop in the guesthouse. It was a little awkward, as a couple of guests were staying there when we showed up en masse. Those of us who needed to be in the guest rooms upstairs had to wait fifteen to twenty minutes for the guests to leave. I felt bad, but it really wasn't our fault. The village had known for a month or more that we were coming on that day. I wasn't surprised with the mix-up in the slightest, however. Communication in the Solomons had been referred to as coconut wireless; it was sometimes effective and sometimes not.

The guesthouse was a light blue color, and the stilts it sat on elevated it well above ground level. As usual, we set up the triage, registration, and nursing stations underneath the building. On previous trips, Kate Wilson had been set up to pull teeth under the building. Unfortunately, this was our first trip without a dentist. There would be a lot of dental patients who would not get their problems fixed, but I had simply been unable to attract a dentist to join us for the trip.

We had two fantastic nurses with us on the trip. Bill Flanagan and Aliria Munoz were top-notch ICU nurses at their respective hospitals in San Francisco and Phoenix. They spent the majority of the first clinic day hunkered down under the guesthouse. They managed the triage station, gave injections, and cleaned and dressed wounds whenever needed. I assured them they wouldn't be stuck under a building throughout the entire trip.

Our first ever summer intern for Marovo Medical Foundation, Catherine Lok, served as the runner for the first couple of days. She probably climbed close to 1,000 steps that first day, taking patients up and down from triage to the doctors' offices and back again. She was young and energetic and was the perfect person to scale the staircase all day long. She earned her keep for the entire trip before lunch that first day.

Upstairs, the doctors had to share rooms as usual. Brooke Myers, our first real pharmacist, and I set up the pharmacy out on the verandah outside the exam rooms. We had a couple of villagers nail some sheets from the ceiling of the verandah, as I had experienced the sun's sinister angles and heat before at that spot. We didn't want to cook, and we definitely didn't want the medicines to cook. The flow was good for us because the docs didn't have far to go to ask the pharmacist questions.

Stephanie had her own surgical room at the end of the building in the event of needing to do a minor procedure. It didn't take long before her surgical skills were needed. A teenage girl arrived at the clinic with a massive boil in her heel. I wasn't aware of the situation until I needed some translation help from Jason. I looked for him below the building but couldn't find him. I walked outside the doctor's rooms and didn't see or hear him. Then, I found him. I heard painful noises coming out of the girl with the heel abscess. As I walked into the surgical room, I saw Jason lying on top of the girl to keep her immobilized. My next, gut-wrenching, view was of Stephanie burying a scalpel deep into the young lady's heel. It wasn't what I had been expecting to see as I peeked around the corner. There were many times during the trips when my needs had to take the backseat, and this was certainly one of them. I had no problem continuing on past the room. I didn't need to see that scene any longer. It was perfect that Stephanie had been there to work on the young lady, especially because she identified the need to send the young lady to the OR because the foot was going to need another round or two of surgical debridement. Evidently, large boils could develop additional pockets of pus inside the main boil. All these areas must be cut open to ensure that the entire volume of pus can properly drain. Local anesthesia was not going to cover the amount of digging and exploration that the surgeons would need to do to fix the problem. A nerve block or general anesthesia would be necessary for the amount of cleaning that her heel required to get back to normal.

As the first week went by, I found myself in a mental place I had not been before on any of the previous trips. I was thoroughly enjoying myself and actually having fun. Having a real pharmacist on the trip allowed me to have a nearly carefree experience. Not only was Brooke there to lead the pharmacy team, but the entire trip was running without a hitch. The team members were working together flawlessly. Everyone did what was asked without incident. Nearly all the team members were on their first trip, but they worked as if they had been there multiple times. I felt like I was in a dream world. The team blew me away! After ten trips, I finally felt like I wanted to party all night long at the upcoming barge party. I was known for turning in shortly after the barge returned to Uepi. Not this time. I planned to dance the night away!

The first Friday of the trip was at Ngari Ngari, which had historically been a slow day. As a result of the planned slow day, Suzanne and Jason decided to visit with the surgical team for the day. We had been visiting Ngari Ngari for the past three trips. Ngari Ngari was located within the same village as Vakabo but located on a different Island. We had visited Vakabo before, until I had witnessed an unfortunate and reckless act by a teen male toward one of our doctors. The female doctor had been writing in the patient registry at the front of the school building when the teen had clandestinely approached her from behind. The doctor had been unaware that the teen had been standing behind her, thrusting his pelvis back and forth toward her rear end. He had turned around and caught the eyes of his friends who were watching and laughing. Sadly, the doctor had paid $5000 to fly halfway around the world to take care of that little shit, along with his entire family. He was a teenager, but come on! Little did the perpetrator know I had witnessed the entire event. At the end of the day, I had shared the incident with Jason. I was pissed off, to say the least. I wanted something done about this and considered anything less than swift punishment unacceptable. I didn't tell the doctor, and to this day, I don't think she is aware of the incident. Some time after our departure, Jason had shared with the village our disgust and anger regarding what had transpired. The leadership void at Vakabo had precipitated no corrective or punitive action toward the youth. As a result of nothing being done, we had decided not to visit Vakabo again. This was why we now found ourselves visiting Ngari Ngari. Both villages were part of the same tribal group, so some people from Vakabo attended the clinic, but not many, as it was a fairly long canoe paddle between the villages.

It was an uneventful day for us at Ngari Ngari, but Jason, Suzanne, and the surgical team had a different experience. Upon prepping for the first surgical patient, who had a hernia, Theresa Fletcher had noticed a man in the outpatient clinic with a severe laceration on his forearm. The slice was nearly two inches wide and close to eight inches long. Theresa, a fantastic nurse, walked back to the surgical team and said, "I think we should take a look at the gentleman in the outpatient clinic. He has cut his arm."

Suzanne told me that she had initially been a little skeptical about needing to bump the hernia patient out of line. As she had looked at the arm wound, however, she had instantly known it was a no-brainer. This guy was heading to surgery first. Evidently, forty-five minutes earlier, he had been carrying some sort of metal box and part of the box had either fallen apart or slipped out of his hands. As the box had fallen to the ground, a sharp edge had sliced through his forearm. The gaping wound was so deep and extensive that three of his tendons were completely severed. This was a serious injury anywhere in the world.

With the assistance of Nigel's portable ultrasound machine, Kevin, one of the anesthesiologists, was able to do a nerve block on the patient's arm. From there, Douglas took over with Stephanie assisting. Before long, the patient was sewed up and in recovery.

What would have happened had the operating room and our team not been there? The nurses would have done a great job dressing the wound and would have put the wheels in motion to have the patient transferred to Gizo or Honiara. If he had been lucky, he would have been on a plane that afternoon. Even had he arrived in Gizo or Honiara that afternoon, the chances of him getting into surgery would have been slim. With time slipping by, the risk of serious infection rises. Also, the longer the tendons are severed, the harder it may be to reattach them. For that man on that day, it was truly a miracle that we were there in a brand-new operating room. Suzanne commented that the wound had been so fresh the tendons had not retracted back into their sheaths. Forty-five minutes from accident to the OR was incredible timing and probably would have never happened in the United States or Australia.

The surgical group had a second interesting case that Friday. A local man was scheduled to have one of his breasts removed. The condition was called gynecomastia. He had an abnormal amount of benign breast tissue growth that made one breast very large. Obviously, this had been a challenge to live with in a culture that knew so little about the human body. With the heat and humidity raging every day, men often toiled shirtless in their gardens or while out fishing in their dugout canoes. I couldn't imagine the ridicule and joking he must have faced throughout his life.

The procedure went off without a hitch. Strangely, a few days after the procedure, he returned to the hospital with blood pooling behind the sutured wound. The team cleaned it out, and yet the blood returned. Here was one of the difficulties of doing surgeries without having a good family history and also without advanced lab capabilities. The man later mentioned that his father and uncle had problems with bleeding. That would have been good to know prior to the surgery. Kevin Fukuda took some of the blood in a test tube to do a poor man's coagulation test, as he called it. He walked around with the blood for quite a while; it took much longer than normal for the blood to coagulate. The man had a hematologic disorder that we could not adequately identify or address. Fortunately, this happened at the end of the trip. Douglas took him on the plane to the National Referral Hospital in Honiara to continue to keep abreast of the issue.

Ah, the weekend had arrived. It had been my best trip so far. Suzanne seemed distant, but everything was running so smoothly, it was hard for me to understand why I was finally able to unwind and she didn't seem to be enjoying herself. I figured her sense of remoteness was solely related to issues between the two of us, but I wasn't positive. The seriousness of the project and the amount of responsibility I'd had to take on to make the project a success had taken away from my ability to be happy, light, and spontaneous with Suzanne. I hope I'm not writing an obituary for our marriage, but time will tell.

Traveling the world, not having a care for anyone else was easy. Living only for me, me, me, had been a dream. Who cared about anything else as long as I, I, I had been happy? I don't think I could ever go back to that type of life. The thought of spending weekends on the golf course makes me want to chew my arm off. The world is sick, and for those of us with the means to not assist those in need is utterly reprehensible to me. The minute I had seen the need at Seghe and felt called to rectify the situation, my life had taken on a serious note. I think that was a good thing, but letting it be one of the chinks in the armor that has degraded our relationship has not been something I would have foreseen or wanted. I hope it will not be so.

The final week of the tour was going well. Jason commented that he had never seen the nurses at Seghe walking around with so much pride in their voices and demeanor. Hovering around the surgical registry, we could tell they knew they worked at a special place now. They knew the operating room at Seghe was the nicest in the entire country. They knew that people far beyond Seghe cared deeply about the facility. They knew they had purpose and that their skills and talents were valued. They had every reason in the world to walk around with their heads held high! When Jason shared the news of the level of pride at Seghe, I had a hard time holding back the tears. True meaning in one's life can be hard to find, but it had just smacked me in the face.

With the last day of the trip upon us, the medical team was going to Tinge. It also meant someone would clandestinely put a cooler full of beer on the boat to celebrate at the end of the clinic day. The weather at Seghe that morning was uneventful. The ride to Tinge took us across the widest part of the lagoon past Seghe. The water at Seghe was so clear and calm that I asked Jason to stop the boats over top of the sunken P-38 Lightning at the end of the runway. There it was. The water was crystal clear, and the outline of the wings and dual fuselages were vividly on display. After the two-minute stop just for fun, we quickly headed toward the open ocean.

Theresa Fletcher was with us. She was the only member of the team who had not had a chance to visit a village on the tour. She had been a vital asset to the surgical team with prepping and recovering patients along with myriad of other tasks. She was excited to help us and also to have a chance to explore a village. It would also be her first day working alongside her husband, Dr. Mark Fletcher. Mark and our friend Peter Fletcher were brothers and in practice together in Brisbane. Mark was having a blast on the trip, and his funny antics were part of the reason I was thoroughly enjoying the experience.

The boats weaved back and forth between small islands surrounded by the most enticing colored water in the world. We hadn't proceeded beyond the islands before we encountered the first ocean swells. The robust swells at this location seemed to conflict with the calm winds and beautiful skies surrounding our journey up until this point. We passed the last protected island, and boom! There was an angry ocean in front of us. The swells were large, and white caps adorned the waves as far as the eye could see. We had so many people with us that we actually had three boats this day. Jason sent the small tinny in for a closer inspection of the landing area. The beach at Tinge was unprotected. There was a small reef, but it didn't extend far enough along the beach to provide a sheltered anchorage.

The other two boats full of people sat out in the ocean, bobbing up and down. The swells were so big that people in my boat were putting their hands up in the air as we crested the swells as if we were on a roller coaster. The conditions were not good for folks who had issues with seasickness. As the sun baked and the waves rolled, we waited nearly fifteen minutes for the tinny to come back. As the boat approached, I had a sinking feeling that the news wasn't good. Jason conversed in Pidgin with the driver and then discussed the findings with me. It wasn't safe. There were always a lot of sick babies at Tinge for us to treat, so it was a hard decision to make, but we had to take account of our safety first, and so we decided to turn around. That was the first time in ten trips that we had ever not made it to Tinge. There was no way to notify the village, but they knew very well the location of their village and how difficult it could be to access if the weather didn't cooperate. Hopefully, the seas would cooperate on our next trip.

At the end of the trip, Jason, Suzanne, and I sat on the welcome jetty and opened a bottle of Dom Perignon that I had bought at Duty Free in Brisbane especially for this moment. We reflected on the past several years with a lot of joy and pride. We were all tired. Surprisingly, Suzanne commented on how she felt she wasn't really needed anymore. Jason and I sharply rebuked her because it was nonsense. She was the chief medical officer of

Marovo Medical and the solid core of the medical side of things. She was the medical pit boss with the medical goods, and she always delivered. It just so happened that the team members were perfect and thus this trip had run without a hitch. It wasn't that she wasn't needed but that this baby that we had raised had grown up. We weren't losing control, and it wasn't as if we weren't needed.

The maturation of the project from trip one until trip ten was smacking us in the face. So much fruit had been produced from the Marovo Medical Foundation tree, it was astonishing. We were seeing the results of a properly planned and executed third-world medical mission project. We hadn't sent the children to elementary school and then forgotten about them. We had nurtured them all the way to college graduation and had lovingly enjoyed the commencement address at the opening ceremony of the new operating room. We had succeeded with an international aid program where so many others had failed. Lives had been changed for the better, and the project was alive and well. Our quest to make Seghe Hospital a facility that the local people would want to visit continued full steam ahead.

Reflections and Pitfalls

*W*atching a culture change before my eyes has been interesting, scary, hopeful, and sad all at the same time. Seeing the people of the Solomon Islands move toward the ways of the western world has been scary to watch. What the future holds for these villagers is uncertain. They'll definitely be affected by rising sea levels—that's a given. They already have been. But the more subtle and seemingly benign changes are the ones that concern me more. From a health and nutrition perspective, the Solomon Islanders are headed off a cliff of epic proportions. Western food is novel and exciting. It shows prestige and affluence if someone is able to buy a lot of soda or candy bars. Education regarding the evils of these foods has barely made an inroad in the community. We can see bodies changing for the worse before our eyes. High consumption levels of rice and soda are ruining lives through diabetes and tooth decay.

When we first visited the Marovo Lagoon in 2006, there were no cell phone towers. As of the summer of 2013, there were two towers, with more installations planned. As I mentioned, it's been hard to watch the community skip toilets and head straight for cell phones. I hope that choice doesn't come back to haunt the people of the lagoon.

We couldn't have provided consistent health care to the people of the Marovo Lagoon over the past seven years without the help of willing participants. People who didn't know us stuck their necks out and opened their hearts and wallets to join us in a faraway and very foreign land. I send a heartfelt thank-you to them because they enabled us to provide physician-based health care in a community where it didn't exist without us.

I think things will have to change culturally for the Solomon Islands to move forward as a nation. At least within the health care system, dealing with egregious behavior among employees is met with sheer impotence. Solomon Islanders seem incapable of actually firing anyone who truly needs to be fired. I have seen the health care system rife with incidents, just in the past seven years, that in any hospital in the developed world, would have led to employees being terminated immediately on the spot. Not in the Solomon Islands.

Through all this, we have served the people of the Marovo Lagoon out of love and a true desire to improve the health care offerings and system for the benefit of its people. Cultural differences have brought progress to a halt from time to time. There have been many instances when I have wanted to throw my hands up in the air and never return. *Forget it! I'm done!* That hasn't happened yet, but it gets harder and harder to repel the draining attacks and bureaucratic impotence that threaten the viability of our participation with improving things in the Marovo Lagoon. I can't forget that the nation's health system is relatively in its infancy. Nevertheless, launching a three-month investigation regarding criminal and dangerous behavior on behalf of an employee is the definition of impotence. If those are the policies that are in place and must be followed, then it is time to revisit and change the policies to be able to be more effective and efficient in dealing with personnel issues. It leaves me scratching my head, to say the least. The Solomon Islands are making positive but slow progress with their system, but if they do not make basic changes with regard to employee conduct and enforcement/termination, they will never create a health care system like those in the developed world. Never.

By failing to deal with bad apples, they embolden others to behave badly, and soon, the entire batch will be rotten. The health system in the Solomon Islands will never improve if bad apples are dealt with by moving them from facility to facility. They must be fired! That concept is completely foreign to them, for some reason. The bad apples just keep being moved, and from time to time, we hear that one we dealt with years ago is coming back to Seghe. That has happened more than I care to remember. Maybe the concept of firing someone is taboo. I don't know the answer. What I do know is that firing almost never happens.

For anyone looking to go down the road we have tread, there are issues to consider. Unless you plan to move to your area of focus, you cannot achieve your goals without responsible, trustworthy, and active people on the ground. Without the Kelly family, we could not have achieved what we've achieved. The Kellys have managed the day-to-day issues and coordinated in-country logistics, which we couldn't have done. They had the resources to assist, which we didn't have. Without a trustworthy partner, you'll have a much harder time succeeding. Without competent local capacity, you are dead in the water. If you don't have it from the start, it will likely take a long time to develop.

There are groups that venture into the developing world with great intentions. I applaud them for their desire to make positive change, but I wonder if they have thought enough about the long-term viability of their endeavors? For example, some groups go around setting up Internet access and providing computers to schools and communities. I applaud the idea, yet a good idea is only the beginning. This happened at Seghe, and of course there was no consideration given to how the people were going to pay their Internet bills; thus, the Internet has been shut down. Think, people, think! Don't just give out carrots. Aid recipients need to know how to plant and maintain the entire garden.

Also avoid trying to be the "first-world savior" for a one-and-done project. I was contacted by a flying humanitarian group a few years ago. They were looking for information regarding the Marovo Lagoon because they were planning to do their trip there during that year. I asked them flat out in an e-mail if they planned a one-and-done trip or if they planned to make a long-term and lasting commitment to the people of the Marovo. Surprise, surprise, they didn't respond to my e-mail. Swooping in with your airplanes and helicopters one time to give out bandages is a nearly useless approach to helping a developing culture improve its health care situation. As hard as it is for me to say this, the people would have been better off if such aid groups had never left the comfort of their country clubs. Such groups may be interested only in returning home with sexy short-term success photos. They'll never have to show the images of the decay that likely ensued shortly after their departure. Think long-term, not short-term.

That's the problem with international aid. Giving communities gifts that require additional long-term funding can be a self-defeating endeavor, unless the long-term funding is planned into the project. Ask about an aid group's long-term plan before you donate. Our long-term plan is to hire our own full-time physician to be posted to Seghe Hospital. Once this happens, we can cut back to one trip a year and then slowly phase ourselves out of the picture. The government has said it will take over paying the physician's salary in a couple years' time. We will have improved the hospital and left it with a full-time physician, which we consider to be successfully working ourselves out of a job.

Let's face it, international aid workers are hired to spend money in the short term. They aren't hired for long-term project monitoring and maintenance. They are hired to spend a budget and to get on to the next project. That way of doing things creates a lot of instant bang for the buck but, long-term, promotes a lot of decay in the community. I've seen the decay at Seghe Hospital and other clinics around the Marovo. I'm sure a lot of nice pictures were taken when the facilities were built, but when I saw them years later, their conditions were inexcusable.

If you are interested in going on a short-term medical mission, make sure you are able to work well with others. You need to go on the trip for all the right reasons. You have to leave your mental and emotional baggage at home, or you won't help the team achieve its objectives. Your inability to fully be there for the right reasons will turn toxic within the group, and it will get ugly, believe me!

To everyone who has made commitments to us and followed through with those commitments, I sincerely appreciate your talents and gifts! To those who made commitments and haven't followed through, know that it takes a lot to recover from false hope.

In the end, I've been an outsider throughout this entire process. I'll always be an outsider in the Marovo Lagoon. Maybe it's easy for an outsider to write the things I've written, but also, maybe that's why businesses and governments often hire outside consultants to shed new light on problems within systems. Things will never change unless someone calls attention to improprieties or deficiencies that are not being addressed. My inner being strives for social justice and genuinely wants to see improvements within the health care system of the Solomon Islands. That's why I haven't said, "Forget it!" and walked away. I hope that never happens, but the line is unfortunately not as thick as I'd like it to be. The line between staying for the long term and saying, "Screw it, I'm out of here!" is very, very thin. Jason has dealt with more staffing issues than I could ever imagine. I applaud and thank him to the point of exhaustion, because I know it has been exhausting for him. There are important constructs and codes of conduct that need to be upheld for the welfare of the project as well as for maintaining the trust that our financial donors have imparted upon us. As long as we continue to work in the Marovo, we will continue to press for accountability from the various stakeholders to ensure that important constructs and codes of conduct are maintained.

It's been my love for God and love for my fellow man that have driven my passion toward improving healthcare for the people of the Marovo Lagoon. Love has driven me to write pointed letters to government officials. Love has driven me to have candid, sometimes not happy, conversations with church officials at home and in the Solomons. Love has required me to not give up thus far on a society that is so vastly different from my own but not inferior in any way. Love is as strong a force as there is in the universe. Sometimes I have to fight the urge to tell people that I've had it with their crap and I'm going to throw in the towel. Love has won out with these struggles thus far. I hope it continues to win, but we'll have to wait and see.

I've benefitted greatly from having a cool head to keep me in check. By no means am I referring to my own head. Jason has helped me to keep an even keel in tough times. He has been around Solomon Islands culture for so long that he has a much better gauge for understanding how things go and how situations are likely to pan out. We joke about me sending off another Daly Special e-mail to someone. Without a doubt, the e-mail is going to be a hot one! I guess my passion for success and providing better health care options for the people of the Marovo gets the better of my diplomacy from time to time. A lot of people in the Solomon Islands have no idea what we go through in the United States with trying to provide them continuously available physician-based health care. It's completely exhausting of time, emotions, and money. Even though I've never been paid a dime for my work, it has been a full-time job for the past seven years, full of intrinsic benefits that I would never trade for all the money in the world.

Seven years of involvement with a medical project in the third world has been enlightening and rewarding, to say the least. The blinders that so many people wear concerning the needy are solid and strapped on tight. It's those people whom I want to join us in the Solomon Islands to assist our medical team. It's those people who need to vacation in a developing country. It's those people whom this world so desperately needs to remove their blinders and to see that the world is not all right just because they got a great bargain at the local big-box store.

There's a world out there waiting for those of us with capable and caring hands to simply open them and embrace the needs of those less fortunate. Please, just one day a month, devote your time to helping someone totally unrelated to you. You will change lives, and maybe, most importantly, you will change your own life ... for the better.

To see photos of our involvement in the Marovo Lagoon, please visit www.marovomedical.org

CPSIA information can be obtained at www.ICGtesting.com
Printed in the USA
LVOW13s0403240814

400576LV00004B/438/P